The Cameraman's Cut

The Cameraman's Cut

A Life through the Lens of a Documentary Cinematographer

COLIN CLARKE

Copyright © 2025 Colin Clarke

Web: colclarke.co.uk

The moral right of the author has been asserted.

Apart from any fair dealing for the purposes of research or private study, or criticism or review, as permitted under the Copyright, Designs and Patents Act 1988, this publication may only be reproduced, stored or transmitted, in any form or by any means, with the prior permission in writing of the publishers, or in the case of reprographic reproduction in accordance with the terms of licences issued by the Copyright Licensing Agency. Enquiries concerning reproduction outside those terms should be sent to the publishers.

This book is an independent work and is not affiliated with, sponsored by, or endorsed by the producers, rights holders, or any individuals associated with the films. All photographs included were taken by the author or crew members during their time on set and are presented as part of a personal memoir for historical and educational purposes.

Every effort has been made to respect the rights of individuals depicted in these images. If any copyright or publicity rights holders believe their material has been used inappropriately, they are invited to contact the author or publisher to discuss proper credit or resolution.

Troubador Publishing Ltd
Unit E2 Airfield Business Park
Harrison Road, Market Harborough
Leicestershire LE16 7UL
Tel: 0116 279 2299
Email: books@troubador.co.uk
Web: www.troubador.co.uk

ISBN 97 81 83628 416 1

British Library Cataloguing in Publication Data.
A catalogue record for this book is available from the British Library.

The manufacturer's authorised representative in the EU for product safety is Authorised Rep Compliance Ltd, 71 Lower Baggot Street, Dublin D02 P593 Ireland (www.arccompliance.com).

Front cover photo by Tim Maurice Jones

Printed and bound by CPI Group (UK) Ltd, Croydon, CR0 4YY
Typeset in 11.5pt Minion Pro by Troubador Publishing Ltd, Leicester, UK

Hey Tim,
So glad you're in our team.
Happy Christmas 2025

from secret santa!
X

For Jack and Azra, with love
Born in the year of writing, 2024

Contents

1	Fifty Words for Snow	1
2	North to the Pole	19
3	The Beginning	30
4	Film School	46
5	Garden of the Emperors	55
6	Editing the Hangul Story	67
7	A Bridge Too Far	71
8	Scene 1, Take 1	82
9	I Am Now a Lighting Cameraman	90
10	Mentioned in Dispatches	97
11	It's Not Only Rock 'n' Roll	104
12	Two Weddings and a Funeral	108
13	On Angel's Wings	114
14	By Royal Appointment	126
15	Madagascar Crocs	131
16	Dark River	142
17	1989	147
18	This Land is Ours	151

Contents

19	Words on Film	157
20	The New Europeans	161
21	State of the Ark	167
22	The Land of all Impossibilities	180
23	Congo	185
24	First Taste of Japan	195
25	Lost Tribes	204
26	Meeting the Korowai Tribe	212
27	Living with Cannibals	223
28	The Price for Sorcery	229
29	Korowai Post-Production	240
30	America Flies	246
31	Soviet Sport, Space Race and Oligarchy	260
32	Presenter-Led	272
33	Quest for the Lost Civilisation	281
34	The Quest Continues	293
35	Tech Moves On	311
36	Death, Deceit and the Nile	318
37	Nefertiti Revealed	328
38	Docudrama	337
39	A Life in Higher Definition	346
40	Looking Back	355
	Acknowledgements	358
	Filmography	360

1

Fifty Words for Snow

I am standing at the axis on which the Earth spins. All meridians of longitude converge; every direction I look is south, and the sun rises and sets just once a year. It is a unique spot that holds immense geographic and symbolic importance. The air is still, and the low sun casts a golden glow over the exquisite, pristine landscape—a vast expanse of ice that stretches to all horizons. This humbling experience fills me with a sense of awe. I reflect on my good fortune and privilege to have a vocation and career that require me to experience remarkable situations and travel to extraordinary places. On this occasion, it's the Geographic North Pole.

It is mid-May 1989, and I am still just on the right side of forty years old. At a balmy minus 20° Celsius, this is the mildest weather we have experienced since the beginning of filming. The sea ice beneath my feet slowly drifts with the tide as I walk towards the three Twin Otter aircraft resting on their skids, engines running to avoid freezing. Aboard are eight exhausted and frostbitten men who have just completed a gruelling expedition, walking from Canada's Cape Columbia to the Pole. My colleagues and I have been documenting their progress from the start of training.

At eight o'clock one morning, three months earlier, I awoke to the familiar ring of my travel alarm and looked out of the twelfth-floor hotel room window onto a curious sight. Below was the mighty Ottawa River, and a steady stream of rush-hour commuters, smartly dressed and carrying briefcases, were skating downtown to the business district. The river regularly freezes over for three months each winter despite Canada's capital city being six degrees of latitude south of London. This was day one of a Channel 4 and Discovery Channel documentary shoot—the first stage of the on-site preparation for the *Icewalk* expedition. Here, the walkers, the support team and the film crew were being kitted out for the three months to be spent in the High Arctic.

A few of us flew on to Iqaluit, now the capital of Nunavut, but at the time, a small Inuit town nestled on the shores of Frobisher Bay, Baffin Island, in Canada's Northwest Territories. Its population was just a few thousand. Before heading further north, this would be our home base for six weeks. Others in the crew were my regular assistant, Mike Marmion, and sound recordist Dave Keene, whom I had come to know and work with only recently and would continue to do so for some years after. Dave is a Kiwi with polar filming experience in the Antarctic. Simon Normanton, the film's director, was also travelling with us.

Our assigned apartment was basic but comfortable: a bedroom each, a communal lounge and a sparsely equipped kitchen. The heating was excessive, seemingly the standard for every indoor space. So, coming in from minus 40ºC was quite a shock to the system.

We ventured into town, crunching through the snow and ice past rows of stilt houses elevated above the permafrost, though not above the February snowpack from which the remains of last season's hunt protruded. The walls were thick and the windows small. Television satellite dishes were bolted to smoking chimneys, and heavy-duty power cables ran out to the parked four-wheel-drive vehicles to prevent their engine blocks from freezing. To familiarise ourselves with the alien environment, we made our way to the beach, weaving through speeding snowmobiles. Stepping onto the frozen sea with our newly acquired skis resting on our shoulders, we clambered over small pressure ridges where shifting tides had heaved the ice upward. From here, we ski-walked out to the 'Churchberg,' a small yet striking iceberg sculpted by elements and locked in the bay by the winter sea ice. When we returned to base, we were thoroughly exhausted—and we hadn't even been carrying any film equipment.

The 'Churchberg'

'Skidoo' is a brand, but, like 'Hoover' for a vacuum cleaner, locally, it had become the generic name for a snowmobile. We were supplied with a couple of basic ones for our personal use; they were a great deal of fun as well as useful tools. The serious high-powered machines were to be handled by our local Inuit helpers, Johnny, who spoke good English and Jacob, who spoke none—and my mastery of the Inuktitut language left much to be desired!

As the walkers ventured onto the ice to test their equipment and start acclimatisation, we tagged along. We pitched our two-person tents to prepare for our first night of sleeping on the ice. I was with Mike. While I fired up the kerosene stove in the middle of the tent (not advisable in anything other than extreme conditions where every joule of heat is treasured), Mike filled a mess tin with snow for water, and we cooked the first of many freeze-dried noodle meals. All hot food tastes great in this environment. I removed my Canadian Army mukluk boots and down-filled parka. Still wearing multiple layers, I climbed into my inner sleeping bag, followed by a Gore-Tex vapour barrier and an outer down-filled bag. I pulled the vital pee bottle inside and the camera batteries to keep them warm. We extinguished the stove and zipped up until nothing but our noses and mouths were exposed, and we tried to sleep. As the tent quickly cooled, there was always some point on the body where the cold would find refuge, and I struggled to adjust layers of clothing to cover the gap—a phenomenon that would taunt us day and night over the coming months.

I woke in the morning cosy in my 'mummy' bag, which was frosted from head to toe. It crunched and crackled as I sat up to relight the stove. Breakfast was a mug of tea and muesli topped with milk powder, then steeped in boiling water from fresh snow. Made my first gaffe and learnt the lesson—do not put your pee bottle outside of the sleeping bag during the night; a flask filled with frozen urine has no further use!

As we were breaking camp, a mushing dog team came thundering towards us and pulled to a halt. The dogs settled to relax in the snow, and the musher, Brent Boddy, introduced himself. His is a name synonymous with polar travel. He is a Canadian married to an Inuit, and he is a renowned explorer, hunter, husky breeder, and authority figure in all things Arctic. I asked him whether dog sleds had any advantages over skidoos in this day and age. His reply was, "There aren't many parts of a skidoo you can eat." He also pointed out that they are handy for distracting bears in an encounter. As the trip progressed, I was pleasantly surprised by the large number of dog teams we came across. Also, the number of igloos that were used as temporary dwellings on hunting trips. They are much warmer than tents and more secure from predators.

On the second night, I decided to try sleeping out in the open, as did the walkers—why? I don't know. I guess it would be my only chance to do something so silly. The first thing that struck me was the extraordinary soundscape. It was a still night, and there was the muted quietness unique to a deep snow environment. Yet, as soon as I lay with my ear to the ice, albeit via snow, groundsheet and sleeping bag hood, I became aware of an eerie cacophony of creaks, cracking and moaning as ice floes for miles around rubbed against each other. Turning on my back and wrapped snugly in my cocoon, I listened to Tomita's "Snowflakes are Dancing" (electronic Debussy) on my Walkman. I stared at the magnificent night sky where the dominant North Star shone brilliantly, virtually overhead. Eventually, I drifted off to sleep. At around 4:00am and 36ºC below, common sense won, and I crawled back into the tent.

Now, it was time to test the camera equipment. We brought two 16mm Aaton cameras, a selection of lenses, my tripods, plus loads of extra paraphernalia that always accompany camera kits. I also had my 1952 Bolex 100ft load clockwork 16mm camera. I had done my homework before leaving the UK. A significant concern was batteries losing their potency in the cold. We had a stack of the prototype lithium, single-use 12V batteries which had been assembled in the Aaton factory. They cost approximately £150 each (£465 equivalent today, 2024). They were reckoned to handle between forty-five to fifty 400ft rolls of film under normal conditions, and we managed fifteen rolls out of each, but that was OK as we had plenty. I had been worried that the oil in the fluid head on my tripod would freeze. It did thicken, but it was fine as long as I kept the resistance settings at the minimum.

The cameras and lenses had been winterised, primarily by disassembling them and removing all lubricants that would stiffen in the cold. I had a heated barney (a soft camera cover with battery-powered heating elements), space blankets, chemical hand-warmers and 'Crewsaver' heat packs which automatically triggered at -8ºC. We carried an insulated bagful; the outside packs would go off, protecting the inside ones for later use. It was now -28ºC, and, despite all this clever stuff, the camera was struggling to get up to speed, and the focus, zoom, and stop rings were extremely stiff. It was back to base and thinking caps on to solve our cold camera problems. So was born the concept of 'The Sauna'. Fortunately, among Johnny's many skills was carpentry. This enabled us to build a plywood box with a sliding panel at the bottom, on which was bolted an MSR kerosene stove. Above was a metal plate, a gap of a few inches and suitably vented cut-out spaces for a brace of ready-to-shoot Aatons. On top was a lid, and after all this had been carefully insulated, it was lashed onto a komatik, a substantial sleigh that is towed behind a high-powered skidoo or a dog team. The Sauna would only be of use while based on Baffin Island; in a few weeks, we would be heading further north, by which time we should be wiser and more experienced in Arctic filming techniques.

The *Icewalk* team consisted of eight men from seven countries, led by Robert Swan, a charismatic and renowned British explorer and campaigner for environmental awareness. If successful, he would be the first person to walk to both the North and South Poles. Rupert Summerson, another Englishman, was deputy leader and navigator and was to collect snow and air samples for a scientific programme. As a Royal Marines Instructor, he had substantial field service in both the Arctic and the Antarctic. In this period of Glasnost, six months before the Berlin Wall would come down, Dr Michael (Misha) Malakhov, the team medic, had had ten years of polar experience, having been on many Soviet expeditions. Darryl Roberts, at twenty-four, would be the first American and youngest person to walk to the North Pole, as well as the first black man and only the second black man to get there at all. The first had been the unsung Matthew Henson. He was on Robert Peary's dog sled expedition in 1909, and they were the first people to reach the Pole. Henson is believed to be the very first person to 'sit on top of the world' (it is disputed as to whether they ever accurately found the Pole). Hiro Onishi from Japan was a professional expeditionary and renowned mountaineer. Graeme Joy, an Australian sportsman and adventurer had spent the previous two years helping Summerson coordinate the logistics. His vital role on the walk would be as radio operator. Arved Fuchs would be the first German to walk to the North Pole. He was an accomplished mountaineer and explorer and had kayaked to the Magnetic (as opposed to Geographic) North Pole. Canadian Angus 'Kaanerk' Cockney was an Inuit from the Northwest Territories. He was a former cross-country ski champion and coach. He had produced video programmes to promote public understanding of environmental issues; we provided him with a winterised and adapted Sony Sports Video8 handycam, the latest in home-movie cameras, to shoot some extra footage on the walk.

The most light-sensitive film stock available at the time (Eastman 7292) had a speed rating of 320 ISO, which you could 'push' (in the processing lab) to 640 ISO. Today's equivalent broadcast quality digital cameras have an ISO rating of 800, which you can push (in the camera) to 6,000 ISO plus. In simple terms, we needed four times as much light to get an exposure, so to film their interactions in the dimly lit walkers' house, we had to add our own lighting, pushing the minimal power circuits to the max.

As an integral aspect of the story, we needed to document the endless discussions on logistics. There were arguments about whether to take Russian or Australian stoves, how best to balance their loads between backpacks and sledges, and how to optimise their vast calorie intake. Was it really necessary to add pemmican—ground meat with melted fat and berries—to their morning muesli? These, along with countless minutiae, were details that needed to be sorted out in advance and between folk with varying command of the English language.

There were inevitable misunderstandings and ego clashes

to overcome. These were areas of the narrative that I felt to be powerful and was eager to shoot more of, but Simon, the director, whom I considered rather conventional in his approach, was not so keen. He restrained me with the aid of his much-favoured catchphrase, "Let's have a gloriously idle moment."

The walkers' house cook was Speedy Eddy. His brief was to feed them enormous amounts of calories, fat and protein. They would eat large chunks of cold butter like they were biscuits. Back at our house, Johnny had been out hunting and delivered us a whole leg of caribou. As we all fancied ourselves as cordon bleu chefs, we took turns to cook dinner. One night, we would have caribou curry; the next, caribou steaks, and then caribou in grape sauce.

The purpose of these weeks in Iqaluit was for the walkers to prepare, train and get fit for their upcoming journey. This involved spending extended periods trekking on the ice, developing the techniques for man-hauling 115-kilo sledges over steep 30ft pressure ridges caused by the ever-drifting ice floes, currents and tides. We shot the process, always being one step ahead. The film was important to the team, and they were very cooperative, but this was life-or-death training for them, and they did not want to compromise on that.

It was our most productive period in terms of capturing vital dramatic footage of the guys in action. We also experienced the harshest weather conditions of the trip, with temperatures dipping to 69.5ºC below zero, including windchill. Factor in a further 35mph of chill if we were bombing along to windward on a skidoo—that was very cold by any standard.

Naturally, the choice of clothing is critical and is all about layers. It's vital to regulate your temperature constantly.

Hanging around—quite a lot of that when filming—you need to be well wrapped up, but if you are trekking or skiing and the body is creating heat, you have to unzip or de-layer. Sweat is your worst enemy, as it will freeze and leave you vulnerable to frostbite. For this reason, the Inuit people have evolved to sweat mainly on their faces. We wore synthetic thermal vests and long johns, which wicked sweat away from the skin to the outer layers to evaporate. Then, fibre-pile salopettes and jacket, a fleece and a down-filled parka with a fox fur windbreak on the hood to protect the face. We added heavy-duty Gore-Tex over-trousers and jackets if there was strong wind or snow. We wore four or five layers of socks under our Canadian Army mukluks and balaclavas and faux-fur lined hats on our heads. We had several options and combinations for our hands, which were down to personal preference. Mine was first silk gloves, then fingerless wool, another wool, and mitts with a slit to get fingers out when necessary and, in the more extreme temperatures, large over-mitts with a string through the sleeves like toddlers wear. Despite all this clothing, there was always some infuriating, hard-to-access area of skin where the cold would creep in.

A common question is: "How do you pee in such icy conditions?" The answer is: "Very quickly!" Also, heed well the wisdom shared in Frank Zapper's renowned album track, *Don't Eat the Yellow Snow*.

There are so many different textures and properties to the air-bound and ground-bound conditions that you soon understand why the Inuktitut language has over fifty words for snow.

I already had ten years of experience filming in extreme environments, but nothing compared with shooting in these bitter temperatures, winds, blizzards, ice and deep snow. It was not friendly to man or machine. Every action was an energy-sapping struggle.

So, let's take the scenario of an 'up-and-past' sequence. It's blowing a bit of a blizzard—all very nice for dramatic shots but not necessarily for getting the whole operation to work. Fitting in with their training routine, we have a word with the guys, requesting them to head to a particular point and on into the pressure ridges. We bomb ahead on our skidoos to an elevated vantage point on a mini berg, leaving ourselves plenty of time as we have learnt that everything takes at least twice as long as usual.

Out comes the tripod; the adjustment bolts are frozen solid, so we are stuck at the minimum height of the legs. OK, that's not too big a problem. We can now see our subjects in the distance. We plan to leave it as late as possible to get a camera out of the 'sauna'. The stove is burning, and I dread to think what effect it is having inside the cameras' works—they should now be at a temperature of about plus 35°C. At the given moment, Mike removes the lid; smoke comes billowing out as he grabs a camera. We then activate five hot-gel packs inside the barney to keep things as warm as possible for as long as possible. A short rubberised power extension lead already velcroed to the cover links to a brown lead that is attached to the lithium battery, which, in turn, is buried deep under many layers of clothing as close to my skin as possible. Test it; the camera runs—that's a start.

All this is happening whilst wearing innumerable layers of gloves and mitts, making it very difficult to handle anything. I point the camera towards the walkers. Let's take a look; close my left eye and hope my eyelashes won't fuse. Looking through the viewfinder with my right eye, the body warmth from that causes condensation on the eyepiece glass, which freezes as soon as I take it away. So, I have to clear the frost with a half-gloved finger. Although I can see the walkers approaching in the distance, it's going to be another couple of minutes before we run the camera. I can already feel the focus and zoom rings on the lens stiffening up.

The walkers are reaching the right distance. OK, let's turn over. Switch on the camera. It is already struggling to get up to speed; it's not there yet, moaning a bit, but I think it'll just make it. The sync light is flickering; yeah, it's all right. We are actually running to sound speed. Let's hope it lasts the length of the shot, although there's a good chance it won't. On goes the clapper board. In his headphones, Dave can hear the walker's dialogue from the radio mics that he had attached earlier. They appear through the mist at the long end of the zoom as they head towards us. It's looking atmospheric through the viewfinder. Still, I am unsure whether this is because of the haze or because the eyepiece is frosting over again. I've taken a couple of layers of gloves off my left hand to be able to operate the zoom and focus and so that I can stick my finger in every so often to scrape the ice from the eyepiece.

This would be the simplest of shots under normal circumstances. I try to walk around the tripod as I pan, but the snow underfoot is deep and sticky. Because we're standing around, we are vulnerable to the cold. Everything is starting to freeze. The condensation from my breath turns to ice in my balaclava. It feels like a metal plate moving around my face; it slips and obstructs my vision. At least we are getting dramatic images through the driving snow. It will be a good sequence if the camera keeps running for the duration. They are heading away from us now. Maybe we can get ahead and catch a couple of close handheld shots in among the pressure ridges. Onto the skidoo—Mike is driving, and I am riding pillion, battered by the bitingly cold wind, clutching the camera wrapped in a space blanket. A little way behind is Johnny's skidoo pulling: the komatik with Simon, Dave clasping his sound kit and, of course, the 'sauna' with the backup camera. We pull up alongside the line of pressure ridges, find a good position to get some dramatic angles and beckon Robert and the team towards us. The rush is exhausting, but we need the material. Handholding creates its own problems because, apart from the difficulty of making smooth in-shot moves, I now have to remove the over-mitts from my right hand to hold the grip and operate the on-off rocker. A standard feature of the Aaton is a wonderful moulded walnut wooden hand grip, so at least that doesn't get icy cold. The position of my right hand is now above my shoulder; consequently, the blood is draining from the hand, making it prone to frostbite. Wiggling my fingers helps until it gets too painful, and I have to hand the camera to Mike and warm myself up. We have shots, but I want more variety.

While Robert and the gang, carrying weighty packs and hauling heavy sledges, are in training and moving slowly over the trickiest route, we can take a more direct one to get ahead. In position, sitting on the snow for a low angle as they appear over a ridge, I try to run the camera, but it is just not getting up to speed, so we try plugging in our 16V battery for that little bit of extra kick which sometimes does the trick but, in this case, it doesn't. Wish I had the Bolex handy. So, of the two set-ups, one works and the other doesn't. That's what it is like most of the time.

It is a case of returning to the komatik and sticking the camera back in the sauna, and when we are ready for the next shot, we pull the other one out and see what we can do.

While Simon is having a 'gloriously idle moment,' Dave is with the walkers recording wild tracks of skis and crunching ice and a myriad of sounds that can be used in the edit to supplement the sync sound. Mike heroically puts his minimally gloved hands through the light traps of the film-changing bag, offloading and loading the 400ft rolls of film. It is a job that requires dexterity. The cold makes the film stock very brittle, so it must be handled delicately.

L-R. Myself, Johnny and Mike, with the camera protected by a space blanket

Time for a brew and a light bite. The idea of eating uncooked meat is synonymous with the now pejorative term, 'Eskimo' (meaning 'eaters of raw flesh', though disputed by some etymologists), but I can highly recommend raw caribou. A thin slither freshly cut from a frozen chunk of meat melts in the mouth and is delicious and wholesome. Another vital on-the-go snack is GORP, '**G**ood **O**ld **R**aisins and **P**eanuts'. Then there are the 'Amway Bars', specifically manufactured for the expedition by the primary sponsors. We had a tasting at room temperature in Ottawa. They were disgusting, sickly sweet, glutinous, and horrendously calorific. They were heavy with chocolate, butter, and peanut butter and had the consistency of a Mars Bar forgotten in the sun—a nutritionist's worst nightmare. Out here in the cold, the consistency is perfect; they taste amazing and fuel the body with calories and sugar to confront the elements.

Back on flat-ish ice, we do tracking shots of the team from the skidoo-pulled komatik—handheld to absorb the bumps—low angles and close-up skis from lying flat on the base, and wide shots and close-up faces from sitting atop the sauna. Ahhhh!

Later, we come across a large crevice about 5ft wide and 5ft deep. I see the prospect for an unusual angle by positioning the camera at the bottom, shooting towards the sky as the guys, sledges in tow, cross overhead supported by their ominously bending skis. Think I will close the eyepiece—otherwise, light gets in and fogs the film—and shoot this one 'blind'. Great shot. The weather improves for the final images of the session—the team heading off into the sunset (which they won't be doing on the expedition proper as it will be twenty-four-hour daylight by then). Simple set-up from behind; got that. Let's rush ahead of them to make the best of the good light. I ride pillion, this time facing backwards (more comfortable when carrying the camera in the more benign conditions). We are towing a lightweight plastic sled, carrying odds and ends. My heels are secure, and I'm leaning against Mike's back for stability. Feeling a little unsafe on the bumpy ride, I shout to him to slow down, but he goes faster. I push back on the footrests to secure myself. I keep yelling, and he keeps going faster. I push back harder, yelling at the top of my voice to be heard over the roaring engine and the whistling wind, and we are still picking up speed. In fear for my life, I decide to jump clear, but the sled is bouncing around behind us. I have to go for it. I make an almighty leap off to one side, cradling the camera as if it were a baby to be cushioned from the impact. More by luck than by judgement, I execute a roll on the soft snow that any stunt person would be proud of, and man and machine live to fight another day.

Satisfied that the camera and I are intact, an exasperated Mike points out that each time I pushed further back against him, it squashed his body and hand up against the throttle. He could do nothing to rectify the situation without losing control.

The walkers, with us in tow, alternately camped and travelled on the ice, then returned to base to revise and adapt their kit and provisions. They fixed clothing with help from local seamstresses, and they agreed on Inuit-style sealskin mukluks for their all-important footwear as they were warmer, more comfortable, and waterproof than the high-tech Canadian boots. There were women in town whose speciality was chewing the skin to make it supple and to seal the joins.

Poor Daryl was already suffering severe frostbite on one of his feet. Whether black skin pigment is a factor in susceptibility,

I don't know, but ill-fitting boots were a contributor. There were serious concerns as to whether he would be fit to go. Misha was an amazing doctor with much polar experience and what appeared to be a bag of magic tinctures and ointments. When asked about them, his stock answer was, "It is zee Russian system." He certainly did an excellent job of fixing the frost nip on my nose and treating my sprained wrist from a slip on the ice.

Simon became impatient with the guys because he felt they were spending too much time at base for his filming interests, but their priorities differed.

We had our own kit problems as one of the Aatons had packed up. Being thousands of miles from the nearest camera workshop, we had to have a go ourselves. We reckoned it would be a simple fix; there was a broken electrical joint to one of the pins on the cannon socket that connected to the battery. But could we get to the back end of it? We had to disassemble the camera body, reducing it to hundreds of delicate components, in order to achieve access. Thankfully, Dave is a wizard with Allen keys, precision screwdrivers and a soldering iron. Miraculously, he reassembled the camera, leaving only one mystery component on the table.

A few days before everyone was due to head further north to the advanced base camp, Simon Dring, our producer and employer, arrived in Iqaluit to see how it was going and was not totally happy with what he found. Simon Normanton had a good track record, having worked for nine years on *The World About Us*, a recently finished BBC2 high-end Science and Natural History series headed by David Attenborough. Still, Dring felt Normanton's approach was "too old school." He wanted a style more suitable for the American audience—

younger, "… more rock 'n' roll." Also, he demanded extra footage for promotional films and training clips. Personally, I would have liked to have gone for more 'fly on the wall' material observing the team, but I was just a 'gun for hire'. We only had a few days before heading north to start the actual expedition. We were behind schedule on our filming, but to appease Dring, we did squeeze in an under-cranked (speeded-up) clip of Robert out in the snow, naked but for his underpants, then dressing item by item into full polar garb. Rather he than me.

2

North to the Pole

*I*cewalk was Robert's brainchild. After completing his walk to the South Pole, *'In the Footsteps of Scott'*, in 1986, he had spent a couple of years travelling at his own expense to raise £3,000,000 in sponsorship, find suitable members for the expedition, and promote his environmental message. If successful, he would be the first person to walk to both poles.

> "Respect for the Arctic's power and vulnerability is also the key to global survival. The Arctic graphically illustrates the irrevocable impact of industrial man.
>
> Thousands of miles from the nearest industry, the Arctic soft snows are awash with chemicals and pesticides and a seasonally premature breakup of the northern icecap, which threatens to thwart our expedition, is almost certainly global warming.
>
> The Arctic gives me one graphic and terrifying message. The natural world is striking back, and we

have everything to lose. Unless we join together now, maybe not this month or next year, but certainly within the lifetimes of our children. This is an emergency and all the rhetoric and well-intentioned political accords in the world are not enough. We must begin now."

Robert Swan *(1989).*

The operation was enormous, as was the publicity machine and media attention, which was now beginning to grind into action.

We all left in preparation for the main adventure. Equipment and people were crammed into a rather old Boeing 748. It seemed to struggle into the air, but once it settled, everything was fine, and soon we were far from Iqaluit. The view through the porthole was awe-inspiring—virgin white snow from horizon to horizon over a massive, deep, frozen archipelago. The islands are made up of mountain ranges with glaciers flowing down every valley. The low sun shone, casting long shadows of the peaks and their rugged outcrops to windward and silky smooth sloped to leeward. We flew the 1,600km to Resolute on Ellesmere Island, an Inuit hamlet at 75°N with a good airstrip and suitable accommodation for High Arctic travellers. It was here alone that I saw the only evidence of a polar bear, and it was a pelt stretched out on a drying rack. But I was well aware of local wisdom that stated: "If you don't carry a gun, the only way to survive an encounter with a hungry bear is to have a companion who is a slower runner than you!"

A radio station was set up here for the expedition, and a storage warehouse for resupplies. It would be a stop-off point for us a couple of times further down the line. For now, it was a refuelling stop before heading on to the Eureka High

Arctic Weather Station at 80°N, the furthest point a medium-sized plane can land. We had a brief stopover before using the smaller Twin Otter planes to ferry all the expedition's paraphernalia and personnel to the advanced base station at Cape Colombia.

Two and a half hours after leaving Eureka, we started our descent. A blizzard engulfed the peninsula, and visibility was minimal. The aircraft bounced and skidded to an abrupt halt along this last snow-covered promontory, Canada's northernmost point of land. Beyond was nothing but the frozen Arctic Ocean—774km to the Pole. We left the comparative warmth of the plane to be hit by bitterly cold winds and a feeling in the air that told us we were truly in the very High Arctic.

The 'Polar Haven' was a large, well-anchored, standing-height tent that would be home to the four-man advanced-base support crew for the duration of the expedition, but for a few days, it housed about twenty of us. As well as extra logistics crew, there was a Japanese photographer, a couple of journalists, and us. It was stacked high with provisions, and soon the moist air became heavy with the stench of kerosene heaters and the closeness of men living and working in the three small plastic-walled rooms. Initially, there was a buzz of excitement among the expedition members as they made last-minute preparations, checking radio communications and weather forecasts. The timing of their departure was vital for success.

Such was the expedition's high profile that dozens of messages of goodwill were pouring in from the likes of President Bush, Prince Charles, and Prime Ministers Thatcher, Mulroney, Gandhi, and Ryzhkov. The walkers were writing letters to their loved ones, and a kind of hush ensued as they contemplated the enormity of the task ahead. Of course, all the while, we were filming and, undoubtedly, being considered pests in their eyes.

A major technical hurdle for us, as if there were not enough, was condensation. The cameras were all metal and glass, so moving from the cold outside to the warmth inside was a nightmare. The issue had been a problem from the outset, so we devised a system to deal with it. When we came in from the cold, we would put the camera, complete with lens filters and film magazine, into a thin plastic bin liner, suck out as much air as possible and seal it as best we could; the idea being that the condensation would form on the outside of the bag. This put the camera out of action for a while, but we did have another.

On the second day, there was a total whiteout. After attending to a call of nature, I was returning to the haven when I had the most beautiful encounter with an Arctic wolf. It just stepped into vision from about four metres away. His or her immaculate whiteness all but blended into the surroundings, apart from a jet-black nose and bright blue eyes. It was magnificent. We just stared fearlessly at each other for about five minutes until it gracefully wandered off, melting into the mist. I have had a few close encounters with potentially dangerous wild animals over the years, usually resulting in one or the other or both of us running for safety. Yet, on this occasion, it was something akin to a Zen experience.

It was late morning on the 20th of March 1989, the temperature was minus 55°C, conditions were suitable, and the walkers had enjoyed their last meal in the comfort and warmth of the haven. Robert stood up and, with a dramatic flourish, said, "Well, gentleman, I'm going to the North Pole. Is anyone coming?" (wish he had briefed us so we could have filmed his quip). We rushed outside to catch the moment as they exited. Then I shot actuality of all the excitement as they donned their packs and hitched themselves up to their sledges. Robert and Arved had opted to haul their 60kg personal loads on large sledges, and the others split theirs between backpacks and smaller sledges. Moving around in the deep snow to get the best shooting angles was a struggle. My right hand was freezing up, but there was no way we could compromise these vital moments of the story, so I kept wiggling my fingers and gritting my teeth.

After exchanging farewells with the support team, they lined up on the frozen beach, looking out over the miles of massive pressure-ice ridges extending to the horizon. The first of many daunting challenges.

Our naive notion of getting ahead of them to film their departure from the mainland had thankfully been abandoned. The images of them from behind as they ventured into the Arctic expanse were far more emotive. By now, the camera was on the tripod as we watched eight intrepid men head north at a tortuously slow pace, clambering and clawing their way over 12 to 13m 'ice-scrapers', passing packs and sledges to one another, then disappearing over the other side. I used my telephoto lens to squeeze out as much good footage as possible until eight red dots vanished into the haze. We would next encounter them on a resupply flight.

The Eureka Weather Station was home to six full-time staff and had accommodation for many visitors, as it was a temporary base for scientific and environmental research projects. Now, it was about to house the most significant influx of guests yet. It was mid-April, and the *Icewalk* 'Student Expedition' consisting of twenty-two students from fifteen countries with their escorts, leaders and tutors started to arrive, increasing the station's population sevenfold. In addition to monitoring the walkers' progress and chatting with them via radio, they were here for the High Arctic experience. Their primary task was to carry out environmental studies. Their findings were alarming. This is one of the cleanest places on the planet. There is no industry within 1,000 miles, yet they found pesticides in the snow, signs of acid rain and greenhouse gases, as well as evidence of a thinning ozone layer and global warming. They launched balloons to take readings in the atmosphere, collected and analysed ice-core samples, and discussed their findings and conclusions. We also filmed them ski-trekking across the bay and learning how to build igloos.

We were now experiencing 24-hour daylight, which was somewhat disorienting but gave a fascinating insight into the planet's geography. When the haze cleared, the light was beautiful—good low sunshine and long shadows. Apart from a distinct yellow haze of pollution on the horizon originating from both North America and Russia, all was pristine white.

Dave and I boarded a laden Twin Otter for a resupply flight. We flew from Eureka via Cape Columbia and landed at the 'Ice Island', a mid-ocean landing strip marked out on the ice. Two Inuit men were stationed there, along with numerous drums of fuel that had been flown out in advance. 'Leads' are narrow, linear cracks in the ice that form when floes diverge or shear as they move parallel. When they refreeze, they create flat ice, making them ideal for a temporary runway, but, as it's an ever-changing icescape, there is a limited window before having to relocate. Landing here created an opportunity to step onto the icecap without having a head full of cinematographic calculations and to enjoy this unique environment in its awesome grandeur.

Back in the air, the skilled and specialised pilot and navigator set about locating the team. GPS technology was in its infancy and only available to the US military, so the most sophisticated system was Omega radio navigation, which used a network of land-based radio beacons rather than satellites. Visibility was poor, and even if the walkers had managed to scout and mark a suitable landing strip, the captain was not prepared to land due to insufficient contrast, making it impossible to spot irregularities on the ice sheet.

Once radio contact was established and they were located, the flight crew circled the area and reported the position of opening leads and other hazards ahead of them that they could not observe from sea level. The ice was constantly on the move and, unfortunately, in a direction that was counterproductive for the walkers. They would camp to sleep for six hours, only to wake up four miles further south than when they had stopped.

We prepared for an airdrop. This involved pushing the supplies, such as food, stove fuel, replacement skis, and anything else they had requested, out of the plane as close as possible to the guys' camp. In anticipation, the rear starboard door had been removed and left at the Ice Island. As we flew lower and in tighter circles, it was no longer coloured specks in the whiteness but tents, sledges, and enthusiastically waving men. The plane banked steeply as two support team members hurriedly pushed out the supplies; I was filming over their shoulders, leaning against the port-side door for support, when it flew open. The thought darted into my head: "This is it. I'm going to end up being part of the airdrop!" Thankfully, the plane's slipstream wouldn't let the door open enough for me to fall out, but my heart very nearly did. (I must add that I was wearing a safety harness.)

We were now heading back south, and the weather cleared as we flew over the Arctic Archipelago. The views were stunning. Eerie shapes were created as the low sun cast long shadows of a multitude of icebergs trapped by the frozen ocean. Mesmerised by the Daliesque vision, I was wrenched from my stupor as I realised we were flying dangerously low. Before I could contemplate my second existential threat in one day, the pilot calmly announced that we should belt up for landing. He taxied the plane, pulling to a halt alongside a beautiful berg, disembarked and started to hack away at it with a small axe. He climbed back on board, grinning from ear to ear, announcing that he had just collected some 10,000-year-old ice for our scotch on arrival at base. And it was special; it effervesced as the ancient air was released from the trapped bubbles. An excellent way to finish what had been an extraordinarily long and adventurous day—or was it night? Hard to tell.

Robert Swan was nothing if not a publicity hound. After all, the whole project, including the student expedition and the significant environmental message, meant nothing if it was not well publicised. For the duration of the expedition, there was media coverage of the progress. At one stage, there was even talk of flying out live breakfast TV crews from multiple countries to cover the arrival at the pole, an idea so impractical that I am surprised it was ever considered. As it turns out, the story would be eclipsed by the biggest news event of the time, the tragic Tiananmen Square massacre in Beijing, in which the Chinese Communist Party military killed several hundred protesters.

However, a grand media reception and press conference were to be held in Resolute. Every hotel room had been booked, every caterer and their neighbours hired, and crates of wine procured. Specialists arrived to install dozens more telephone lines and reactivate Resolute's tiny satellite station. A Boeing 737 was chartered to carry seventy international TV, radio, and press journalists, technicians, and equipment.

Three days of lost radio contact with the expedition fuelled speculation of drama and loss of life on the ice. Weather conditions were unusually harsh, and uncharacteristic warming meant that leads were opening up the ice sheet earlier than usual. Also, Darryl's frostbite was severe, and Hiro had a serious bout of flu.

It was our time to leave for Eureka, where we would be on standby to fly to the Pole. While we were on the taxiway, there was an almighty roar as a Lear Jet touched down on the runway. It was Bill Nicholson, the CEO of Amway, the primary *Icewalk* sponsor. The jet was also due to buzz the walkers at the pole but could not, of course, land there.

May 14, 1989, 03:30am. Eight men from seven countries reached their destination at the North Pole after fifty-six gruelling days of clambering and walking with heavy loads and losing distance every time they stopped to rest or sleep. Exhausted, frostbitten, and weak, they would have been delighted to be met by the evacuation team, but the weather had closed in, making flying conditions impossible. After their embraces and celebrations, they searched out and marked a suitably flat landing strip and then pitched camp.

The following day, we receive the all-clear and the three Twin Otters take off. To accommodate the walkers and their kit on the return flight, there is space for only eight passengers: a couple from the expedition support team, a one-person Canadian TV news crew, the official photographer, a journalist, Dave and I, and Bill Nicholson cradling a jeroboam of champagne. So many disappointed hopefuls are left behind, including the two Simons and Mike.

Six hours into the flight, I am shooting over the pilot's shoulder, camera trained on the instrument panel, when the confused compass starts behaving erratically and spinning like a top—we are flying over the Magnetic Pole.

Soon, we have sight of the team, and after a couple of circuits for aerial filming and photography, we bounce along the 'runway'. It is a mild -20°C, the sun is shining, and there's no wind. Still, to Dave's annoyance, each plane must leave one engine running—not ideal for his sound. Everyone disembarks, and there's much excitement, greetings and toasts, followed by a flurry of interviews and photo opportunities, flag-planting and waving. We shoot observational footage of it all. Then comes the most cringeworthy, embarrassing moment of my professional life. Following strict instructions from Simon N, I have to ask the guys to harness up their sledges, don their skis and backpacks and reenact their moment of arrival at the pole. They begrudgingly oblige. It is not a fine performance.

Frostbitten, exhausted and joyous, Robert and the team board the aircraft along with what remains of the heavy kit they have dragged and carried across the Arctic ice, ridges and leads. I have a few minutes for my own 'gloriously idle moment'.

I am in awe of my surroundings. The stark beauty of this pristine wilderness moves me deeply. It brings home the importance of mankind's responsibility to protect our fragile world. The planet will survive in some form for billions of years, but how long will it be habitable for humankind? Thirty-five years have passed since that moment. Despite endless political posturing and rhetoric on environmental issues, little has been done, and much has been lost.

3

The Beginning

Rewind twenty-six years to 1966. School had not been my forte and, at the age of seventeen, my hard-won four 'O' level GSEs were not going to launch me into a conventional career for a middle-class private school boy. (It was twenty-five years later when my son was assessed that I had myself tested and was found to be dyslexic.)

Many a similar memoir would lead with something like: "At the age of ten, my granny gave me a Box Brownie camera, and I had an epiphany." Not in my case. Photography was my mother's idea. She felt I had an artistic flair, but my draughtsmanship abilities were basic. I didn't know one end of a camera from the other, but this was the mid-sixties; London was swinging and the world's fashion centre. Photographers such as Brian Duffy, David Bailey, and Terrance Donovan had rock star status. It sounded like a pretty cool idea.

Extraordinarily, my father, an able salesman, accompanied me to my first interview and did most of the talking. He played the 'Jewish' card. I got the job at Jeff Vickers Photography as a £5 per week gopher (go-for) and general dogsbody in a thriving advertising studio in the heart of Soho. I absorbed some basics of studio photography and the darkroom, along with tea making, floor washing, tidying and errand running (on a 50cc moped—a great thrill). Perks were the use of lower-end camera equipment and out-of-hours access to the studios and dark rooms. One weekend, I took home a 35mm camera and an out-of-date roll of Kodak Tri X film and photographed my best friend Greg, an aspiring folk musician. I sat him on a stool and carefully positioned a free-standing mirror from my parents' room. Lit by a single naked 100W bulb hanging from my bedroom ceiling and, using an exposure of about a quarter of a second, I took a few handheld shots of him strumming his guitar. I had little technical understanding of the finer points of photography. Despite the long exposure that would normally require a tripod, miraculously, one negative was sharp with correctly exposed highlights. Fifty years later, the resulting moody shot, neg-digitised and cleaned up in Photoshop, was included in a panel of fifteen 'Portraits of Artists' that won me an Associateship of the Royal Photographic Society.

Despite being a hopelessly shy young man, I plucked up the courage to invite a girl I met at a party to the studio for a session. We rendezvoused at Piccadilly Circus Station, and while chatting, she told me that the previous evening, she and her mother had been to see the new and controversial Michelangelo Antonioni movie *Blow Up*. The central character, played by David Hemmings, was a successful photographer, and there were explicitly sexual scenes, including a romp with a couple of visiting models. We did our proper and tasteful photo shoot, packed up and readied to leave. I secured the doors of the penthouse studio complex, and we took the lift down to the lobby, only to discover we were locked inside the building. The rag-trade premises below us assumed they had been the last to leave. One can only imagine what was going through Mum's mind when she received a phone call from her daughter saying she was locked in with the photographer! I sheepishly called Jeff; he contacted the police, who had access to a set of keys, and, in due course, a bobby arrived. With a 'wink wink, nudge nudge' look in his eye, he let us out.

One of the company's clients was *Penthouse* magazine, the UK's answer to *Playboy*. It was mainly darkroom work on editorial stories and technical layout stuff. Their 'glamour' shoots were usually shot on location, but this was the facility they used on the rare occasion they required a studio. It would be a closed set and, as some sort of rite of passage, my first assisting job was on such a shoot. The beautiful naked model had an all-over body tattoo of a fox hunt with the potential prey escaping down a hole. My role was to shift studio flash units, load and change Hasselblad film magazines, and warm Polaroid test shots under my armpit to accelerate the self-processing, all the while attempting to hide my blushes and to act blasé.

To supplement my income, I earned twelve shillings and sixpence (62½ p) per show, working backstage at the iconic Golders Green Hippodrome, initially as a stagehand and later as a lighting technician. The theatre was among the biggest in the UK and specialised in lavish variety shows and pantomimes, meaning there was much in the way of sophisticated stagecraft and dramatic lighting. It had been known for a while that the theatre would be closing in 1968, so there had been no attempt to upgrade any lighting equipment; consequently, there was all this wonderful old heavy-duty hardware. The 'Grand Master' sixty-eight-channel lighting console was a magnificent specimen of Edwardian mechanical engineering with rows of gleaming throw switches, levers, valves and wheels. A complicated cross-fade lighting cue could involve presetting several locking devices. The senior operator would spin the shiny brass wheel at the right speed, causing each linked fader to move to a precise predestined position. At the same time, his number two (me) would be sat on a stool manipulating up to four other faders using hands and feet.

My favourite role, though, was that of follow-spot operator. The 'limes' room was high up at the back of the auditorium. Inside were three enormous carbon-arc beasts. I would insert two carbon rods and throw the high-voltage DC power switch to ignite my lamp before the show. Looking through a densely filtered peephole, I would tweak the metal knobs to manoeuvre the rods until they touched. That would strike the arc, and as I slowly drew the heated tips apart, the carbon vaporised to produce a dazzlingly bright light. Throughout the show, I continuously made adjustments to keep the shape of the spotlight circular. In front of the arc-unit shutter was a massive lens, and in front of that, the iris and a set of framed colour gels, gobos and effects, operated by a row of levers. There was a soft-edged pink spot for the fairy godmother and a flickering hard-edged green one for the wicked witch. The other operator and I would align our spots by projecting them onto the luxuriant red velvet proscenium curtains before the auditorium opened to the public. Despite the extractor hoods above each lamp, the room would get baking hot; our work clothes were shorts only, whatever the weather outside. To amuse ourselves, we would occasionally swing the lamps one-eighty degrees, point them through the window and spotlight some poor, bewildered soul picking his nose at the bus stop outside Golders Green Station. I would encounter similar carbon-arc technology a few years later in the form of 'Brute' lamps on the set of the Hollywood blockbuster *A Bridge Too Far*.

Working in the theatre entitled me to join the trade union NATTKE, the National Association of Theatrical Television and Kine Employees, which, in turn, enabled me to accept freelance work from their employment list. Hence, my introduction to the world of television. I had one day's work as a props assistant at the Thames TV studios in Euston, where much of the live daytime TV was shot. I was greeted with grunts by the staff prop gang and instructed to keep a low profile. There was much hanging out in the crew room, drinking cups of tea and reading the tabloids. The idea was to do the minimum amount of work and make sure that what little was done was done during the designated lunch hour so you could claim an additional 'no lunch break' allowance. I sneaked onto the studio floor as often as possible to absorb the atmosphere and get some small insight into what was going on.

Today was Thames Television's first regional news magazine programme. It was hosted by Eamonn Andrews, the famous frontman of *This is Your Life*. The floor manager announced, "Going live in five!" As I recall, the only instruction I received from the prop master all day was, "You see those two red chairs; you see those two black tape crosses on the floor—chairs on crosses." What he neglected to tell me was that Eamonn gets the swivel chair so that he can turn to camera to talk to the viewers, and the guest gets the fixed one. Don't think I need to spell out the end of the story.

After a year at Jeff Vickers Photography, I launched myself onto the market as a freelance camera assistant, working for various studios and individuals and in multiple genres—advertising, high fashion, catalogue fashion, catalogue products, room sets and cars. I worked for many photographers varying from mediocre to brilliant, but the pinnacle had to be a few extraordinary weeks with Norman Parkinson in 1972. He was the quintessential English eccentric. He lived on the tropical island of Tobago, making annual work trips to London and New York. Over six-feet-five inches tall, debonair, witty, charming, flamboyantly attired and sporting a now grey handlebar moustache, he cut a commanding figure. But more importantly, he was a photographic genius. He had revolutionised portrait and fashion photography in the 1950s and was still at the top of the game. As the Photographer Royal, two of his assignments that year were Princess Anne's twenty-first birthday portraits—she had never looked so glamorous—and an in-camera double exposure of HRH Queen Elizabeth & Prince Philip to grace their Silver Wedding Anniversary postage stamp.

He sent me on a delivery errand, pedantically detailing every single step from the spot where I stood in the Savile Row studio to the recipient's desk in *Vogue* magazine's head office in Hanover Square—a familiar route to me. That same afternoon, 'the master painter with light' requested me to rig the studio with an evenly illuminated white backdrop, a backlight and a key-light 'brolly' for a model's portfolio shoot. He came in, sat cross-legged on the floor wearing his pearl-studded Kashmiri wedding cap and meditated for a few minutes. He then positioned the girl in front of the motor-drive Hasselblad that I had set up on a tripod, with the exposure and focus settings that I had calculated and, engaging only with her, fired off the first two rolls of film without even looking through the camera.

A Comex loo stop

Most of my generation recall watching the Apollo 11 moon landing live on TV—why can't I? Oh yes, I was trundling over rough, pot-holed roads through Yugoslavia (when such a country existed) in a packed short-wheel-base bus with my new friends and enough loo rolls strung up beneath the heaving luggage racks to satisfy twenty-five folk for three months. It was 1969, and five hundred young people from twenty UK university towns set off in twenty suitably adapted Duple buses on an extraordinary 16,000-mile overland drive to Delhi, beyond and back. The expedition was called 'Comex 3'. The patron was Prince Philip, and it was the idealistic and ambitious brainchild of one Lieutenant Colonel Lionel Gregory, a friend of India's President Nehru. He was promoting a future where barriers of culture, religion, race and inequality had no place. By bringing young people from across the globe together, Nehru and the Colonel hoped to encourage a society in which there would be greater mutual understanding, friendship and peaceful cooperation among people of all nations.

Somehow, my two best buddies, Greg Parfitt and Pat

The Beginning

Townley, and I passed the selection process. Pat joined the Norwich contingent as he was a student at Norwich Art School, and Greg and I were on the London bus. Each contingent needed to be self-sufficient, so a variety of skills were required. Training courses were arranged for HGV drivers, navigators, mechanics, radio operators, medics, cooks, quartermasters, etc. No course for me—I was to be the expedition photographer.

Many months of preparation followed—fundraising, route planning, logistics, and writing and rehearsing our cultural offerings. London's was street cries, essentially the "Who Will Buy" scene from the musical *Oliver*, and a selection of songs from the progressive 'hippy' musical *Hair*, in which my guitar and I played a significant role. I must say that some other contingents made more weighty contributions, such as scenes from Shakespeare's plays, traditional dancing, and classical recitals.

This trip was a profound experience for everyone involved. The conditions were harsh at times, but we all had a glimpse of otherworldly lifestyles and travelled through countries that have no overland access to today. We crossed from Europe to Asia by boarding the Bosphorus ferry, as the bridge had not yet been built. We drove from Turkey through Iran and Afghanistan, via the Kabul Gorge and the tribal, lawless Khyber Pass, where we were under strict instructions to lock the bus doors and not to stop under any circumstances (five years later, I was to return and get a closer look). Then we continued through Pakistan, over the Murree Hills and on to India.

We were a bunch of young, largely middle-class Brits on our first big adventure, speeding through the East. Hence, interactions with the locals were on a pretty superficial level, but I found the Afghans to be the most intriguing people. They were proud and dignified, friendly and helpful. Nevertheless, it would be unwise to get on anybody's wrong side. We were advised that should the worst occur and we were to be involved in an accident, whatever happens, do not stop to offer help, or you could well be lynched—'an eye for an eye'.

There were only a few places en route where we were all expected to meet up. Each bus was independent and, theoretically, within radio distance of the bus in front and behind. There were reception parties and cultural exchanges in which to participate. Memorably, a Tehran sports stadium was one such venue. We parked the buses in a big circle. We pitched our tents in the most sophisticated of many alternative configurations, a large traditional-style ridge tent with an open frame in the middle into which we drove the bus. This system was deemed the most secure and a convenient way to separate the sexes (by parking a bus in between?).

On reaching Delhi, there was a full convoy drive-through and a grand reception, where Nehru gave a welcome address. The twenty contingents made camp in a large park, and thousands of visitors came. Concerts, performances, and cultural exchanges were organised, and the press and TV were out in force. It was a great success.

Delegations were encouraged to briefly visit other universities in the region. Arguably a step removed from the Comex spirit, a handful of individuals took this opportunity to do their own thing. My girlfriend Sue, from the Bristol bus, and I took a ride with the Exeter crowd as far as Agra to see the stunning, white marble Taj Mahal and on to the captivating 'Pink City' of Jaipur with its rose-coloured buildings, Red Fort, opulent palaces, and intricately decorated temples. From there, we made our own way to Bombay (now Mumbai) by train. It was a twenty-six-hour ride, and we took a third-class sleeper—an experience in itself. The 'sleeper' bit was a plywood-hinged shelf in a communal carriage packed with individuals, families and livestock. We were the centre of much interest, especially Sue, who was a novelty with her blonde hair and fair skin. We enjoyed some fascinating interactions with our fellow travellers but were also subjected to some very disapproving looks when we shared our bunk to sleep. In town, we booked into a hotel as a married couple. We handed over our passports, and the manager challenged the fact that our surnames differed. Generally, I am not one to fib, but I found myself backed into a corner and saying that we had just married and hadn't had time to update Sue's passport. I breathed a sigh of relief, happy that the awkwardness was over. That is, until an hour later, when we entered the dining room to a standing ovation for the newlyweds!

I was both thrilled and daunted by the responsibility of visually documenting the expedition. I carried my two second-hand Nikon F camera bodies, one for colour and the other for monochrome, plus three lenses. Kodak was a sponsor and supplied us with large quantities of film. I dutifully covered as much as I could. The film cassettes were regularly shipped back to the UK for processing and used for newspaper articles, general PR, and the monthly magazine. Regrettably, all those transparencies and negatives have been lost to time.

Fifty years later, in 2019, there was a grand reunion in London. With an expedition to my attic almost as challenging as Comex itself, I dug out a folder with black and white fifteen by twelve-inch prints that had been used in an exhibition shortly after our return. They were grubby, yellow and creased, so I rephotographed the images, applied my twenty-first-century Photoshop skills and revived them for an Apple Keynote presentation and a booklet for the event. Looking at them with fresh eyes, I think that maybe my mum was right, and I did have an eye for a picture.

I met someone who had worked as a cruise shipboard photographer, and the idea appealed to me, so I investigated how to go about it. I visited a company called Marine Photo Services, a Colchester-based firm that serviced the industry. Nothing immediately, but in due course, the call came, and I was to be a 'Number 3' on the Greek-owned cruise ship *Queen Frederika*, plying the Mediterranean. 'Number 2' was a mild-mannered chap who, after a few months, had something akin to a nervous breakdown brought on by overwork and bullying from 'Number 1'. He was a charming slave driver who did minimum work and maximum womanising as well as creaming off the profits, which, in turn, negatively affected our commission. He got a bad ulcer, so within a few months, I rose to the dizzying heights of 'Number 1', and my support crew were flown out to meet the ship.

I had compromised my hippy-style persona with a smart uniform during the day and a dinner jacket in the evenings. We had officer status, and we were free to mingle with passengers and use their facilities (e.g., bars, dining room, loungers, and swimming pool). Not that we had much time for frivolities; the work was arduous, and the conditions in the two darkrooms left much to be desired. Unlike today, the passengers had no instant access to their holiday photos, and those they took would not be seen for at least a week after their return. There was a likelihood that many would 'not come out', so the desirability of our professionally taken, card-mounted colour prints was high. This had to be exploited to the full—lifeboat drill shots, deck shots, dining room shots, gangway shots, bar shots, tour shots and the big one: the captain's cocktail party.

Two of us would be poised with our Rolleiflex TLR cameras and Courtney Courier flash guns (with their smart leather enclosed power pack, housing two massive 240V disposable batteries) to snap each passenger shaking hands with the skipper. When the first had shot his twelve frames, he would speedily reload while the other took over. That was just the start. We had fifty rolls of exposed film. First, they had to be loaded onto spirals in total darkness (nine to a rack) and go through a six-tank process, washed, hung to dry, and then each roll and frame manually numbered. Every negative went through the very basic enlarger—no filter wheels, just a tray in which to insert colour correction gels, then exposed onto individual sheets of paper with the corresponding number on the back. They, in turn, went through a five-tank process, one hundred and twenty sheets at a time, dried on a rotary glazer and put on the display boards outside the dining room for sale at breakfast time the following morning.

The trick for controlling colour balance and exposure in bulk colour printing was a high degree of consistency at every stage. This vitally included chemical temperatures and a steady power supply, neither of which the ageing Frederika could offer. The voltage was unpredictable, and temperature control relied on three taps—hot (very), tepid and refrigerated. Our tanks were in large sinks, and these taps gave us control over the chemicals' temperature. This experience would not develop my creative photography, but it certainly was a great lesson in colour control, speedy working and discipline.

The final cruise of the season returned to Southampton,

where I planned to finish, but I was tempted back with an offer of a 'command' for a further six months, sailing to Sydney, Australia and then cruising the Pacific. So, after a couple of days visiting my parents in Sussex and meeting my brother's new American fiancée, I was back in port overseeing the restocking of photographic materials for another voyage. The *Queen Fred* blasted her whistle as she left the quayside with great ceremony, music and streamers. She was crammed to capacity with 'Ten Pound Poms'. This was towards the end of the era when Australia actually wanted (white) immigrants.

The Beginning

The Commonwealth funded the passage, apart from the £10 processing fee, for those in search of a new life in the Antipodes. These were not going to be good customers for our expensive photos.

No longer cruising in circles around the benign Med, I had been advised to storm rig the darkrooms—a job for tomorrow. I woke in the middle of the first night as the ship pitched and rolled heavily in a force-nine gale. I got up and staggered to the dark rooms to find the door jammed. There was a sort of unused serving hatch that I forced open, and I looked through to see the enlarger all smashed up on the deck and a dozen, one-hundred-sheet boxes of colour photographic paper floating around in a turbulent pool of spilt chemicals—not a good start.

These were not the biggest seas we would encounter. Rounding the Cape of Good Hope at the southern tip of the African continent, where the Atlantic meets the Indian Ocean, we experienced an extreme swell with a very long wavelength. These are known as Cape Rollers. The *Queen Fred* was steaming parallel and, if you were inside, you were barely aware of the motion but, if you looked through a window or porthole, you would see nothing but sea for about twenty seconds, then the horizon would appear for a short while followed by nothing but sky. On another occasion, when we had reached the Pacific, we rode the edge of a typhoon (known as a hurricane or cyclone in other parts of the world). Virtually all passengers, crew and officers were extremely seasick, and the decks were empty. I have been blessed with very good sea legs, and it was like a fairground ride to me. I staggered to the forward observation deck and delighted in the experience of watching the massive waves crashing over the forecastle, feeling this large ship being tossed around, and marvelling at the power of nature. In retrospect, while I was in the observation lounge obliviously revelling in the spectacle of the storm, Captain Papadopoulos and his crew were likely overworking their worry beads on the bridge directly above.

When the ship was built back in 1926 as *SS Malono*, she was the pride of the Matsonian Line, carrying a few hundred passengers in luxury around the West Coast of the USA and the Pacific. By this time, she had changed hands and been laid up and refitted a few times. She was now run by the Greek shipping company, Chandris, and carrying a couple of thousand hopefuls to their new lives. She was definitely suffering from old age. Stuff was forever breaking down, and unknown to the passengers, there were frequent fires in the engine room.

After offloading the human cargo in Sydney, we were back in the business of cruising. This was more like it—while folks back home were enduring a bitter winter, we enjoyed glorious summer weather and travelled to interesting ports such as Aukland, Wellington, Perth, Tonga, Apia, and Pago Pago. In Singapore, immigration would not let me off the ship because my hair was too long.

There's a saturation point for passengers' desire for photos, so the three-week cruises sold similarly to the ten-day Med cruises. The pressure was off, and we could relax a little.

Shipboard lifestyle for the non-Greek, officer-level crew was different to any other I can think of. Our gang consisted of musicians, entertainers, dancers, junior pursers, shop managers and assistants, hairdressers and we photographers. Many were aboard for the experience and adventure; others were 'lifers' who were on for the security and the duty-free booze. After all, you were fed, clothed and accommodated. As long as you did your job and were not seen to be

The Beginning

misbehaving, everything else was looked after. Work was hard and creatively ungratifying for the photographers, but it was lucrative—a new experience for me—and we had a good social life. There was enough behind-the-scenes drama for a soap. In fact, a couple of years later, when at film school, I tried to get a below-decks observational documentary off the ground, but for some reason, I failed in the negotiations for access!

Back on terra firma, the UK population was in confusion. There were no longer 12d (old pence) to the shilling nor 20 shillings (240d) to the pound, but 100 new pence (each worth 2½d) to the pound. British currency had switched from imperial to decimal!

I returned to freelancing. Some assisting, some run-of-the-mill corporate shooting, weddings and the like. I had to think seriously about my future. I looked around at who was thriving. Some very talented photographers were doing well and making names for themselves, and some mediocre ones were doing equally well and doing even better. There were many very gifted photographers falling by the wayside. Why was this? Networking. That's what it's about—chatting with the right people, making conversation, selling yourself, ensuring that you are in the right place at the right time, laying on the charm, being outgoing, hail-fellow-well-met. All attributes that I lacked.

I had been considering a move to cinematography for a while but needed to figure out how to go about it, so I did some research.

4

Film School

It was 1973. Two years previously, the National Film School had taken over the recently closed Beaconsfield Film Studios. It had generous funding from the film industry and the Ministry for the Arts. Under the stewardship of the founding director, Colin Young, it was destined to become an educational centre of excellence. If I was going to make the move, this was where I needed to be. There were approximately four hundred applicants for twenty-five places that year. It was a post-graduate level course, and I had graduated from nowhere. I submitted a portfolio of my photography and a ten-minute 'standard form' action drama screenplay, which, fortunately for me, they lost. Although the panel was friendly and welcoming, I felt intimidated at the interview and far outside my comfort zone. After a couple of months, the inevitable letter arrived: "We are sorry to inform you…" It also stated that I was twenty-ninth on the list and that they would be in touch if enough people pulled out. I heard nothing more.

I carried on scraping a freelance living supplemented with more backstage theatre work, specifically on *Behind the Fridge* at the Cambridge Theatre with Peter Cook and Dudley Moore (the name was a pun on *Beyond the Fringe*, a groundbreaking satirical review that had catapulted them to stardom ten years earlier). Now, they were not on talking terms off-stage and trying to befuddle each other on-stage. It was an open set, and my role was to help effect scene changes, wearing grey overalls and a bowler hat. This was interspersed with crew trips to the fire exit to smoke spliffs. When it closed, I moved to *The Max Bygraves Show* at the Victoria Palace Theatre. During a long set with no cues, we would be invited up to the flies, where the fly-men projected silent Super8mm porn films onto a sheet. Most memorably, one involving a girl and a donkey accompanied by Max's big hit, "You Need Hands", drifting up from the stage below.

In an act of desperation, I drove out to Beaconsfield and wandered into the film school common room/canteen, where I bumped into Colin Young queuing for his lunch. To my delight, he remembered me and my photography. He offered me a place on the spot. Apparently, two of the chosen students had dropped out, and for reasons best known to itself, the school hadn't contacted anyone on the shortlist. I was over the moon, though I felt sorry for the three others who had been ahead of me on the list—a lesson in being a little pushy. Also, these were the 'good old days' when the government not only paid for your further education tuition fees but also gave you a maintenance grant sufficient, in my case, to flat share in NW London, feed myself and run an old banger of a car—how things have changed.

My mind was made up. I was moving into the world of television, so had no need to carry on freelancing. I had a time gap to fill, so I reconnected with Marine Photo Services and was offered a six-month contract. I spent a short while on the P&O cruise ship the *SS Aronsay*, and then I found myself back aboard the good old *Queen Frederika*, which was now certified as only suitable for cruising the Mediterranean. This was my means to accumulate a little cash and breathe some sea air before becoming a student for the next three years.

I fell for Chrissie, a delightful 'pursarette'. She was petite and cute, with dark curly hair and a turned-up nose. We developed a beautiful relationship, only slightly marred by the fact that the staff captain (number two on the ship) had the hots for her—not the officer to be on the wrong side of. Fortunately, the Greek men did have a code of honour regarding such things. My contract came to an end, and Chrissie's had another six months to run. We sat outside a café in Cannes, saying our farewells and agreed that she would move in with me in London at the end of her stint.

Film school was quite a culture shock. Discussion and conversations were laden with intellectual rhetoric that went over my head. Party politics was not uppermost on my agenda, but I suppose mine could be labelled left-of-centre. The mood here was far-left Trotskyist, and the Socialist Workers Party had a heavy presence. I felt like an outsider. These things aside, the facilities, equipment and calibre of the faculty were excellent.

Today, it is known as the National Film and Television School (NFTS) and is considered by many to be the world's top film school. Its alumnus includes many names renowned throughout the film and TV industry. The courses are highly structured and specialised.

In '73, it was new, vibrant and innovative and had little

apparent structure. This 'open curriculum' was Young's philosophy, building on his previous role as chairman of the School of Theatre, Film and Television at UCLA in California. Teaching or, more accurately, 'learning' happened in open-ended conversations, the discussion of ideas and guidance from high-calibre industry professionals.

I spent months going in circles, wondering when someone was going to teach me something. What was organised was a 16mm film exercise where we were each given a couple of 400ft rolls of stock to make a short film. This was to see if we had a basic idea of camera and editing techniques. I buddied up with my new friend, Paul Miller. He directed, and I shot. I went to the camera store and took out an Arri BL, a couple of lamps and a 'sun-gun' battery light. We filmed *Pork Chop* on location in the Wall's Pig Improvement Centre. It included a discreet sequence in a slaughterhouse and a graphically shot scene of semen being collected—did you know that boars have an extremely long corkscrew-shaped penis?

Assuming that the bigger of the two batteries was for the camera, I shot the whole film using the 30-volt sun-gun battery instead of the 12-volt one. Impressively, the external crystal unit, designed to run the camera at precisely 25 fps to keep it in sync with the audiotape, kept to speed without blowing up the unit or the camera. Paul cut the material to the soundtrack of speeches by the Tory Prime Minister, Edward Heath, and to the music of the Beatles' "Piggy Song."

The heads of department were all eminent in their fields. In charge of the script department was Stephen Frears, who was already established as a movie director and went on to become one of Britain's leading independent filmmakers. Head of Camera was Charles Stewart, a top documentary cameraman. If six or more students got together and requested a specific type of workshop, the HoD would arrange it. The school's reputation was such that the cream of the industry would be happy to oblige. I was in a group of budding cinematographers eager for a lighting workshop, and Charles came up trumps with Ossie Morris. He was a prominent Director of Photography in the UK and Hollywood. We gathered around a 35mm Steenbeck (a flatbed editing and viewing machine), and he talked us through every shot in *Oliver!* and *Fiddler on the Roof* (for which he won an Oscar). These were all massive lighting rigs, the likes of which we were unlikely to encounter in the near future, but we were spellbound.

There were plenty of other workshops, screenings, and discussions, but, for me, learning was primarily achieved by working in a variety of roles on other students' productions, and there were always mentors at hand to help out.

The school had two large sound stages (soundproof studios) and a MOS stage (for mute filming), as well as scenery workshops, etc. There was a well-equipped editing block, sound dubbing studio and production offices. Let's not forget the equipment stores, brimming with camera, lighting, sound and grip equipment (camera dollies, mounts, tracks, cranes, etc.). Also, there was money. I recall the production budget figure was around £7,000 per student for the duration. Considering that all in-house facilities were free and that external suppliers such as Kodak and film processing labs gave generous discounts, that sum could go a very long way.

I had missed Chrissy so much and was thrilled that she was on her way. She stopped off at her parents' house in Kent for a few days, and we arranged for me to meet her off the train in London. Excitedly, I got into my battered old Cortina and headed for St. Pancras Station. We embraced at the ticket gate, both flushed with the anticipation of making a life together. I grabbed her bags, and we headed for the car. Driving towards home in Willesden Green, the first thing she said was that she didn't expect me to have this sort of car. I didn't give the comment much thought.

We arrived at the Victorian terraced house where I shared a first-floor flat with my good friend, Bill. It was tiny—basically two rooms. I led her through the front door, which opened directly into Bill's bedroom, which doubled as a kitchen. He was lounging on his mattress on the floor. He greeted Chrissy with his charming smile. We walked through to my bedroom, which doubled as the lounge. There was a small two-seat couch facing the door with a TV set tucked behind it that could only be watched when the door was closed. The bathroom, which we shared with another flat, was out of the front door and up a couple of steps. "Don't forget to take the front door key with you." Apparently, love is not blind. It hadn't struck me that the Colin she had 'fallen' for was a smartly turned out, monied, cool guy, not the scruffy, strapped, and hippyish student that I now was. After a couple of months, she ran away to sea.

Paul had created a film noir screenplay from a Jorge Luis Borges short story, "Death and the Compass", and I was the camera op. Set in 1940s Borgasia, a fictional South American Town, Hasidic rabbis are murdered. Detective Llonrot follows clues in mystical Hebrew texts that lure him into a deadly trap laid by Red Scharlach, his master criminal nemesis. Llonrot was played by Nigel Hawthorn, who was an established theatre actor but with minimal film or TV exposure. Within a few years, he was to become an internationally loved household name as Sir Humphrey Appleby in *Yes Minister*, followed by a sparkling career in film, TV and on stage, plus a knighthood for his efforts.

Nigel Hawthorne in character   *Paul and I at work*

It was my first drama shoot. We shot 16mm black and white in the grand-looking foyer of the London Polytechnic, on location around Beaconsfield and London, and in the studio. This was my chance to master the 'wheels'. The Warrall head is a marvel of precision engineering used mainly on feature films and commercials with 35mm and 70mm cameras. It sits atop a tripod or dolly and is a geared head with several settings. You pan with a wheel on the left and tilt with another at the back—can't be that hard. I was advised to practise by painting a large figure eight onto a studio flat and to trace it while looking through a camera viewfinder. It's a bit like simultaneously rubbing your tummy and head with circular movements and changing direction with one. I practised this for many hours until I mastered it.

The very first set-up of the shoot is a complicated tracking shot. A period limo pulls up in London's Regent Street. Protected by his military-style security guards, The Tetrarch of Galilee and his posse of rabbis disembark and stride through the revolving doors. Develop from a wide to a medium shot and follow them through the foyer. I oversee the time-consuming job of rigging straight steel tracks to pass through the glass door next to the revolving ones, followed by two opposing curved sections to bring the camera closer and back to the parallel. The Chapman dolly with the Worrall head fitted is lifted onto the tracks, and on goes the Arriflex 16BL camera with a 12mm Zeiss Distagon lens. The focus puller and I take our seats on the dolly for a walk-through. It works well as we go past the revolving door; we hit the curve, and suddenly, the camera was facing backwards with a window view of contemporary Regent Street traffic. I try to compensate by frantically spinning the pan wheel, by which time I am back on the straight, pointing 180 degrees towards the lights and crew. I learnt three things at this moment:

1. Only use a curved track in one direction at a time, 2. Leave the 'wheels' to the specialist operators, 3. You are unlikely ever to be asked to shoot a figure of eight!

We dreamt up plenty of interesting and more successful dramatic scenarios. Paul wanted a shot as the cops got into a jeep, with the camera tracking past them into a carnival poster that seamlessly burst into life, thus transitioning into the next sequence. We had filmed footage of the dragon dance at the Chinatown New Year celebrations. I took a single frame from the negative to the darkroom and enlarged it to create the poster. There was no way to align the end of our tracking shot with enough precision for a smooth transition, so we shot the whole thing in reverse, with the camera upside down. We started on the poster and tracked back, revealing our three actors climbing backward out of the car and walking backward as the camera moved. Paul flopped the print in the edit, and the illusion actually worked. Such were the days of analogue.

The final sequence was of cryptic dialogue followed by Llonrot's death sprawled across a railway track. The penultimate shot culminated the chess game motif we had been using. Having painted a giant chequered board onto the floor of Studio 1, we precariously rigged the camera high in the lighting gantry, pointing vertically down as he is shot dead by Scharlach. Then the final shot, Scharlach, gun in hand, leaves the spreadeagled Llonrot and walks down the centre of the single-track railway, saying in voiceover: *"The next time I kill you, I promise you that maze consisting of a single straight line."* The camera tracks back, accelerating until he is a distant dot. This was achieved by half a dozen helpers pushing a railway cart carrying me and the focus puller. I kept yelling, "Faster! Faster!" The poor guys eventually collapsed in a heap, but the shot was in the can. "It's a wrap."

5

Garden of the Emperors

My aspiration at the time was to shoot ethnographic documentaries along the lines of *Disappearing World*, a prolific TV series that focussed on specific traditional tribal communities. I was eager to find something for my graduation project to reflect that. Brian Winston, the senior tutor, was a renowned journalist and academic within the media and documentary world. He was my mentor and together we looked for a suitable project. We discovered an expedition that was being planned by the Cambridge World Wildlife Study Centre (CWWSC), so I set off to Cambridge University to meet the instigators Dewar Donithorne-Tate and Jeremy Robinson. They told me of their plan to drive a twelve-person team overland to Kashmir in NW India, there to study the status and range of the critically endangered Hangul Stag. Ok, It was not ethnography, but it ticked other boxes, and I was thrilled when they agreed to include me. It was in their interest to have a film, and there was an added incentive when the film school offered the use of one of their two long-wheel-based Land Rovers. I was given a choice as to which vehicle to take and, in my ignorance, chose the more powerful and sophisticated Series 3, six-cylinder petrol model rather than the basic diesel 'tank'. Big mistake!

In due course, I met with everyone else, and much planning and preparation ensued. Their newly serviced and adapted Bedford van and the film school Land Rover were loaded to the gunwales and beyond with two and a half tonnes of camping, scientific and filming equipment, vehicle spares and food. We had rations for twelve people for ninety-nine days, packaged in three-day boxes. The loaded roof rack added a metre to the clearance height of the Land Rover.

Setting off on my second overland drive to India in the space of five years, I was already concerned as the vehicle was so top-heavy that it was swaying from side to side, making it tricky to steer. And this was before we reached the cross-channel ferry. Aggravated by rough roads in Yugoslavia and northern Greece, the steering developed a nasty shudder at all speeds between 30 and 40mph. It was a severe problem that would intermittently dog us all the way to Kashmir despite our two very competent engineers, Jeremy and Rick, dismantling and reassembling the steering and the front suspension a few times—once with assistance from a local Land Rover guru. It was permanently fixed ten weeks later in Rawalpindi, Pakistan, on our return journey, by a roadside mechanic with a big hammer. I won't bore the reader with a list of Land Rover woes, but the fact that I, a non-mechanic, have one phrase indelibly burnt on my brain to this day: 'phosphor bronze helical gear on the distributor drive shaft'.

We followed a similar route to that of Comex, but by now, the Bosphorus Bridge had been built. In fact, the team drove it three times. I wanted to film the mini convoy crossing from

Europe to Asia. So, I convinced my travel-weary companions to drop the team's postgraduate botanist, Kristina, and myself off at a suitable hilltop vantage point on the east side, drive back to the west and back again so I could film them crossing the Strait of Istanbul. We found a high vantage point some distance beyond, leaving plenty of time to rig the Arri ST and shoot wide shots of the impressive new bridge. In bright sunshine, pupils dilate, causing the image in the viewfinder to appear very dim. I changed to my longest lens as Kristina trained her binoculars on the stream of crossing traffic. Cellphones were yet to be invented, and we had no walkie-talkies, but the Land Rover had a bright orange hap covering the loaded roof rack so it would be easy to spot. Kristina saw the brilliant colour approaching the bridge. I lined up my shot with a composition that the vehicle would drive into, then panned with it. It was a tricky shot for a novice cameraperson to operate, and I was chuffed that it was working well. It became bigger in my frame as it advanced, but where was the blue Bedford van that should be right behind? That is when I realised that ours was not the only orange hap in town. We frantically searched for our vehicles, and I managed to grab a few usable seconds of material. There was no way I dared ask for a take-two. As it turned out, I used none of the outbound journey footage in the final cut.

The progress across Asia was both thrilling and gruelling in equal measure. The wonderful and varied sights, the contrasts in the landscape from the magnificence of the snow-capped Mount Ararat in Eastern Turkey, through Iran, the deserts of Afghanistan and the swamps in Pakistan. The people we encountered were so different in character, but poverty, to varying degrees, appeared endemic among the majority. Pre-revolution Tehran, in Iran, seemed to us an oasis of westernisation. We crossed the Alborz Mountain range, where the thinner air was a great relief, before descending to the hot and humid Caspian Sea coastal road. We travelled via the city of Mashad, with its sublime holy shrines, and onto the Afghan border, where we camped for the night. As at most border posts, there was a thorough investigation into all we were 'importing', especially camera gear and film stock. I had a Carnet de Passage, the internationally recognised, detailed customs document for temporary importation or transit, which customs officials love to plaster with rubber stamps. Invariably, there was an element of baksheesh to smooth negotiations.

As with my experience five years earlier, I loved Afghanistan. The bustling, dusty towns such as Herat and the proud demeanour of the people. Perhaps my youthful observations were coloured by the fact that, unlike other places on the trip, we weren't continuously stared at or pestered.

We sped through the vast desert with its one good straight road from east to west; half had been built by Russia, with asphalt, and the other half by America, with concrete—that's what you call advance planning! In this apparent wilderness, it was an ongoing mystery as to where the man and his two goats purposefully walking along the road had come from and to where he was going. It is tragic what history had in store for Afghanistan's future.

In the Hindu Kush mountains, the highway between Kabul and Jalalabad is considered one of the most dangerous in the world. On the Comex trip, I had taken a dramatic top shot of the bulk of our convoy descending the Kabul River Gorge, a 2000ft chasm with a narrow winding road that periodically disappeared into tunnels. A fantastic vista, but there was no way I would even suggest leaving me there to film and returning to pick me up, so I opted for putting the camera on a car window mount.

Now came our big adventure. The Khyber Pass, nestled in the mountains dividing present-day Afghanistan and Pakistan, often referred to as 'The Wild East'. It was known as the gateway to India (Pakistan only came into being after the Partition of India in 1947). As well as being a major trade route, it was a vital strategic location and a nightmare for the British colonial military.

With its footplates and roof rack, the Land Rover was perfect for locals to hitch a ride. At one stage, we had a dozen kids sharing our progress, and I could barely see through the windscreen. It was a lawless place, where smuggling, gun running, drug trafficking and illegal money changing were the norm and carrying a gun was a man's birthright.

Though leaving the comparative safety of our transport was not advised, the temptation was strong, and with two of us guarding from within each vehicle, we took turns to visit Landi Kotal. We walked into the bustling bazaar. The air was filled with the earthy fragrance of spices and sizzling street food. The sights and smells were intoxicating, and the atmosphere electrifying; maybe adrenaline had a part to play. Most of the men sported weapons and had bullet belts slung across their chests, and the women all wore burqas. We watched out for one another and protected our wallets and cameras carefully as we were being hounded from all directions to buy drugs, jewellery and all sorts. Our biologist, Fran, was subjected to hard sell on a silver handbag pistol. She resisted. I must say the foreign exchange rates were excellent. We then drove along the winding road past camel caravans, goat herders and mountain cliff faces plastered with old British military plaques.

In stark contrast, Pakistan was very green and swampy (the rainy season was upon us). The poverty and population density were very apparent. Through the flooded streets of Lahore, we literally had to part the mass of humanity and animals with the Land Rover bumpers as kids and beggars pleaded at the car windows. Onwards towards our final destination, we passed ornately painted trucks tightly packed with turbaned passengers.

One month and one day after leaving the UK, we drove the three-kilometre Jawahar Road Tunnel that connected the Jammu region with that of Kashmir. As we exited the noise and fumes of the tunnel, we were greeted by sweet, warm air and the faint sound of goat bells as we cruised along the road to Srinagar, the state capital.

At 5,200 feet (1,600 metres), the lakes of Srinagar and the Jhelum River that connects them were the historical waterborne section of the Himalayan caravan route. The British Raj popularised this stunningly beautiful area as a high-altitude escape from the oppressive summer heat and dust of the Indian plains. The area has had many euphemistic names, such as 'Garden of the Emperors' and 'Venice of the East'.

In the days of the Raj, many local Hanzi artisans adapted their boat-building skills to building palatial residential barges that would navigate the waters, man-propelled by long quant poles and offering luxurious accommodation. More recently, they had evolved into permanently moored craft due to a demand from a broader tourist demographic (predominantly Indian). As soon as we drove into town, we were mobbed by young men promoting their houseboats, some on mopeds, some cyclists hanging on to the Land Rover shouting ever-reducing deals. We ended up aboard the 'Khuroo Palace'. We each had a bedroom with an en-suite, and there was a dining room and a spacious lounge with a veranda looking onto the lake. The ornamentation and decoration were lavish, as is the Indian way, and the food was plentiful and pretty good. After five weeks of roughing it, this was a breath of fresh air (maybe not such a good metaphor, as the unsanitary plumbing left much to be desired). A constant stream of shikaris, the local wooden boats, came alongside, offering regional crafts and produce.

Being in Kashmir, one of the optional extras was hashish, and as I was the only group member with a predilection in that direction, I had just happened to have packed some rolling papers. As I recall, only Rick had dabbled, and despite it being 1974, the others were novices. I eagerly rolled up a five-skinner, lit it and passed it on. Tim, our quartermaster and cook, took a hefty drag and announced that it had no effect. Treating it as though it were an after-dinner cigar, he proceeded to sink his six-foot-five frame into an armchair and puffed his way through the whole thing while devouring an entire large bowl of Bombay mix. I rolled another.

The area was beautiful, and the local environment fascinated me. I would have to return and film some local everyday life.

After a couple of days of recuperation, tourism, and permit finalising, we set off for the Dachigam Wildlife Sanctuary, which used to be a hunting ground for maharajas and, later, the British Raj. On arrival, we were met and directed to our prearranged campsite. At the end of a very rough track, it was at the furthest point we could reach with the Land Rover; the Bedford had to be left further back. We arrived at a rickety footbridge over a river and parked up. On the other side was a large clearing that had been an area for workers' base camps for centuries. I say 'clearing'; in fact, it was chest high with now-wild marijuana. We set about it with machetes and, apart from a very small bag for personal use, lit a large bonfire and proceeded to erect our tents—all the while inhaling deeply.

Up until the end of British rule in 1947, the Hangul stag had been highly prized, only second to the Indian tiger, as the most royal of Indian game and, as such, great effort was put into making sure they were plentiful. They were now a protected species in this, their last habitat. But it was being shared with the Gujar nomads, who herd buffalo. Buffalo are traditionally valley feeders and cumbersome in this hilly environment, churning up the ground and encouraging soil erosion. Similarly, the Bakarwal nomads with their goats and sheep. These indigenous wanderers, a proud and rugged people, were being squeezed out of their traditional grazing grounds by encroaching 'civilisation'.

Passing near an encampment, we heard a shrieking child. On investigation, we became aware of a toddler being lowered onto the embers of a fire. A man was cauterising a nasty wound on his son's foot. Richard, our team medic, came to the rescue with our Western medicine, first aid and antibiotics. The family were very grateful and invited us for some tea. Today, London's fashionable tea rooms will serve you Kashmiri Chai, and I daresay it's delicious. This concoction of stewed local tea leaves, salt, and bicarbonate of soda was bright pink and hard to keep down. The short time spent interacting with this small family group in their modest, nomadic home environment was a humbling and memorable experience. As we bade our farewells, I snapped a photo of a beautiful young girl with an enigmatic smile. She looked straight down the lens. She has looked at me from all my living room walls ever since. She is my Mona Lisa.

Nomads were not the biggest problem for conservation. Within this government-sponsored sanctuary was a government-sponsored experimental sheep breeding project with well over 2,000 sheep. Supplement that with significant human activity and noisy dogs, it was startling all the wildlife. Gangs of grass cutters collected vast amounts of winter fodder that would otherwise feed Hangul and other wild animals. A conflict of interests. I filmed a sequence there.

On this trip, I had three close encounters with dangerous wildlife. Why was I up a dead tree with an axe? Naturally, I was gathering dry firewood. In the process, I disturbed a hornet's nest, and they were not happy. I fell to the ground before the swarm could engulf me, but one managed to sting me on the lip. There's some sort of tight membrane down the middle, and my lip swelled up like two balloons on either side. It caused agonising pain for some days, which was expertly alleviated by Gill, the team nurse.

The Arri camera, with a lens and a 400ft 'Micky Mouse ears' magazine attached, was lying on top of my sleeping bag. I lifted it to find a bright green viper coiled underneath, having a nap. I called for help and in charged the cavalry consisting of Richard and Tim armed with a fork-ended stick and a hammer. A battle of wits ensued, and the snake slithered its way into the gap between the tent and fly sheet. There was much to-ing, fro-ing and thrashing, but it eventually met a messy end. It spent the following week drying out on a rock—a gruesome trophy.

I was walking along the track on the other side of the bridge, dreaming of Marmite, when I rounded a bend and came face to face with an adult Himalayan Black Bear—maybe seven metres away. I had done my homework and knew that they could be highly aggressive: Stand your ground; you cannot outrun them. Speak in a soft, monotone voice and wave your arms slowly to let the animal know you are a human. So, I turned on my heels and ran as fast as I could! Fortunately, the bear had the same idea. He was as startled as I was. When my heart eventually stopped pounding, I thought, "There are bears around here. Maybe I can get some good shots." The following day, Richard and I set off with a jar of honey, smeared a couple of carefully chosen rocks and positioned ourselves and the camera with a long lens at a good, sheltered vantage point. After three days of nothing, we gave up. Have I got it wrong? Is it only Winnie the Pooh who can't resist honey?

Though I loved the great outdoors and operating in remote environments, I had no particular interest in filming wildlife, and it's a very specialised field, so I am happy to leave it to the specialists. That said, I was here for a purpose, and we hadn't yet encountered any Hangul. With help from porters, there were mini expeditions on foot to the higher slopes, and the only wild deer we saw and filmed were small in frame on distant hillsides. This was a testament to their rarity but not very gripping documentary material. I got close-up footage of a captive stag in a conservation enclosure and archive photos of dead stags, many with proud hunters posing with their kill. These I would rostrum back in the UK. I filmed birds, insects, flora and scenery. I shot team members going about their individual projects. Fran and Kristina were pressing undocumented flora and collecting seeds for a UK seed bank, and Rick collected soil samples on behalf of ICI antibiotics research. I wasn't well-equipped for synchronised sound, and the Arri ST was too noisy anyhow. I had a Nagra quarter-inch tape machine (the industry standard). I had a basic microphone kit and a new-fangled parabolic ultra-directional microphone for singling out specific birdsong. With assistance from other team members, I recorded 'wild' sound and atmosphere tracks. These I would cobble together in the cutting room at a later stage.

Though the expedition team was frustrated with the bureaucracy, they completed their habitat surveys and photographic records and succeeded in gathering sufficient information to report on their findings. With this data, they could initiate strategies for future improvements. I, on the other hand, had a rather weak documentary. I needed fresh material to give the story more context and to lift it visually.

As we were breaking camp in Dachigam, news came through that the Kashmir border with Ladakh, the Indian-administered Tibetan territory, had opened for the first time since Partition, and this was a unique opportunity to visit the region before it would be developed for tourism. How I was tempted, but if others were extending their trip by a week to take the two-day bus ride from Srinagar, this was my chance to spend some time filming the Jhelum River and Nagin and Dal Lakes.

Team members Sylvia, Tony, and I stayed behind. We hired a self-paddle shikara and spent a few days exploring the waterways. I did some filming from the shore and aboard a moving barge but shot mostly from our boat—long, slow tracking shots of life on the water and the banks. I fear it may be different today, but this was an otherworldly place. Most of local Hanzi life unfolded along the waterways. The people had strong features and weathered faces. Life was difficult but industrious. Some cultivated floating vegetable gardens, while others collected lotus seeds and leaves to feed their livestock. Shikaras and larger hand-propelled boats went about their business. Goats felt at home being paddled along the river in the narrow, punt-like crafts. A man irrigated his fields on the banks using an ingenious pivot and lever system. Nothing motorised could be seen anywhere. Rickety storehouses lined the water, and women laundered clothes while children played on the banks. Oblivious to the hubbub, brightly coloured kingfishers stood on their perches, watching for prey. The soundscape was equally remarkable; a blend of lively chatter, cocks crowing, children playing, paddles paddling, shikaras bouncing off each other as they plied the narrow channels, and the muezzin calling the faithful to prayer. It was a feast for the eyes and ears. Every direction I pointed the camera, there was magic. From my point of view, this material was much stronger than the story I was there to tell. Integrating it into the documentary will be a problem to face later.

The road trip back to the UK was a two-week dash, often driving through the night. Inevitably, all of us had suffered varying degrees of stomach problems. Early on the journey home, it was my turn to have a nasty one. A berth was made up for me behind the front seats of the Bedford, where I lay feeling sorry for myself. At one point, I roused from medicated slumber to a sight still vivid in my memory. It was a beautiful sunny day; the sky was an azure blue, and fluid yellow dunes stretched to the horizon. An Afghan horseman in immaculate, flowing white robes and headdress upon a dazzling white steed with equally flowing mane and tail galloped in slow motion across our path. I don't know to this day what was in that blue pill that Gill gave me.

6

Editing the Hangul Story

I don't understand how any cinematographer can hone his skills without some experience in the cutting room. I learnt more about camerawork in the edit suite than I did on the shoot—mainly from my mistakes. For example, how to reliably cover a sequence, how to frame shots so that they will cut together smoothly, how long to hold a static shot at each end of a pan, tilt or track, how to match eye-lines, how to match lighting and exposure. The list goes on.

At my disposal was a well-equipped cutting room, all the time I needed (a lot!) and the invaluable mentorship of Roger Crittenden, the head of editing. Thankfully, my rushes (the uncut work-prints) were technically acceptable. I invited the gang to sit through an eight-hour viewing in the film school theatre. When you are not used to it, all the wobbly bits, like when shooting the clapperboard, reframing and searching for focus, seem endless, and the controlled, useable bits seem fleeting. I shrank into my seat with embarrassment, though they seemed happy to see glimpses of themselves on the big screen. Note to self—never view uncut documentary rushes with people unfamiliar with the process.

Logging and marking up the material was a massive task. As a one-person operation, I did minimal paperwork in the field. All the audio was transferred to mag stock, which is 16mm wide magnetic tape with filmstock-like sprocket holes. This means the sound and picture are physically the same length and can be aligned and extended or shortened for sound overlaps, mixes, and fades. As the edit developed, all these bits of picture and sound could be cut up and taped back together as often as necessary.

I spent a few months juggling the material to make the story work, much of which was building the soundtrack. I had recorded too little on the trip, so I supplemented it with a selection of recordings from the massive BBC sound library, which came in the form of a stack of twelve-inch vinyl records. I was careful to keep all clips authentic to the location; a bird song could be a two-second recording of a tweet followed by a twenty-second verbal tag saying the species name, location, date of recording, and the tech spec. I chopped up these tiny lengths of magnetic film and assembled them on a dozen alternating parallel tracks, plus another with my atmosphere recordings to smooth the joins. On top of that, and a rare luxury on documentary films, I had three days of foley recording in the school's state-of-the-art dubbing studio, overseen by the head of sound, Tony Gurrin. This was a great deal of fun. I had broken the cut picture into a series of loops. They were laced up by the technicians in the projection booth above and operated from Tony's mixing desk. Using all sorts of footwear, surfaces, props, and tubs of water, we recreated synchronised effects for everything we could see on the screen. We even did butterflies' footsteps. Also, shikara paddling, creaking and bumping, and birds' flapping wings effect using leather gloves.

I needed to write the narration and find the right person for the voiceover. A young radio journalist presented the 'Super Saver' shopping slot on Chris Tarrant's breakfast show on London's newly launched commercial radio station, Capital Radio. She had a great voice with resonance, befitting the mood I wanted. I didn't think she would go for the meagre rate I could offer from my depleted budget. I was wrong. Sue Cook came to the recording studio and did a great job. She went on to become a prominent BBC TV broadcaster, and I found myself working with her a few years later.

I added an occasional music track from an album of Paul Horn's haunting flute music recorded in the Taj Mahal and returned to Tony's studio for the final dub. I now had sixteen synced tracks and several sound loops from location-recorded atmosphere tracks. These were 25ft lengths of 16mm mag stock tape joined into loops that went in circles over playback heads. The high-tech, soundproofed projection/audio room had an array of interlocked mag stock players that, to contemporary eyes, must look like a 1950s sci-fi mad professor's lab. As picture and sound rolled back and forth, the clatter was deafening. Meanwhile, we sat at the gleaming Neve mixing console in the peaceful theatre below, sipping our coffees and watching the images on the giant screen as Tony weaved his magic on the desk. At last, the labour of the previous six months came together into something resembling a documentary film.

By this stage, the work print looked incredibly grubby and smothered in chinagraph pencil crosses and lines that designated sync marks, crossfades, etc. At this point, the professionals stepped in. Neg cutters wearing white silk gloves, lab coats, and hair nets, armed with a detailed edit decision list (EDL), went back to the original negative and spliced each edit in a dust-free environment. The final stage, the colour grade, supposedly overseen by me, making scene-by-scene adjustments to the colour balance, brightness, and contrast for the release print.

The film opened with the Hanzi section to introduce the area and segued into the Operation Hangul story. When assessing the film, Colin Young commented that the visual style was reminiscent of the photographs I had shown at the interview four years earlier. I was flattered that he remembered my pictures, and I took it as a compliment. Ironically, forty-five years later, in my retirement, I returned to still photography, and now, people comment that my images have a 'filmic' look.

Garden of the Emperors was shown at the National Film Theatre as part of a graduation screening. It was no masterpiece, but the whole experience had been astounding, and I learnt an enormous amount.

I reworked the Hanzi waterways section into a thirteen-minute short. It was tranquil, almost meditative, featuring long, slow floating moves and an evocative soundtrack. It received some acclaim and was a more gratifying film for me.

Shortly before graduation, I had been in discussion with a young producer about making a Super8mm film on Tibetans in exile. We were to stay in a variety of monasteries as guests of the Dalai Lama in Dharamshala. What a fantastic project, and what a way to launch a career as a documentary cameraman! Filming was set to begin the following autumn. I was ecstatic.

7

A Bridge Too Far

A Bridge Too Far is an epic movie based on the true World War II story of a failed Allied attempt to break through German lines at Arnhem by taking a series of bridges in Nazi-occupied Holland. It featured a cast list with the cream of British and Hollywood royalty, and when it was shot in 1976, it was the highest-budget film ever made. The director was Sir Richard Attenborough, one of the film school's governors. He offered a three-week work experience attachment to each of that year's graduates. Of course, it was too commercial a production to interest most NFS students and, being a war film, was deemed too politically incorrect (though the term had not yet been coined).

Extraordinarily, only two out of the twenty-five took advantage of this unique opportunity. One was with the production department, and he spent much of his time as a 20th assistant director, directing traffic on the periphery of the shooting area. The other was me, embedded in the action with the main camera crew. The Director of Photography

(DoP) was Geoffrey Unsworth, then in his mid-60s, with a string of Oscars and BAFTAs to his name, and the camera operator was Peter MacDonald, also at the top of his game. Thirty miles downstream from Arnhem is the small town of Deventer, where there is a similar bridge that had sufficient available space surrounding it to reconstruct the 1940s town and, later, to destroy it. The three-hundred-strong unit was based here—a significant boost to the local economy.

What an experience. Stepping from film school productions into a world of extreme professionalism, extravagance, and make-believe was intriguing. I walked through deserted streets with barricades, burnt-out war machinery and life-like fake corpses.

I was keen to absorb as much as I could of all that was going on with the camera and lighting. My assigned tasks were to keep the camera crew supplied with cups of tea and to deliver the correct rigidised aluminium cases containing lenses and filters to the focus puller. As the name suggests, he is responsible for ensuring the correct parts of the shot are sharp, either through a geared ring and knob on the lens or a wired remote system. It is no easy task, as both the action and the camera are on the move and not necessarily in the same direction. Often working with a depth of field of just a few inches, he uses a tape measure and tables showing how much leeway there is for each focal length lens, at which aperture, and at what distance. Today, they use monitors, wireless remotes, laser devices, and apps. The focus puller is also the first assistant responsible for keeping the film gate clean, engaging magazines, lacing the film camera mechanism, and changing the lenses and filters, etc.

All the big boys' toys were on hand, most importantly, the magnificent Panavision cameras with the full selection

Above: Richard Attenborough directing James Caan

Right: Four Panavision-adapted cameras mounted on a single tracking vehicle

of 'anamorphic' lenses. These lenses horizontally squeeze the image onto the standard 35mm frame, which, in turn, is stretched on projection to produce a widescreen image (a lo-tech explanation). I was awe-struck by the efficiency and professionalism of Peter and his crew, as well as the ingenuity of the grips, who offered inventive solutions for every camera move or position required.

On my first day on set, there was an action scene of foot soldiers and jeeps rushing through woodland. A wide choice of sophisticated tracking vehicles, with specialised suspension and elaborate camera rigging options, was standing by, so I was astonished to see a Citroën 2CV (Deux Chevaux), with its bodywork replaced by a wooden frame from which a camera was dangled on a rope. This contraption was used for a jeep driver's POV (point of view). The 2CV was an extremely cheap and basic two-horsepower car that was first rolled out in the 1940s and had changed little since. It had spongy suspension that had been designed to handle rough farm tracks. The scene had been mapped out, and the actors and extras briefed. Unsworth lifted his pan glass to his eye and looked skyward to check cloud movements for the optimum light window. On a cue from David Tomblin, the 1st. AD (assistant director), a convoy of Land Rovers with large cracked-oil smoke machines weaved in and out of the trees in the middle distance. This was not for war carnage smoke but a way of creating separation and depth in the forest. The camera was rolling, and the 2CV, rolling even more, drove into the scene with Peter and crew hanging on for dear life.

Attenborough was a delightful man, and I was touched that he made time to welcome and encourage me, though I was a little perturbed when he called me "darling"; that is until I realised he called everyone darling, including each of the twenty-plus megastars. Apparently, he had a tough time remembering names (I can relate to that). He would have played a major part in the production meetings that I was not party to, but on set, his directorial role appeared to me to be focused on dealing with the dialogue scenes and performances. Coordinating the multitude of departments, actors and extras to be ready and in place was an extraordinarily complex task, as was choreographing the action sequences, stunts, effects and pyrotechnics. These aspect were overseen by Tomblin and his sizeable team. It made a strong impression on me—whatever the scale of production, there needs to be an efficient individual with a handle on all of the logistics.

The Director of Photography is responsible for the film's overall look. Unsworth would have been in discussion with Attenborough during pre-production and while scouting locations, and he would have collaborated with set designers and the art department. With McDonald at his side, he'd have been involved with camera, lighting and grip equipment decisions. His main role on the shoot was supervising the lighting and communicating with the sparks through his gaffer, the head electrician. (The No. 2 electrician is known as 'The Best Boy'. I have yet to see a credit for 'Best Girl' or 'Best Person', but I'm sure it is out there).

I had a basic understanding of lighting interiors and simple nighttime exteriors, but what I had been unaware of was the degree of additional lighting needed for day exteriors, especially with close-ups. Daylight can be very unforgiving; it can cast unwanted shadows, and what works well on one character in the scene would invariably not do so on the others. A short dialogue sequence can take many hours to shoot, during which time the natural light will change. Also, you must make sure Robert Redford always looks good if you want to stay employed! The bottom line is that it takes an enormous quantity of artificial light to supplement the available daylight. It was the tail end of the thirty-year reign of the Mole Richardson carbon-arc 'Brute', a powerful daylight-balanced beast with a Fresnel lens, providing an unrivalled quality of light. Powered by a large DC generator, it was similar technology to the arc follow-spot that I used to operate in the theatre. It took three electricians to erect and one to remain with it to strike and continuously adjust the carbons while in operation. Unsworth used banks of them.

A small documentary crew came out for a few days of behind-the-scenes filming, and I helped them out. When they left, the director handed me a Bolex 16mm camera and some stock and asked me to film anything I felt could contribute. I was chuffed.

It is the day of the epic scene of the battle on the bridge. Extra crews have been flown in for a multi-camera shoot. My role for the morning is to deliver cases of kit to each camera position using the Citroën 2CV, which has now been repurposed as a motorised flatbed trolley. As time approaches for the master shots of the main action sequence, my services are no longer needed, so I look around for a potential shot for the doc. The bridge is littered with carefully positioned debris. There's a plywood flat propped between the high kerb and the road. Great—I crawl under it to get a dramatic low-angle of the action while staying out of view of the principal units. I lie flat on my stomach, Bolex with a 10mm lens at the ready. I hear Tomblin yelling through his megaphone to cameras A, B, C, etc., to "Turn over", then cueing "Action!". A momentary silence, then the low rumble of distant vehicles as they kick up dust and billow black smoke from their exhausts. The rumble becomes a roar. At this point, it strikes home that I am invisible to all, and a fleet of armoured cars and Sherman tanks is heading my way. They open fire, shooting flames and smoke from their gun barrels. There are ear-shattering explosions all around. Controlled carnage everywhere. Everything is meticulously planned and choreographed except for one idiot who has taken it upon himself to hide unprotected amid it all. Should I make a run for it and risk spoiling the movie's shots at the cost of hundreds of thousands of dollars and getting a serious amount of egg on my face? Of course, I should. Do I? Of course not. I am getting a cool shot—I just hope it won't end with a shattered lens with my blood running down it. One tank's steel-plate caterpillar tracks pass within a few feet of me. I tremble for hours and must look like a ghost.

Several months later, I saw *The Making of...* on TV and, of course, that shot didn't make the cut, and why should it? After all, they had access to the finished movie. I should have done a shot featuring some filming action in the foreground. Basic!

The end of my stint coincided with a weekend break for the unit. A proportion of the sizeable camera crew had obtained tickets for a Rolling Stones and Robin Trower concert at the Den Haag Football Stadium in the Hague. I was invited to join them, which was great, and from there, it would be an easier and cheaper journey home to the UK. We established our pitch as close as possible, though still far from the stage, and settled with our beers and picnic. The joints came around thick and fast, and by the time the Stones hit the stage, I was well-stoned and remember very little of the musical experience (and arena sound systems were not so powerful back then). I also don't remember my farewells. What I do remember is roaming the streets of the Hague in the early hours, desperate to find somewhere to lay my head. I awoke in the morning in an otherwise empty road workers' shelter. A little worse for wear, I pulled myself together and hitched a ride to Amsterdam.

I had received a message that the Tibetan exile film had fallen through (or maybe just my involvement). I was devastated. My big break was nipped in the bud. I would soon learn that for every worthwhile production that came to fruition, a number didn't. What to do? I had nothing in the pipeline and no strategy in place. It was a beautiful summer. I was in mainland Europe, and I had a bright idea. From a payphone in the youth hostel, I made a costly call to Carina in Stockholm. She was a girlfriend of my friend Bill, and she had stayed in our flat in Kensal Green the previous summer. She invited me to visit, so I stuck out my thumb, and within a few days, which included a two-night stopover in Copenhagen, I had hitchhiked the 900-mile journey.

Carina had a small flat in Gamla Stan, the delightful, car-free, medieval 'old town' island in the centre of the Stockholm archipelago. It was a magnet for artists, bohemians and tourists. Atmosphere oozed from every corner. Carina welcomed me with open arms and introduced me to her friends, and I was having a great time. But it was a costly city and my meagre supply of cash was fast dwindling. I was looking into the options for a cheap flight home when I became aware that every second street corner had a busker performing. Most were British, and many were not that good. I was no maestro, but better than some of them. So began my three-month career as a street musician. I borrowed a guitar, practised a little and went in search of a pitch. I soon discovered that there was a well-defined pecking order, and the best spots had assertively protected rosters.

There are two categories of buskers: those who gather an appreciative audience and get rewarded for their talent and those who passersby pass by occasionally tossing coins into the hat out of pity. I was one of the latter. Nevertheless, playing for a few hours a day, I made sufficient to feed myself and pay my way socially. My repertoire consisted mainly of Beatles, Dylan, Baez, and Simon & Garfunkel, with a few of my own ten-year-old compositions thrown in. I became aware that one song was the best earner: Simon & Garfunkel's *The Boxer*. As it was rare that anyone actually stopped to listen to me, I decided to repeat it. Launching into my fancy finger-picking intro, I sang the penniless boy's tale of loneliness on the cold streets of New York. Mustering all the pathos I could, I sang through all the verses and choruses, seamlessly segueing back to the intro, thus forming a continuous loop. What I hadn't considered was the suffering staff in the nearby shops. One guy came out and politely pleaded, "Do you know any other songs?"

The Great Drought of 1976 was an unprecedented heatwave in the UK, having a profound negative impact on everyone's life. However, the sun-starved Swedes on the edge of the same weather system experienced a heavenly subtropical summer, and the atmosphere was electric.

In this country with abundant land and a small population, everyone seemed to have access to a holiday country cabin or house owned by someone within their extended family. Some were well-equipped, others had minimal amenities. The Stockholm archipelago is massive and has 24,000 islands. On one of them, Carina's father, an architect, had built his own, and I spent some time there. We went out fishing in a dinghy with an outboard motor. Using mini rods and multiple hooks, we caught hundreds of herring. Back on land, we gutted them, then soaked them in a selection of delicious marinades in readiness for a feast to come.

The Midsummer holiday is a big deal for the Swedes. Held over one weekend at the time of the solstice and the midnight sun, they really know how to let their hair down. There are many traditions, such as dancing around maypoles, imbibing large quantities of schnapps, wearing flowers in their hair and little or nothing else (on our island, anyway). All notions of monogamy and sexual restraint are put aside.

I had a wonderful, heady time for a couple of months, but life is not a holiday. My new friends had to get on with their lives, and a brief relationship was turning a bit weird. I had a lot of time on my hands and would sunbathe in the park, deep in thought and worrying about my future. For the only time in my life, I sunk into depression and became somewhat paranoid. It freaked me out. Not so much the practical worries but the fact that I was capable of getting into such a mental state. The lovely Carina had been a warm and generous host, but I felt I was outstaying my welcome, and it was time to return to the UK.

I had temporarily sub-let my room in the London flat and went to stay with my parents who now lived in Wilmington, a hamlet in Sussex at the feet of the 235ft (72m) tall, Neolithic, 'Long Man', carved from the underlying chalk of the hillside. I signed on at the Eastbourne labour exchange and was sent to Newhaven Docks to stand in line for casual work offloading and loading cargo ships. This was a time before shipping containers were commonplace. Early each morning, the foreman would invite in the number of men according to the requirements of that day. Quite rightly, regulars were at the top of the list, and I was at the bottom, occasionally being offered days of hard manual labour. It mostly involved loading pallets with all sorts of merchandise, but I recall one occasion being in a ship's hold dodging rocks dropped from crane grabs and then having to help reorganise them to maximise the space. I have no idea what sort of rocks they were or where they were being transported. Neither do I recollect hard hats or steel-toed boots—all part of life's rich tapestry.

My feet were back on the ground. I was in the embrace of my loving mum and dad, and my mood lifted. But, what blew away my blues, never to return, was a letter I received from the assistant head of film at the BBC. I had been to see him a year or so earlier as part of my push to get a foothold in a very competitive industry. He offered me a three-month contract as a holiday relief assistant cameraman based at the film department's Ealing Studios, the oldest continuously working studio facility for film production in the world (taken over by the BBC in 1955).

This was an answer to a dream.

8
Scene 1, Take 1

The clapperboard or 'slate' is the one piece of technology that has changed little since the first talking pictures. On it is marked all the information needed by each department at each part of the process—production title, date, director, DoP, roll number, scene number, take number, film stock type, day or night, interior or exterior, etc. In a controlled situation, it goes on the front of each shot with an announcement for the soundtrack followed by the clap, which gives a frame-accurate visual and audio reference to synchronise the two. If it's impractical to put it on at the beginning, it goes on at the end, but upside down so that everyone knows, and if it is a shot without sound, the clapstick is left open. There are usually three sizes of slate. Large for wide shots, medium for closeups and tiny for macro. Originally, the information was either chalked up or Sharpied on white or coloured half-inch camera tape; then came velcroed numbers, followed by digital slates. Despite the later rise of timecode, metadata, sophisticated electronics and the digital age, the clapperboard system has endured for its simplicity whenever sound and picture are shot separately. So, whose job is it to make all this happen? It's the clapper loader. He or she must also load and offload film into the magazine, which has to be done in total darkness. In the studio or on big sets, there are darkrooms, but on location, it is done with lightproof changing bags—a skill that has to be acquired, and mistakes, such as mixing up exposed and unexposed film or letting unwanted light fog the film stock, are ever-present risks. Also, there is paperwork with every can. Though it's the junior job on the core camera crew, it carries a great deal of responsibility.

In the world of 16mm factual TV production, the roles of loader and focus puller were combined and referred to as 'assistant cameraman', and the roles of DoP and camera operator were combined and referred to as 'lighting cameraman'. Very few women were in camera departments at the time.

I was twenty-seven years old. I had kitted myself out with the vital assistant cameraman's paraphernalia: penlight torch, blower and magnifying glass to check for and clean away 'hairs in the gate' (not really hairs, but tiny slithers of film emulsion that flit around on the edges of the image), and a lens cleaning kit. I had loops attached to my belt for rolls of camera tape and gaffer tape, a Swiss Army knife, a 66ft focus pullers' cloth measuring tape, leather-encased with a brass winder, and, of course, clapperboards, chalk and duster.

Nervous and excited in equal measure, I presented myself for work and was directed to the department office. The walls were covered with whiteboard planners listing all productions and dates with location details and crew lists. There were whole weeks and months marked up for exotic-looking location shoots worldwide, as well as the day-today where my name would be appearing. I was assigned to whoever was short of an assistant. There were some very accomplished lighting cameramen on the staff, and all were very competent. The more popular ones would be requested for the plum shoots. They had all risen through the system, starting at the bottom and applying for internal training courses as they came up and then for the next-level job when a vacancy arose. This usually happened when a cameraman retired or died, and everyone on that ladder moved up a rung. A successful guy who had entered young could make cameraman in his mid-thirties. This was the BBC way.

TFS (Television Film Studios) employed fifty-six full-time film crews along with support staff, office-based coordinators and maintenance technicians. There were four sound stages for the big film drama productions and numerous cutting rooms and dubbing theatres. Apart from news, the Natural History Unit in Bristol and small local programming units in the regions all filming was crewed from here.

Video production, mainly out of TVC (Television Centre), was recorded on two-inch tape with very limited editing capability. It primarily relied on live cutting with multi-camera setups, many engineers and technicians, miles of cables, and heavy-duty equipment. It was perfect for live TV, such as studio news (with film-shot stories inserted) and outside broadcasts for sporting events and stage shows. When it came to soaps, studio drama series and comedy shows, the interiors were shot on the TV studio sets. As soon as a character stepped through a door into the open, it switched to film that had been shot beforehand and converted to videotape (complete with the odd spec of dust). The 'clean', low-contrast studio images were flat-lit so that they worked for multiple camera angles, whereas the single-camera film footage was punchier with more lighting options and nuanced colour. Viewing archived shows today, the difference in look and style really jars, but at the time, the audience was accustomed to it, and everyone was happy.

At TFS, each cameraman would have his allocated camera. The workhorses at the time were the Arriflex BL (German) and the Eclair NPR (French). The zoom and fixed lenses were Zeiss (German) and Angenieux (French). The supplied vehicle was a large estate car with an equipment security cage in the back and a solid shooting platform on the roof.

I spent a lot of time packing and driving. Every member of the production team and the crew would receive a call sheet with all the necessary information for the following day's filming. Each day was crewed and equipped according to the demands of the shoot. The core crew consisted of the lighting cameraman and assistant, a sound recordist and a spark. When deemed necessary, there would be a sound assistant or boom operator, e.g. if they required more than one radio mic at a time or had to record music or a large meeting with dialogue. Likewise, a more complex lighting setup would require a second spark. A car mount or camera dolly required a grip or two and kit.

The ABS was the BBC's trade union and strictly controlled the hours worked and the breaks prescribed. The very nature of filming, especially documentary, made it difficult to stick to, so there were penalty payments to compensate us. It was in production's interest to minimise these, but they were inevitable. Although BBC rates were low compared to the rest of the industry, which was controlled by the ACTT union, the income from penalty payments meant that I could make a satisfactory living for a single person.

The ACTT was a closed-shop union, meaning that you could not work (outside of the BBC) without a ticket, and you could not get a ticket without a job. A catch-22 that was a feared obstacle for anyone trying to get a foothold in the industry. There were very few ways in. The most common being an entry-level job in a film processing laboratory. Fortunately, the BBC did have an affiliation with the ACTT, and since I was also an NFS graduate, my application was granted.

Towards the end of my stint, I was thrilled to be offered a further three-month contract.

The work was hard, but every day was different. I learnt a great deal and gained much experience and confidence.

Post BBC, I spent eighteen months freelancing as an assistant on various productions, ranging from low-budget corporate films to lavish TV commercials. I found the world of advertising uncomfortable. Exchanges between agency creatives, producers, directors and DoPs were more about award-winning potential than selling the product. Excesses and waste went through the roof, and despite charging double my TV assisting rate for working as a clapper loader, invoices were sometimes rejected by the production company, insisting that I charge more. Their income was a percentage of their spend and 'cheap' did not impress in that world. It was, and still is, an attractive field for DoPs and directors. They get to flex their creative muscles and often work with 'anything you want' sized budgets. Every thirty-second ad is packed with visual 'excellence', and it can be a segue to making movies. Not to mention that DoP's rates, even then, ran into thousands of pounds per day. Though I dabbled a little in later years, it was not a career path that attracted me.

I was getting by, but there were more gaps in my diary

than I would have liked. I received a call from Hannen Foss, an ex-tutor at the NFS, inviting me to a meeting. Visnews was a sizeable international TV news agency based in Park Royal, West London. It had a separate production department. This was where we met, and Hannen made a surprising proposition. He was setting up a film school for third-world filmmakers (that was the term for 'developing countries'). Would I like to be 'Head of Camera'? A grand title for someone who wasn't yet a cameraman. I went for it, and before long, the first intake arrived, mainly Africans and mainly individuals who had acquired jobs within government film units—not because they were passionate about filmmaking, but because they were relatives of ministers within a pertinent department. So, no philosophical discussions about Buñuelian themes then— simply lessons in loading a Bolex camera, changing lenses and filming interviews.

I recall picking up the first group of Nigerians from Heathrow Airport. They were overwhelmed by the unfamiliar sights and sounds. As I drove them to the Visnews complex, there was a jaw-dropping moment for the young man sat next to me—he could not conceive of what he saw—a white man was sweeping the road.

They were a likeable crowd, and it was an enjoyable experience. After a few months, a vacancy arose, and I was offered a six-month contract in Nigeria as 'Chief Cameraman at the Rivers State Ministry of Information and Communications', Port Harcourt. This was a good call. A chance to travel to Africa, hone my shooting skills and earn good money to help finance a camera kit on my return.

I was greeted by the friendly face of one of my ex-students and shown to my office. I was honoured—it had an air conditioning unit. OK, it didn't work, but it was still prestigious, and there were three telephones on my desk. They were not connected, but… I was given the tour. First, the equipment store, filled with the latest in 35mm and 16mm camera equipment and lenses, much of it in its original packaging, most of it un-operational because the necessary peripherals were not there. Then on to the fabulous dubbing suite with the latest Neve mixing desk that no longer worked because the maintenance department had got their hands on it.

Supposedly, a substantial film processing laboratory was being built, taking over the ministry's ground floor. All the machinery was there in large shipping crates. It was like a building site, but no building occurred during my six-month residency. Temperature control is vital for developing film, but all the air conditioning units had mysteriously disappeared. For the time being, all exposed film was shipped to the Visnews lab in the UK, and the occasional vital stories were edited there and returned.

My staff were amazed that I wanted to leave my 'plush' office and film 'stuff'. In fact, in the unlikely scenario that 'stuff' needed filming, surely, I would delegate. They were disinterested, and I was there to gain filming experience, so I dreamt up my own project—a travelogue/promo for the area.

Ian was a British film editor on a contract similar to mine. I showed him how to operate a Nagra, and he would record sound. I gave call details to the rest of the crew, knowing they would be hours late, invariably with the same, sometimes true, excuse—they couldn't get fuel for their government-owned vehicle despite being in the world's fourth-largest oil-producing nation. We shot some interesting material. We hired a boat to take us upstream to a remote village where we were treated like royal visitors, and the locals put on a traditional dance performance for our benefit. We went to other villages and interviewed chiefs and locals. On the way home from one such shoot, our Range Rover driver was going at breakneck speed, swerving around the potholes and throwing us and the kit all over the place. I asked what the hurry was. "We are low on petrol, and I want to get back before we run out!"

We booked a helicopter and removed the port-side door to shoot aerials using my 'ColiMount Mk 1', an improvised, vibration-absorbing aerial filming rig. It consisted of a spiderweb-like contrivance with bungees attached to every possible anchor point around the door aperture, with the camera secured in the middle. Over the decades that followed, I would develop and simplify this system.

My ministry team undoubtedly thought me mad. I was spending government money, which was plentiful, shooting a film that no one had asked for. We shipped the exposed negative to the UK for processing and printing. Nothing I shot ever came back. No one seemed bothered.

It was a good time. Ian and I shared a comfortable house, which had a housekeeper, a gardener, a driver, and gate guards. Our closest ex-pat friend was a French chef for the Presidential Hotel, so we ate very well, and it was not just pepper soup or fermented cassava (gari).

I was invited to perform a couple of songs on NTV's local live magazine programme. I expressed to the producer, an ex-student of mine, that I was flattered and asked how they would fill the spot if I were not interested. He told me he'd go to the airport when an incoming flight was due and find some other foreign visitor. All the European ex-pat community tuned in. I rehearsed with my guitar in the living room and nervously waited for the NTV driver to collect me. He never turned up.

9

I Am Now a Lighting Cameraman

In 1979, having just turned thirty, I was back in London. I rented a small basement studio flat in Islington. My bed was a foam mattress atop packing boxes containing my belongings, newly released from storage. It was time to set myself up as a broadcast lighting cameraman.

A freelance in the TV world was expected to come as a fully equipped package including an assistant, a sound recordist, and transport. I could have bought a second-hand BL or NPR, but if I was to make my mark in this competitive environment, I needed to push out the boat and have the latest kit.

Aaton had built a beautiful 16mm camera. It purred like a cat; it was light (7kg with a zoom lens and battery), had a low centre of gravity, and was moulded to sit comfortably on the shoulder. Add the stylish sculptured walnut grip, and it was way ahead of the competition for handheld filming. It ran at sound-sync speeds of 25 fps (frames per second) for Europe or 24 fps for the Americas, plus variable rates from 6 – 32 fps for slow or fast motion. As a sweeping generalisation, it was the new camera of choice for owner-users, whereas the rental houses preferred the more robust Arriflex SR. I bought a set of rechargeable batteries, three film magazines, two zoom lenses and three prime lenses, exposure meters, a tripod, and many accessories such as colour correction and effects filters. Then there was a basic tungsten lighting kit consisting of eight lamps from 300W 'Mizar' spots, thru 850W 'Redheads', up to 2kW 'Blondes', clamps, flags, colour gels and diffusion.

This equipment set me back over £17,000, not including insurance or a suitable vehicle—a considerable sum in 1979. My savings from the Visnews contract covered one-third of the cost; the rest was a loan from my father at a favourable interest rate. Considering I had no work lined up, it was a significant leap of faith for both of us.

I loathed schmoozing and was extremely bad at it. The thought of cold calling filled me with dread, and I didn't yet have suitable material for a showreel.

The BBC had a system of Film Operation Managers known as FOMs. Each one oversaw the crewing of a particular area of programming, such as music and arts, current affairs, drama, children's shows, etc. Despite all the in-house crews, there was a fair amount of freelance hiring. As I was familiar with the system and had had past dealings with some of the FOMs, they were my first ports of call. Long-form documentaries and music and arts were my main interests, but I was not naive enough to think they would take a risk on me, and these were prime pickings for the staff crews anyway. TFS was home to a few FOMs, but most productions came out of other West London BBC complexes, such as Kensington Grove, Television Centre and Lime Grove, the hub for current affairs and daytime TV. I visited them all. I would make an appointment with one to access the compound and pop my head into other's offices once I was inside. I also visited the Bristol documentary department and the BBC Open University (O.U.) unit in Milton Keynes. The first bite was a one-off interview shoot for the O.U. in a Holiday Inn conference room. I cobbled a crew together. It was a simple setup, and all went smoothly. I was on my way.

Unlike movie and commercials DoPs, we didn't have agents. Technicians had a dedicated diary service with camerapeople, assistants, sound recordists, etc, on their books. I was registered with Carlin & Co., and contacts would phone me at home. The cassette answering machine would give Carlin's number and accept a recorded message if I wasn't in. The client would call them to check my availability and pencil or confirm a booking. If I was unavailable and they didn't have someone else in mind, they may ask who on Carlin's books was free. Likewise, I would check for an assistant and soundperson in the same way. At this early stage, many jobs would be for the next day, so efficient contact was vital. Landline telephones were the only form of communication, so when out and about, I always kept a bag of coins handy and was forever on the lookout for phone boxes in order to check-in. Once pagers became available, it became a little simpler, but mobile phones were still in the realm of science fiction.

The British Broadcasting Company, also affectionately known as 'Auntie' or 'The Beeb', launched the world's first-ever regularly scheduled TV service back in 1936 and had been considered the international gold standard ever since. When I started, the UK had only three TV channels: BBC 1, BBC 2 and ITV. An audience of twelve million for a popular programme was considered satisfactory and, if you missed it, there were no domestic video recorders, so—hard luck. As all viewers watched the latest episode of *Fawlty Towers* simultaneously, it could well be a subject of conversation over a pint in the pub afterwards. My point is that Auntie Beeb was a good place for me to get work. A couple of FOMs based at Lime Grove provided a periodic stream of day-to-day assignments.

I shot several stories for *Nationwide*, a weekday magazine programme that followed the six o'clock news. It was mainly current affairs stories, often with prominent politicians. Also, entertaining interludes, such as filming an eighteen-year-old George Michael and his Wham! bandmate Andrew Ridgeley, buying clothes for their first *Top of the Pops* appearance or riding to Heathrow Airport on a bus full of overexcited, blue-rinse old ladies who made up the British Liberace Fan Club. They were to meet and greet America's 'Mr. Entertainment', the era's most flamboyant showman and a highly talented pianist. He travelled with his bejewelled and equally camp 'assistant', but the 'Liberace Ladies' refused even to consider the idea that he may be a homosexual (the term 'gay' still had its original meaning).

I recall covering one story that was an exposé and involved some undercover filming at a meeting. There were no tie-clip cameras or special glasses. I went to the tech store and picked up the 'secret camera'. It was a briefcase containing an ACL 200ft load camera with a 12mm lens aligned with a three-inch hole hidden by a flap. As I walked back through the corridors of Lime Grove Studios casually carrying the briefcase, a few passers-by commented, "Oh look—the secret camera." By guessing and presetting the exposure and focus and lifting the flap, it was operated via an on/off cable release. Though filming blind, the shoot worked out OK, and I didn't even cut off anyone's head.

I did a number of stories for *That's Life*, a hugely popular consumer advice series with a prime-time Saturday evening slot. Hosted by the charismatic Esther Rantzen, it encompassed a mixture of hard-hitting investigative content with satire and pure silliness, such as skateboarding ducks and the like. I also shot a serious and sensitive long-form doc with Esther about children's hospices.

Jim'll Fix It was a massive, long-running hit—twenty years, to be precise. Jimmy Saville devised and presented the show. He would later be knighted for his philanthropy and charity fund-raising achievements (40 million pounds worth) and was posthumously proven to be Britain's most prolific ever paedophile. Jim would 'fix it' for the wishes of several children to come true each week. Then they would come on to the glitzy live show, where Saville, with his white flowing locks, outrageous outfits and abiding extinguished cigar, would present them with their medals. Most of the 'fixes' would be filmed in advance, sometimes by me.

One child, Charlie, wanted to burn money. The three crew members, two production, Charlie and his mum, went to the Royal Mint, where all British and Commonwealth currency was manufactured. We were shepherded through security, where our personal cash was put into lockers so that we entered with none and exited with none. We proceeded to the incinerator facility, where all paper money due for removal from circulation was reduced to ashes. We filmed Charlie shovelling in some notes, and then I crawled into the inactive furnace and sat crossed-legged, camera on shoulder, as thousands of pounds were thrown over me. That was fun.

Twenty years earlier, aged seventeen, landing at Stansted airport on my return from a Club 18-30 holiday in Benidorm, I had looked out of the window and was freaked to see a load of burnt-out fuselages on the runway verges. I recall thinking that this place must have a pretty awful safety record. Jim fixed it for me when a kid wanted to operate an airport fire engine, and it turned out this was the training centre for airside firefighters.

Not all my shoots were so frivolous. I was now picking up current affairs jobs, mainly for *Panorama* and the newly launched *Newsnight*. Much of it was reporters talking to camera in Westminster or outside 10 Downing Street and numerous interviews with the prominent politicians of the day.

For fast turnaround stories and news, we shot on reversal film rather than using negative. As the name suggests, it used a different type of processing that produced a positive image, so the film that was edited and then telecined for broadcast was the actual piece of film that had run through the camera. There was no room for error in exposure, contrast, or colour balance at the shooting stage, but the post-production process was much faster.

In March 1979, the Irish National Liberation Army assassinated Airey Neave, the British Shadow Secretary of State for Northern Ireland. They had attached a bomb under his car, which detonated in the House of Commons car park. A dauntless *Newsnight* journalist had secured a meeting with the perpetrators to take place in Dublin. This was very hush-hush and potentially dangerous. These were not men to mess with. No staff crews were willing to go, and no danger money was offered.

I was hungry for anything. I gathered a crew, and we flew to Dublin, picked up a hire car and drove away from the airport. We pulled up at a phone box, and the journalist called a number he had been given. A muffled voice gave some convoluted rendezvous instructions starting with the words "From the direction your car is facing ..." It was apparent they had had us in their sights from the moment we had disembarked. These guys were taking no risks. We met three men at an all but derelict apartment building. They were wearing Beatles wigs, blatant false moustaches and dark glasses. They had bulges under their oversized anoraks, assumedly concealing weapons. They frisked us, checked our equipment, and once they were satisfied that we posed no threat to them or their identity, we set up and proceeded to shoot a silhouetted interview with their spokesperson. 'Interview' may be the wrong word as they controlled the content, which was their political stance and reasoning. As pertinent in such circumstances, the sound kept rolling during magazine changes and other 'downtime' in case anything important was said when they assumed they were off-the-record. Also, the device of prearranged coded wording variations on the reporter's cues. For example, he would say "Cut camera" rather than "Cut", and I would discreetly close the viewfinder shutter and look up as if we had stopped filming. Hopefully, that would fool the contributors into believing the camera was off when, in reality, it was still running. Before packing up, I shot cutaways that excluded the mouth, such as close-ups of hands and a defocussed wide shot. These are devices the editor could use to cut around the dialogue. My heart was beating nineteen to the dozen, and I was very happy to be out of there as soon as it was over.

When the story was broadcast the following evening, it caused great controversy. The Counter Terrorism Police called us all in for cross-examination. Why hadn't we informed them of our trip in advance?—that was a very silly question. I feared I would be forever on some secret service blacklist database. Fortunately, computers were not yet monitoring the world, and there was no knock-on effect.

10

Mentioned in Dispatches

Looking through a lens, you are one step removed from the world, especially with a film camera where your right eye must stay in contact with the eyepiece whenever the camera is running. When shooting 'actuality', you develop a technique of using your left eye independently to check what is happening outside the frame, but that only goes so far. In April 1981, the 'Brixton Riots'—later correctly renamed the 'Brixton Uprising'—was a series of clashes between mainly black youths and the Metropolitan Police, resulting from racist discrimination by the mainly white force and their increased use of indiscriminate 'stop and search' powers. I was in the midst of it, filming for *Nationwide*. In close, getting a dramatic shot of a line of police with riot gear and shields, I was oblivious to the approaching angry mob behind me. Fortunately, our reporter was a giant of a man, and he lifted me from the waist and carried me back to the sidelines. I kept the camera running and fortuitously got an impactful, continuous developing shot of the ensuing clash.

This was a lesson for the future. As a documentary shooter, you are often so absorbed with what is playing out in the viewfinder that you can be blind to the dangers surrounding you. I always ensure a crew member is watching my back in such situations.

At last, I received a phone call from the FOM I had been pestering since the beginning. He was responsible for crewing music and arts. It was late Friday afternoon, and there had been a last-minute decision for the first two days of filming to take place over the weekend. A production for the prestigious arts series *Arena,* titled 'Mentioned in Dispatches', it was a profile of the legendary war photographer Tim Page, the inspiration for Dennis Hopper's character in Francis Ford Coppola's classic movie *Apocalypse Now.*

Tim had gone travelling at seventeen and found himself in Laos, documenting the civil war. He moved on to Saigon, where he spent five years mainly on assignments for *Time-Life, Paris Match* and the like. He had no photography background but learned on the job. Unapologetically fuelled by hard and soft drugs, he revelled in the adventure and excitement and captured some extraordinary photos. A quote from his 2022 obituary reads, "He cadged rides in US helicopters, put himself in the line of fire, took LSD and smoked 'grass by the kilo.'" The power of many of his images was due to the fact that he would raise his head when others ducked. He paid for it with a series of shrapnel wounds to his head, back and arms, culminating in an incident involving an exploding mine. He was pronounced dead on arrival at the field hospital but was miraculously resuscitated. He required extensive neurosurgery and spent many years in recovery.

This documentary was a break I was after; I had to impress.

I phoned around all the assistants and sound recordists I knew—none were available. Good teamwork and rapport are vital, so this was not a good start. I booked a couple of guys to whom I had been referred. We filmed Tim in a flat he had been lent in Maida Vale. He showed pictures and talked about them. You could tell that the poor man was in pain. He had a heavy limp and broke into a sweat from minor exertions. Though he consumed quantities of both pain relief and leisure drugs, he was sharp, with a banter that would shock. He came out with lines such as, *"Take the glamour out of war? How the hell can you do that? It's like trying to take the glamour out of sex, trying to take the glamour out of the Rolling Stones. I mean, you know that it just can't be done."*

We filmed him washing and shaving before leaving the house to wander along the canal with his cameras. He stopped to photograph some boys fishing by a half-sunken supermarket trolley. He got them to pose and informed them that they could smoke that hemp instead of using it for bait. My dozy camera assistant put the tripod down among the long grass on the towpath and forgot about it. We arrived at the next location; I asked for the 'legs', and that is when he realised what he had done. We dashed back to the canal and, fortunately, managed to recover them—this was not the sort of impression I wanted to make.

During a tea break, I was chatting with Tim, and he complained that he was out of hash and didn't know where to score. Not the most professional of gestures, but I said I could bring him a small piece the following day, which I did. Possibly influenced by this, he had taken a liking to me and told Chris Sykes, the director, that he would be happy if I could be the cameraman for the remainder of the filming. It was Chris's first long-form documentary, too, and I don't think he had anyone particular in mind, so he agreed. That was a result.

There had been a mass exodus of hundreds of thousands of Vietnamese fleeing communist oppression, mainly in small boats. Approximately 300,000 perished, and several countries took in survivors. Three thousand refugees were brought to Hampshire's recently decommissioned RAF Sopley facility. These 'boat people' were housed and fed in the barracks and happy to be safe. Our next shoot was Tim visiting there to take photographs. This called for some sensitive, minimal fuss, observational filming. Once again, I had difficulty finding a crew. The only sound recordist I could get was an unfit, old-school guy who was also an ACTT shop steward. He was not going to wander around carrying his Nagra and a boom mike. He insisted on slowly setting up his sound cart and stool somewhere central. At his leisure, he put a radio mic on Tim and another for me so that I could cue sound when the camera was running. Oh, and it was "time for a tea break!" I was highly stressed, and Chris was not happy. In due course, we filmed Tim at work. There was a magical moment when he interacted with some kids, and a boy pulled a toy gun from his pocket and posed with it. We did maybe ten days of shooting altogether, and the final result was satisfactory, but the process had been a nightmare for me. I had certainly not developed the working rapport with Chris that I had hoped may lead to future collaborations. Forty years later, upon learning that an acquaintance of mine was his neighbour, I asked him to say hello from me. He did remember me—as "the guy who left his tripod behind by the Grand Union Canal."

Charles Stewart, who had run the NFS camera department,

was renowned as a 'fly-on-the-wall' cameraman. He declared that it takes ten years to master hand-held camerawork. This was an era when it was all about smooth camera moves, tracking shots using 'rubber knees' (walking in a way that absorbs vertical motion), and hitting accurate framing and focus rather than searching for it during a shot. Some years later, it became fashionable to abandon those ideas and call it 'edgy'. He phoned me, inviting himself to my flat for a chat. Sat on one of my equipment cases with a cup of tea (I didn't have the space or money for furniture), he told me about a production he and Roger Graef were collaborating on, embedding themselves with the Thames Valley Police for a year. He proposed I join them in a double role for half of the shooting period. I would assist him when only one story was being followed and shoot when there were parallel stories. It was a next-level opportunity. I was thrilled beyond imagining. I like to think he approached me because he thought I had the talent, though, in reality, it was likely because I had the camera and could strike a 'charge as used' rental deal on it.

Graef was a giant in the field. BBC Bristol had approached him with the concept, and he had negotiated total access to the force. This was to be a real observational documentary series. No commentary, no music, no interaction with the camera, nothing set up and all with available light. Roger and Charles were the industry's number one team for the project. Today, behind-the-scenes cop docs are two a penny, but this was the first.

Moreover, it was not just searching out dramatic action but delving deeply into the investigative processes. This involved catching vital dialogue on the hoof, requiring skill and sensitivity from both camera and sound to capture the content without getting under the feet of our protagonists. Charles self-directed, and Roger tagged along with me, aggressively directing with a growling whisper in my ear. Sure, he was the master and I the tenderfoot, but it made it very awkward for me to achieve a flow. What really disillusioned me was witnessing my two heroes of the genre noisily bickering like an unhappily married couple within earshot of the police protagonists. Nonetheless, it was a wondrous experience, and I learnt an enormous amount.

Each programme was to be a separate story, and "Operation Carter" was one. It was the most extensive operation in the history of the regional crime squads—it was also top secret. Working with the evidence from two major 'supergrasses' and an undercover police operative, they cracked a network of top London crime gangs. On 'D-Day', there were dozens of arrests, and the number one target was the gang's boss, Rudy Cooke. The undercover officer, who had won his confidence, arranged to drive him from London to Reading for a rendezvous with a supposed accomplice. In a locale that Cooke was unfamiliar with, he was driven straight to the car park ramp at the Reading Police HQ. There, he was confronted by gun-toting police officers and arrested. My role, along with sound recordist Dave Motta, was to film from the unmarked car that was surreptitiously following them from London, reporting progress at every stage and pulling up behind to cut off any attempt at an escape. As it happened, I got the most dramatic, tension-building footage of both the journey and the springing of the trap. Charles popped up from behind a wall, getting that angle and followed them into the station. Armed with this footage and the material I shot in the run-up, Roger approached the programme commissioners at Bristol. He convinced them that *Operation Carter* had the makings of its own seven-part series. *Police* won the BAFTA award for Best Factual Series, and one episode (mainly shot by Charles) brought about legislation affecting changes in the way in which the UK police were to handle future rape cases.

11

It's Not Only Rock 'n' Roll

In 1981, America launched MTV. A new film genre was born, and the UK was at the cutting edge. Every record release needed a 'Pop Promo'. This was an exciting new field in which established filmmaking norms were discarded and creativity let loose. It was a refreshing and liberating format.

One of the companies I shot for was Stiff Records, a thriving independent label. Dave Robinson, the CEO, had directed a bio-pic with the ska band Madness, and he took it upon himself to produce and direct the label's videos. He, the band and his production manager, Nigel Dick, would come up with a concept and suitable locations, and what followed was a pretty anarchic affair. He would have two DoPs working together in a sometimes fluid and often erratic way. I predominantly worked alongside Chris Morphet (whom I had assisted a few years earlier and who had offered great support when I started shooting) or Roger Deakins (decades later knighted for his services to film).

"Our House" was the track and accompanying promo that broke America for Madness. We shot in two locations. One was the magnificent mansion owned by Playboy Europe's boss, Victor Lownes. It was a house designed for partying, with jacuzzis, cushioned 'lounging' areas, an electronics games room with more Space Invaders consuls than you could dream of, and a menagerie of monkeys. We filmed everywhere and had a quick plunge at lunchtime. We had a 100ft reach, truck-mounted cherry picker positioned in front of the mansion. I was descending in the platform cage with Suggs singing to playback when it lurched to one side as the truck's outriggers sank into the forecourt—I don't know who ended up paying the bill for that. The second location was the antithesis, a two-up, two-down terraced house under a railway bridge in East London. We had a different type of crane to fly in Kix, playing an East End mum character blasting out a saxophone solo. As well as being superb musicians, they were all prodigious clowns and the resulting zany videos were great entertainment.

Nigel moved on to Polygram Records as a director, and I shot some videos for him. Status Quo's "Margherita Time" was originally to be shot in the Canary Islands, but we ended up in the tropical swimming pool complex at the Heathrow Sheraton Hotel with an extensive lighting rig. For the Boomtown Rats' "Drag Me Down", I shot exteriors and interiors in the old Chislehurst chalk and flint mines with lots of smoke and moody lighting—I loved it. Bob Geldof is a very strong character, and he put his heavy stamp on the two Rats' promos I worked on. For Robert Plant's debut solo single, "Burning Down One Side", Nigel (his 'Hitchcock' moment), head wrapped in a bandage, wearing dark glasses and a dinner suit, sent drinks flying in slow motion as he leapt onto the table, where Plant was having an intimate dinner with a beautiful young lady, and rocked out with a guitar solo.

The rock 'n' roll world also needed live concerts shot on 16mm or 35mm film. There were multiple cameras, and I often found myself shooting handheld up close. We had talkback headsets for communication, but the music was so loud that I couldn't hear directions, so I would do my own thing. The only proviso was ensuring that all operators' magazine changes every ten minutes (three and a half minutes on 35mm) were staggered so there were no gaps in the coverage. What a buzz to be on stage with Eric Clapton!

It is thrilling to be up close when a great musician is performing, whatever the genre. Evelyn Glennie is a phenomenal performer. She was the first musician to maintain a full-time career as a solo percussionist, and remarkably, she has been profoundly deaf since the age of twelve. Performing barefoot to experience the base reverberations, she has learnt to 'hear' with all parts of her body, feeling the upper frequencies from the waist up and the lower ones from the waist down. She had an amazing, converted barn studio at her home. It was packed with every imaginable percussion instrument, stick, brush and mallet. I carefully positioned myself in the middle of the assortment she had set up for this specific performance. From here, I could get a selection of close-ups and wides. Later, we would do a second take for cutaways without the precise sync so the editor could cut the sequence smoothly. Radiating grace and poise, she approached her instruments with a focused intensity. As she started to play, her hands flowed effortlessly across the array of instruments. I was enraptured by the sounds, exploring the entire sonic spectrum, seamlessly blending rhythms and melodies—thunderous crescendos to delicate whispers. She used her whole body to coax out the perfect resonance. I was in the midst of it, immersed in the job at hand yet still absorbing the vibrations and experiencing the surround sound happening of a lifetime. Wow!

Many years later, in the grand conservatory of her secluded holiday home looking out onto the beautiful Bay of Islands in the north of New Zealand, we filmed the legendary soprano Dame Kiri Te Kanawa rehearsing for an upcoming performance. Positioned by her swimming pool with her accompanist at an upright piano, the music was sublime. As if that were not enough, the acoustics, enhanced by the water and glass, took the experience to a higher level. Quite a contrast to the previous week's filming we had done with her thigh-deep in an icy river, salmon fishing in Iceland during a break in her schedule of masterclasses in Reykjavík.

12

Two Weddings and a Funeral

In July 1981, 'The Wedding of the Century' was televised, and the BBC live coverage was estimated to have 750 million viewers worldwide. Prince Charles, the heir to the British throne, was marrying the young and beautiful Lady Diana Spencer. This historical event needed a future-proof record, and Pathé was making a 35mm film for the big screen. There were dozens of cameras along the route. My position was on a rostrum outside Kensington Palace, alongside a number of outside broadcast cameras, news crews and photographers. From here, we would get the first glimpse of the blushing bride and the much-anticipated wedding dress as she and her father boarded the gilded carriage and left for St. Paul's Cathedral. I was responsible for just one vital shot. I had no support crew. The heavy-duty tripod had been set up, and a stack of equipment cases awaited my arrival. I started to assemble the Arriflex 35 camera and found that the 10x zoom, a large and heavy lens, would not lock into its mount. There was no way to contact anyone, so I had to improvise on possibly my trickiest camera operating shot to date. The palace gates opened to reveal the carriage and its mounted escort. My right hand was on the tripod's pan bar, and my left hand was physically holding this monster lens in place. On the telephoto end, I caught Diana and her twenty-five-foot wedding dress train being packed into the carriage. As the retinue moved off, I zoomed out with them, pulling stop to adjust the exposure as they came from the shade into the sunshine, pulling focus as they came closer and panning with them as they passed and finally exited the frame. On a normal 35mm shoot, with the lens secured in place, that shot would have involved three sets of hands. To this day, I don't know how I achieved it. The fairy tale marriage was short-lived, and the next time I filmed a Diana-related story was sixteen years later at the funeral following her tragic death.

In the early to mid-'80s, video was making its first tentative steps beyond the studio and outside broadcast (OB) units. Though a long way behind film regarding picture quality and versatility, it came into its own for Electronic News Gathering (ENG), where the faster editing process got content onto the screen quickly and cheaply. There was also the facility to send stories via telephone and satellite links. In this emerging world of two-person single-camera units, the sound recordist now had the burden of carrying the cumbersome video recorder and being tied to the camera by a thick 'umbilical' cable. Later would come the BetacamSP camcorder, returning bulk to the cameraman. It was a heavy and unwieldy beast.

I did do some local news for Thames TV and TV South. It was staunchly unionised, and the crew often included a staff electrician and driver, so everything was done strictly by the book. With Thames TV, somehow, we would invariably find ourselves in the locale of Waterloo, entering La Barca Ristorante at five past one, just in time to infringe our lunch break (we'd receive a penalty payment for that). There, we would meet with the production crew for a two-hour meal break funded by the PA's bulging wallet. Even better if it was at the end of the working week because overtime started at 3:00 pm as Friday was 'POETS day': '**P**iss **O**ff **E**arly, **T**omorrow's **S**aturday'. Similarly, TV South was a good earner as I had to drive from London to Dover (50mph max—union rules) for an 8:30 am start, so overtime stacked up, often leading to infringement of twelve, or even ten-hour breaks, adding further penalty payments to the fast-accumulating tab—I didn't make the rules.

Where the new technology encroached more on my world was the development of Electronic Field Production (EFP), a small-unit single-camera video. My camera of choice was the Ikegami HL-79E. Apparently, translated from the Japanese, 'HL' stood for 'Handy-Looky', an embarrassment they later tried to sweep under the carpet. It was a three-CRT tube camera. An engineer came in the place of an assistant. He aligned the tubes each morning and, when circumstance allowed, would watch a waveform monitor as we were shooting. With a sharp intake of breath, he would mutter comments like, "You can't do that; it's peaking over one volt." This didn't sound like photography language to me. He was trying to tell me that the highlights were burning out and, even if it was a creative choice (not an option in his eyes), you were at risk of damaging the tubes if you overdid it. Should you accidentally point at the sun or change the lens while the camera power was on, you would wipe out the tubes fatally. Shooting a bright object, such as a light bulb, you get a wavy 'trail' when you pan, and leaving the camera pointing at anything for too long could burn the image onto the tubes.

Over the following fifteen years, video evolved; chips replaced tubes, and sensors became more robust. Formats and tape systems came and went. I adapted my lighting and technical skills accordingly. Many broadcast and corporate productions would follow the video route, primarily for economic reasons, but film endured as the choice for image quality and aesthetics. Fortunately, the bulk of my work remained on celluloid.

In 1980, at thirty-one, I became the proud owner of a two-bedroom flat in Kilburn, NW London. Bill was once again my flatmate, but this time his rent was subsidising my mortgage. A few months in, he left a note and number by the phone saying I had received a mysterious call from a girl with an exotic-sounding name; could I call her back? I did. She gingerly explained that she was given my number in the hope of tracking down a mutual (and unreliable) friend who had agreed to put her up, but attempts at contact had failed. She had just arrived on holiday in the UK, and a vague acquaintance generously offered her the sofa for a few nights. As it happens, she was located nearby, so, gallant that I was, I suggested we meet. It was a glorious August day, and I offered to take her for a walk on Hampstead Heath, the highest point overlooking central London.

Yaffa was a repertory actor from Israel. She was on her first foreign holiday and had arrived in London with a fistful of tickets for the National Theatre and the Royal Shakespeare Company and a train ticket to Edinburgh for the fringe festival. She was beautiful, bubbly, smart and spontaneous. She was enraptured with the big city's history, culture, and beauty. She was passionate in every way, and I was enchanted. We would meet after her theatre visits and stroll hand in hand along the South Bank, getting to know one another. The 'mutual friend' had forgotten the arrangement and rented her flat to a Japanese family. Within a few days, Yaffa moved to my place for the remainder of her stay.

She returned to London during a break from work, and I visited her in Israel over my Christmas break (no such thing there). When her contract with Beersheba Repertory Theatre had run its course, she joined me in London and within a year, we were married. Our backgrounds were very different. Following the formation of Israel, her large family had fled from discrimination in Iraq to settle in the 'Promised Land'. As child number ten, Yaffa was the first to be born in Israel, and Ben Gurion awarded her parents $100 for contributing to Israel's population. My parents adored her and were thrilled that I had found myself "a nice Jewish girl."

For the most basic non-union shoots, I thought teaching Yaffa how to load Aaton film magazines, use a clapperboard, do the paperwork, and act as my assistant would be a good idea. One such shoot was a bit of a jolly (a rarity), a TV commercial for Cotters' Tours, a Glaswegian company running two-week bus tours of Europe. It was a lovely trip, taking in Brussels, Paris, Lake Garda, Venice and Geneva, among other destinations. Our brief was to travel on the bus and get a good selection of shots of the destinations, the bus in transit and the holidaymakers enjoying themselves. We featured two hired professional models about half the age and twice as glamorous as the real holidaymakers. Peter Issac, the producer, was aboard for the first day. He got everyone to sign releases and made a cheery speech explaining what was happening, introducing the models and Yaffa and myself, saying we were newlyweds on our honeymoon.

Not strictly accurate; we had already honeymooned in Greece. They were happy and enjoyed the novelty of having us aboard. That is until we arrived at the French/Swiss border (plus each border thereafter), and rather than being waved through, the bus had to stop to have our kit scrutinised by customs and the carnet verified.

Yaffa assisted on occasional days of BBC current affairs and the like. I don't think she liked being bossed around by me or my irritation at her not keeping up with the unit as she struggled to carry the tripod. I was discovering a grumpy side to her, especially with early morning starts. What neither of us knew at the time was that she was already pregnant with Dan, so all was forgiven. Thus ended her brief new career. As I write, we have just celebrated our Ruby wedding anniversary, so I guess we got something right.

13

On Angel's Wings

Channel 4 was a game-changer. In November 1982, the UK's second commercial TV station was launched. Its remit was to provide programmes for minority interests, arts and culture. It was to be more 'serious' than ITV or BBC1, with quality documentary and drama strands, sophisticated comedy and experimental programming. It revolutionised British broadcasting by commissioning programmes rather than making its own. All production was independent, so, from my point of view, and that of all freelancers, it was a potential source of worthwhile work for the years ahead.

John Gau Productions had been a prolific contributor from the start, and I had been badgering them for a while. I knew they had a series in development called *Assignment Adventure*. I was eager to be part of it, so I was thrilled when my name was put forward for an episode. The final decision was down to Peter Macpherson, the director. He came to visit me at home. I effused enthusiasm for the project, we discussed logistics, and he offered me the job.

Angel Falls is the world's highest waterfall, named by the Western world after the colourful American adventurer Jimmy Angel, who 'discovered' it in the 1930s. In his search for gold in the central Venezuelan jungle, his aircraft crashed on the high plateau where the falls form. He trekked for weeks to return to 'civilisation'. *On Angel's Wings* was to be a documentary following two British hang glider pilots recreating the journey, but in reverse—climbing to the top carrying their gliders and flying back down.

Even though it was the type of assignment I had dreamed of for years, I was torn. The timing was far from ideal as our son Dan had just turned one year old, and it was a six-week shoot in a remote location. I loved fatherhood, and I was pretty hands-on. Yaffa did not yet have a network of close friends in London; my parents, though doting, were seventy-five miles away, and her family was over two thousand miles away. It was a tough decision, but passing up this opportunity could have jeopardised the career path I aspired to. Yaffa selflessly encouraged me to accept.

Our base camp was Ucaima, a small collection of lodges at a beautiful spot on the banks of the Rio Carrao, a tributary of the Orinoco. It looked onto a magnificent panorama of tepuis, flat-top mountains that are the remains of a massive primaeval sandstone plateau that once covered the area. Rudy Truffino had established the camp as a base for exploration, scientific expeditions, adventurers, and the occasional documentary film crew. 'Jungle Rudy' was a well-known figure in certain circles. As a young man, he had left his family home in Holland in search of wilderness and was rescued from starvation by Pemon tribespeople. He tells us, on camera, how he traded his clothing for a bow and arrow and a blowpipe, learned from observing the fauna, what berries to forage, and from locals, how to dam rivers to catch fish. He became immersed in the indigenous culture and stayed. In due course, he was elemental in establishing the Canaima National Park. When we arrived, he had lived in the jungle for thirty-three years. He was an extraordinary character, and I would have been happy just to make a film about him (someone else did some years later). He is no longer with us, and today, *'Jungle Rudy's Ucaima'* is a lodge for adventurous tourists run by his two daughters.

It was a great spot to gather and organise all our kit and for the pilots to do the same. We had a good rest after our journey out. We swam and washed in the river. The water was a reddish brown—not because it was dirty, but because it was infused with tannin from the local flora. Rudy's indigenous staff produced delicious meals from the camp kitchen. We sat in the dining lodge discussing the logistics of the upcoming expedition, with Elvis the parrot briefly looking up from his plate of seeds to contribute to the conversation.

The team consisted of Peter and I, Tim Maurice-Jones as my AC and Paul Nathan on sound. Paul was a good friend, and we had worked together a fair bit. Tim had worked with me mainly on MTV music videos. He was a zany guy and insisted on being photographed standing on his head in as many out-of-the-way locations as could be mustered. Gerry Breen was a renowned hang glider, and microlight pilot and developer. With his *Crocodile Dundee* hat and *Fist Full of Dollars* cigar, he cut a central character worthy of any adventure film. His fellow pilot was Kelvin Wilson, a microlight test pilot and hang-gliding school owner. Of utmost importance, Rudy was our guide, along with his daughter, Lilly, and four of his staff as boatmen and helpers.

We headed upstream in two long motorised dugout canoes, punching our way through the fierce current. Paul had radio-miked Gerry and Kelvin, and we shot boat-to-boat footage and dialogue as we sped through the stunning scenery. We rounded a bend in the river to reveal the most spectacular natural sight. Bathed in a pool of sunlight, Auyán Tepui, a kilometre-high sheer rock face, pierced the heavens. The Angel Falls, in all its splendour, cascaded from its summit, the stream momentarily obscured from view by a small white cloud clinging to the cliff one-third of the way down. Locally, it is known as 'the river that falls from the clouds'.

We reached our destination, Ucaima 2, a basic shack that Rudy had built on the bank, with a perfect view of the star feature of our show. There was no mains power available for lighting or charging, but we had brought with us a couple of gas-mantle pressure lanterns, which pushed out more light than the kerosene-fuelled Tilley lamps that were on site. That evening, as the expedition team gathered around the bush-crafted table to discuss the action plan, I positioned these to get sufficient exposure for an atmospheric glow with which to film this critical discussion. It was followed by the presentation of a thick slice of bread with a single large candle to celebrate Tim's birthday.

The following day was spent scouting potential landing sites for the flight. With fluctuating water levels, the options were limited, rocky, and left little room for error.

We set off at daybreak, navigating the dugouts to the best access point, stopping a couple of times to haul them through shallow rapids. The plan was to carry all the kit across the jungle floor and climb to the summit. Gerry insisted, as a point of principle, that he and Kelvin should lug the unwieldy gliders themselves. A decision they would come to regret.

Angel falls from Ucaima 2

There were rivers to cross with all the equipment, camping gear, and supplies. It had to be carried through waist-high, fast-moving water, and the action filmed from mid-stream. It took all my strength to stay upright and not be swept away by the current, camera and all. This was precarious enough, but there were plenty more challenges to come.

It is not called a rainforest for nothing—one downpour produced fifteen inches of rain in one night. We had anticipated these conditions and were kitted out with weather gear made from this new hi-tech material—Gore-Tex. Despite the jackets, leggings, and bivvy bags (waterproof outer layer for a sleeping bag) to crawl into at night, we were permanently drenched from rain and sweat. For the equipment, we had a large selection of heavy-duty plastic bags and sheets as well as the standard film industry weatherproof paraphernalia.

Supervised by Rudy, bivouacs were constructed nightly. A frame was built from what the forest offered, and plastic

Kelvin and Jerry failing to keep dry

sheeting was used for the roof. It took five insect-infested, wet days of hacking, trekking and lugging through the dense jungle to get to the base of the tepui. Conditions were relentless. We were soaked through, exhausted and despondent, and to top it all, Kelvin had a fever. For Rudy and his team, it was just another day at the office. As a matter of course, the film crew had to deal with the same hardships as the subjects, with the added task of shooting the developing story.

There was rethinking to be done, and we shot an intense discussion around a crackling fire in the shelter of the bivouac. Progress had been painfully slow and torturous, and demoralisation had set in. Gerry was concerned that even if they got to the top, provisions would run low, and they may be forced to take off in unsuitable conditions. The decision was made to return to the advanced base and call in a helicopter to take us all and our equipment to the top of the tepui.

They were extremely disappointed that they had failed in this aspect of their expedition. But this is where the world of television took some licence. We had already planned for a chopper to fly in for a multitude of purposes: aerials of the jungle and falls, ferrying us up and down for different camera angles of the hang-gliders' flight, and taking Gerry and Kelvin up for two extra flights so we could get extensive footage for the dramatic and, hopefully, visually poetic climax to the story.

Close to Ucaima 2, a clearing was cut for the arrival of the Hughes helicopter from Caracas, 300 miles away. Being in close proximity to a landing chopper is always a very windy and noisy experience, but on this occasion, there was loose greenery flying around and a deafening clatter. It turned out that the given specifications for the dimensions of the clearing hadn't been thought through. The downwash from the rotors sucked in the surrounding forest canopy, and a blade struck a tree. This put the aircraft out of balance, but Oscar, the pilot, kept control and landed safely. He decided that the machine was still flyable for the mission. He had been a rally driver and was used to pushing the limits—there would be plenty of that over the coming days.

The guys offloaded the cargo, which was barrels of aviation fuel; Gerry and Kelvin hitched the two collapsed and packaged hang-gliders across the landing skids and clambered aboard with their tools, spares and camping supplies. We filmed them taking off and flying in a spiral up the face of the falls until they were a speck at the top. An hour later, we followed suit. I was in the co-pilot seat filming Oscar at the controls and the point of view through the windscreen. It was an incredible sight as we flew through the cloud to reveal the summit and the water that had been sedately gathering on the high plain, being released into free-fall through gullies in the uppermost layer of rock.

We spent some days at the top, awaiting suitable flying conditions, but there was plenty to do. This was a dangerous venture, and every variability had to be scrutinised. We shot the guys constructing, checking, and rechecking every aspect of their aircraft. They were psyched up and eager to fly, but conditions frustrated their plans.

A sizeable ledge stuck out from the edge of the precipice overlooking where the falls emerged, offering a great variety of shots. Suitably safety harnessed, I positioned myself, tripod and camera at the extremity. From there, I could pan and tilt from the gushing source to the forest valley a kilometre below. I filmed Gerry and Kelvin, enveloped in mist, sitting near the edge, discussing the technicalities and logistics of the pioneering flight they were about to embark on. They questioned whether there was an option to take off in cloud should the weather not clear.

I had two GSAP cameras. These were American military gun cameras designed to be mounted on fighter aircraft and triggered automatically when their guns were fired, filming the target and the consequential damage. They ran for just over a minute on a 50ft cassette of 16mm film. Adapted for civilian use, they had crude wire 'sports' finders to take some of the guesswork out of framing the shot. With clamps and gaffer tape, we mounted one near the wing tip facing Gerry and a battery on a long lead positioned on the opposing wing to counterbalance the camera's weight. We put the other GSAP on the tail, looking backwards to catch Kelvin and his glider as they follow Gerry off the edge. We capped the lenses and wrapped the cameras in plastic to keep them dry. Everything was now ready, except for the weather.

The guys took shelter in a crevice close to the edge, where they ate and slept. We filmed their witty banter, mainly about insects, snakes, and miserable conditions. It was uncomfortable and challenging for them, and more so for me, as I clung to the slippery rocks, trying to execute engaging camera angles. The sequence was wound up by Kelvin closing their lantern's gas valve, creating a natural fade-to-black.

Dawn reveals a beautiful day. The sky is blue with wispy clouds. There's the inevitable haze in the valley far below as the sun's heat reclaims moisture for future downpours, but visibility is good. We can see the river and the island that will be the landing strip. There's an eager walkie-talkie exchange with Rudy regarding the river water level in the valley. It needs to be on the low side for a good landing. Through the static crackling, the message comes through: *"All is good"*.

This is it—the culmination of all the planning, setbacks

and hardships. Adrenalin runs high. For them, it is the danger, the test of their skills and the unpredictability of the unknown as they are the first to undertake such a flight. For us, it is the challenge to get coverage to create a sequence worthy of this unique event. Without it, there is no film.

Although it will be repeated, the first flight is the one with all the excitement of the unknown. Peter briefs Gerry on the requirements of the GSAP shots. I shoot last-minute checks and the buzz around getting harnessed to the hang gliders. While Peter shoots on the plateau with a second camera, I rush to my perch on the ledge, where the tripod awaits me. Tim sticks a fresh film magazine on my Aaton with the 15x Angenieux zoom lens and carefully hands it to me.

I have a clear, head-on view of the two aircraft lined up for take-off. Gerry lifts his bright yellow 'kite' and runs towards the precipice. He leaps off the edge, momentarily falls and then gets lifted by the updraft, Kelvin hot on his tail. I have the perfect position to get a shot of them against the gushing water and then zoom out to reveal the epic vista below. The pilots lift their legs into the cocoon harnesses to provide maximum aerodynamics. They skilfully manipulate the control bars to optimise their flight options as they search out thermals to lift and soar—surely, these men are in heaven. They are whooping and shouting at each other; exchanges are recorded by the Pro-Walkman cassette recorders that Paul had rigged on board. I hope that Gerry remembers to trigger the GSAPs. It is a beautiful sight as I get a variety of shots from my eyrie, following them till they are specks on the river-island landing strip.

Time for a celebratory beer? No way. Conditions are good, and we must squeeze all we can from them. While Gerry and Kelvin dismantle their gliders below, Paul, Tim and I board the chopper and spiral down to the valley floor. I say 'floor', but the only place suitable to actually land is in the clearing at Ucaima 2, which is too far away. Oscar has to precariously hover above some rocks as we pass gear, clamber onto the landing skids, and jump off, being wary not to twist an ankle. The flyers do the reverse, and we set up to film them from below.

Peter has stayed at the top for the second run, and I am at the landing strip with my beloved 600mm lens. I follow them most of the way down, letting them first fly into shot, pan with them for a while, and then fly out of shot, giving the editor plenty of options. It is a magical sight as they sweep past the free-falling cataract, dipping in and out of the cliff-face shadow. They climb, stall and dive as if in a dance. We do a swift magazine change. They are really large in the frame now. It looks great, but I can't risk being stuck with this big lens for the landing—a quick change to the zoom as they approach.

First comes Gerry. He stalls his aircraft and makes an impressive landing, running across the rocks. With a beaming smile, he punches the air, then carries the glider to the edge to make room for his friend's approach. I go handheld to get his first comments. *"Where's Kelvin?"* We hear the sound of splintering wood coming from the riverbank. *"Are you OK?"* While trying to give Gerry time to clear, Kelvin experienced a 'sink' over the trees and crash-landed, suffering only a broken wing. I get him on the long end of the zoom as he struggles to untangle the glider.

A quick repair and we are up to the top for a final run. I am shooting from the helicopter. The door has been removed, and we have had a Tyler gyro-stabilised mount fitted at a significant cost. I get a good aerial shot sweeping over the plateau moments before our guys take off, but it all falls to pieces once they are in flight. Oscar cannot manoeuvre into the correct positions without disturbing the flyer's air. Maybe it is a communication problem, combined with my lack of experience using the Tyler mount, but the result is a washout. I am mortified. I could say nothing and let them discover at the rushes viewing in London, but that would not be professional. I tell, and Peter is understandably furious.

Undoubtedly, with a big "Daddy's coming home" buildup, Yaffa and Dan come to meet me at Heathrow Airport. I catch sight of them behind the barrier as I exit the arrivals gate. I rush towards them with arms open wide, and to my dismay, Dan bursts into tears—not of joy but of terror—as this bearded, jungle-weary, mosquito-ravaged apparition looms large. I guess six weeks is a long time for a one-year-old.

A couple of months pass, and I am invited to a preview. Simon Rose, the editor, and Peter have done a great job putting it together. The flight sequence runs for a spell-binding eight minutes with a rousing score written and produced by Rod Argent. Everyone is happy.

14

By Royal Appointment

The standard film crew uniform is jeans (or shorts) and a T-shirt, but on this occasion, I dusted off my outmoded suit and headed to Buckingham Palace. It was the year 1985, and we were there to film HRH Princess Anne, the Honorary President of the British Olympic Association. She was making a campaign submission for Birmingham to host the 1992 Summer Olympics.

After a basic security check, we were ushered through the imposing cast-iron gates and directed to the West Wing. I drove my Ford Granada Estate, jam-packed with kit and crew, to a loading bay, and we trollied lights, sound and camera gear through the grand corridors to HRH's suite of receiving rooms. Her equerry briefed us on protocol, and he pointed out a precious antique vase with delicate porcelain flowers and warned us to keep well clear. It already had a couple of headless stems, and breakage was deemed bad luck.

The director and his PA had yet to arrive, so we started setting up. This was an era long before LED panels or softboxes, so it required a 2kw tungsten lamp through a trace diffusing frame to create a soft, flattering key light, a small spot for hair light and further lamps to lift the shadows and give shape to the background.

As I stepped out of the door to move some of our flight cases to the adjoining room, I heard a forceful voice bellowing instructions to an aide at the other end of the corridor. The owner of this voice strode out of the door opposite and almost bumped into me. She was as startled as I was. She had a face that had been dominating the front pages of the tabloids for weeks—it was Sarah Ferguson, soon to be married to Prince Andrew. The press had not been kind to her, and she probably feared that this encounter with a long-haired, scruffy outsider was about to hand them more ammunition.

The production department arrived; the PA sat in for a final lineup and for the director to approve the shot. At the prearranged time, the Princess Royal made a magical entrance through a 'jib' door concealed in the wall. She greeted us all and was politely directed to her seat. As our director talked her through the plan, I did my final tweak of the lights. I stepped behind her to adjust the hair light. She instinctively turned towards me to check what was happening, constantly wary of potential attacks, even on her home territory.

She was charming and very professional in delivering her message. The shoot ran smoothly. She rose and disappeared back through the wall.

At the end of any sequence, it is standard practice to record the 'silence'. Every environment has its ambient background noise, which our brains normally filter out. This 'atmos', 'buzz-track' or 'room-tone' can be used during post-production to smooth audio transitions on edits. With his microphones in the same position and the lights still on, the soundman called for thirty seconds of silence, announced a verbal ident on to tape, and we all remained still. Ten seconds in, there was a distinct cracking noise. All heads turned as one of the porcelain flower heads popped off its stem—no one was close, and it was undoubtedly the result of heat from the lights.

Barcelona won the bid for the '92 Olympics.

A more momentous occurrence in 1985—our daughter, Tali, burst onto the scene and lit up our world. I now had a fully-fledged family to house and feed. I was getting a reasonable amount of work but certainly had no reason to be complacent. There was always that nagging feeling that the phone would never ring again. I loathed the idea of bugging all the people who had 'forgotten' me and, even worse, cold-calling producers, directors and production managers. What do you say when you get through to someone? The competition was doing the same, and many had the gift of the gab.

It was essential to have an up-to-date showreel; producing one was expensive and time-consuming. At least it was no longer necessary to have a reel on 16mm film. Still, you had to source a second-generation Umatic video copy of each included film, rent an editing facility with an operator, and have a run of top-quality VHS cassette copies made. Then, add a sleeve graphic that would stand out and hope it would find a dominant position on production companies' shelves. I don't understand the contemporary approach to showreels, where the cinematographer fast cuts all their best shots to music, and it's over in a minute. Surely, a director wants to see that the cameraperson is empathetic, can create a sequence, and match lighting as well as make pretty pictures. Aren't they prepared to invest ten minutes of their time to understand whether this vital crew member can help them express their vision? Maybe not. This was not the case in the 1980s and '90s, and I updated a couple of nine to twelve-minute reels every few years.

They were vital when someone contacted me via a recommendation. I also sent a number out more randomly, with follow-up calls. These had minimal success, except on one occasion—and that is all it needs. I usually would not consider a natural history production company a target as it is a specialised field. I don't recall why I sent a reel to Partridge Films; maybe it was because their offices were local to me, and I could save on postage. It just so happened that they were planning a shoot a little outside of their comfort zone. They had put in a successful bid to National Geographic Films for an expedition documentary accompanying a conservation research team penetrating the remote Ankarana Massif in Northern Madagascar.

Phil Chapman, a naturalist, was to be both expedition leader and director. Today, a producer at the BBC's Natural History Unit, this was his first film. Partridge's CEO and senior producer, John Rosenberg, was eager to have a suitably experienced cameraman to support him. Fortuitously, my new showreel, which included a substantial clip from *On Angel's Wings*, had landed on his desk.

These would prove to be the physically most demanding conditions I had yet to work in, so it was of no help that I had had a hospital operation to remove two wisdom teeth a few weeks earlier. A nerve had been damaged, causing pain and total numbness of my tongue. I could not eat.

Even though Yaffa had been devotedly preparing nourishing smoothies for me, I had lost a significant amount of weight. Furthermore, both kids had chickenpox, and there was a likelihood that I could be incubating the contagious infection. Not the best body or mindset to embark on this assignment.

15

Madagascar Crocs

Madagascar, the world's fourth-largest island, broke away from Africa one hundred and sixty million years ago. Its flora and fauna have evolved in isolation, and approximately 95% of the wildlife is unique to the island. We were there to tell this story primarily through exploration of the all-but-inaccessible sunken forests concealed within the Ankarana massif, an immense and magnificent limestone outcrop located in the north. Because of their inaccessibility, these forests are a sanctuary for wildlife, protected from the effects of the human colonisation that started two thousand years ago. Regrettably, it has led to the extinction of numerous species and continues to do so—initially through overhunting and later through the demand for farming land. There has been continuous deforestation, predominantly achieved through slash-and-burn clearing techniques, with fires that often blaze out of control. Phil refers to Ankarana in the film as *"...an island of plenty in a sea of waste."*

Filming a slash-and-burn fire. Phil is in the foreground

Phil was the project's instigator and leader, and the other protagonists were Michael Rakatonirina, a Malagasy naturalist and conservationist; Blaid Michel, a local guide with knowledge of the cave system, and Sheila Herd, a British caving and abseiling expert. Inevitably, the support and film teams comprised more personnel than the expedition.

Once again, my crew was Tim and Paul. Also with us was Jim Clare, a wildlife cameraman who shot most of the animal footage, which made up a fair proportion of the film. He was happy to be left to his own devices, except for the odd occasion when our stories coincided. The equipment package was sizeable as I would be lighting huge caves. As well as specially adapted and maximised head torches and a couple of 300W 'SunGun' battery lights, I had two 2kW Blondes and two 850W Redheads, each with its own petrol generator and lengths of cable.

While we were filming in Antananarivo, the capital, a

convoy of Land Cruisers set off with the heavy kit on the 1,100-kilometre drive. When we were done, we met them at an airstrip a couple of days' rough-track drive from our destination.

It was a magnificent and daunting sight as we approached the 'Wall of Ankarana', a sheer Jurassic limestone cliff that extends 25 kilometres north to south and rises as high as 280 metres, and we proceeded through a fissure to the furthest point we could drive. This was where we established our base camp.

The massif has hundreds of kilometres of caves—some dry, some with rivers, and some only accessible via squeeze holes. Only a small proportion have been charted. This cave system is the sole access point to the sunken forests.

A simple set-up to ease us into the gruelling exploration ahead. The expedition has inflatable canoes to navigate the underground rivers; I suggest to Phil a sequence in a cave with a calm river and good available light. I stand chest-deep in the water, with the camera on my shoulder and cue them to paddle towards me, skirting close as they pass. Seeing them veer wildly from side to side, it strikes me that I am the only member of this team of 'intrepid' adventurers who actually knows how to handle a canoe. I spend the rest of the afternoon giving lessons.

There is a cave known to be one of the world's largest, and it leads to a sunken forest. How do you show the extent of this cavern and still give the impression that it is pitch black? I use the two larger lamps to skim the beautiful scallops on the walls that aeons of water erosion have created. I conceal the smaller lamps behind rocks to pick out a couple of dramatic formations. Underexposed to the lowest limits of the fast film stock and fast lenses, the sources and beams of the team's head torches burn out, helping the illusion. The most compelling image is a pan, culminating in a wide shot revealing the enormity of the cave with the guys walking through—tiny in the frame. The noise from four generators thumping away in this giant echo chamber is thunderous, so Paul has his own walk-through to record 'wild' sound of the conversation and footsteps.

On his previous visit a couple of years earlier, Phil had discovered a skeleton in an offshoot cave. He believed it to be of a now-extinct lemur species, and he hoped to locate it again. It would make an excellent story for the film, so I volunteered to join the search. He led the way as we clambered over rocks, along narrow ridges and squeezed through tight spaces, turning left and right and climbing up and down. I hoped Phil knew the way back. This little expedition hadn't really been thought through, and we had no provisions or spare batteries. Deep into this labyrinth, he suggested I perch on a rock, conserving my head-torch batteries while he hurried ahead on his quest. We would reunite on his return. The cave was massive. I examined my surroundings as best I could and then turned off the torch.

I thought I had encountered both darkness and silence before—this was another level—total sensory deprivation. It was a profound experience, awe-inspiring and terrifying. After what may have been a quarter of an hour, my mind was taking me to strange places; after half an hour, it dawned on me that something may have happened to Phil. Maybe he was hurt or lost. Was I going to become a skeleton to be found by some future expedition? There was no option for me to retrace my steps—I have trouble finding my way to the corner shop; anyhow, that would negate the possibility of Phil finding me. The other team members would have no idea where to start a search. As I began to mentally compose a note to Yaffa and the kids to be found with my decomposing body, I heard distant panting and saw a dimming sparkle getting closer. Having failed in his search, Phil was rushing back, aided by the dying glimmer from his head torch. What a relief!

Back in the main chamber, we headed towards the threshold and into the comparatively dazzling brightness emanating from our first sight of a sunken forest, where an even larger cave had collapsed probably thousands of years ago. Tropical vegetation had colonised the floor and was reaching towards the daylight high above. Underfoot was no longer hard rock but a tangle of undergrowth. A symphony of nature's sounds engulfed us. We encountered lemurs for the first time as, undoubtedly, these individuals encountered humans for the first time. These elegant and colourful primates exhibited no fear, just wide-eyed curiosity. Lemurs are Madagascar's only primate and of a lineage predating African monkeys. Ranging from mouse-sized to human-sized variants, the number of recorded subspecies had reached well into the hundreds, one-third of which were already considered extinct.

I had, and would later, experience, many jungle environments where you would have to make an effort to encounter wildlife. Here, it was abundant and unhidden—a fabulous experience but also a sign that this was the last haven of Madagascar's unthreatened forest.

Our early forays had been on foot through caves on known routes; now, we were about to search from the top. This karst landscape is stunning, with towers, spikes and obelisks, Consisting of razor-sharp ridges known as 'tsingy', where the calcific upper layers have been completely eroded, and the harder base rock has been etched into channels. This is a remarkable environment unlike any I have seen or tried to navigate. Despite wearing heavy boots and gloves, we all experienced rips, scratches and bruises while clambering over this hostile terrain. Concentration was at one hundred per cent for every foothold and handhold as we progressed carrying our camping, expedition, and filming equipment. We battled to find perches from which to shoot sequences of the search for extraordinary life in the nooks and crannies of this bizarre landscape. Meanwhile, a family of lemurs smugly watched us struggle as they bounded effortlessly from ridge to ridge.

Night was closing in, and we found a small patch to make camp. Suddenly, Paul whispered excitedly, "Over there!" It was a fossa, which is of the mongoose family. There are no cats in Madagascar, and the fossa has evolved to fill that gap. Its appearance is cougar-like, and it's at the top of the food chain. They are elusive and have never been filmed in the wild—until now. I set up quickly. The light was fading and flat. I had the wrong lens on and the wrong film stock loaded, but I could not afford to lose a second. The window was brief, and the shots were not great, but they were in the can. Poor Jim had been getting lovely wildlife sequences but was not around for the unique one.

On the next day, we came to the precipitous edge of a massive sinkhole. One hundred and ten metres below, we could see a forest-surrounded lake that disappeared into a cave. The abseiling gear was broken out, and Sheila was now in her element. This was good action value for the film. For me, it was a challenge to get enough angles to capture the drama. Great as it would be to be spontaneous with such things, the reality was very different. I filmed handheld up close for preparations and point-of-view over the edge, and then we scrambled to the far side of the abyss, from where I could capture a wide-angle vista showing the scale of the situation. Communicating with Sheila via walkie-talkies, we coordinated a variety of long lens shots—an over-cranked slo-mo shot following the 'static' rope uncoiling as it plunged down the sheer face, along with close-ups of Phil's descent. As the whole team had to go down individually, there were opportunities for other shots where faces and outfits were unrecognisable. For our own descents, in the middle of the process, we were happy to concentrate on abseiling technique and safety rather than carrying any kit or trying to film.

Once at the bottom, we carried on shooting from there. This was real *Lost World* territory. Canoes were inflated, and we paddled into the unknown, swallowed up by another of Ankarana's networks of darkness. It was no environment for a claustrophobe; the stream narrowed, and the ceiling lowered. I soon discovered the importance of our helmets. Once again, our only source of light was head torches. It made for some atmospheric POV shots and a good dialogue sequence, with the beams of the team's torches illuminating one another.

We could hear fast-running water ahead—this would be exciting. We disembarked onto the rocks when we neared the white-water rapids and surveyed the situation. Being the designated canoe master, I sussed the options and advised that it was feasible to canoe them and film the action. The nature of inflatables is such that you can feel through your bottom or feet as you slide over submerged boulders; the flexibility of the hull wraps itself around the undulations of the water-smoothed rocks. It was exhilarating paddling, but more tricky was trying to keep a foothold on the slippery stones while setting our battery lights and scrambling to a shooting position. I did fall and nearly dunked the camera but instinctively protected it instead of myself. Tim calls it my 'Excalibur' moment, with an outstretched arm holding the cherished symbol of my professional purpose, rising defiantly from the water. He dutifully relieved me of the camera as I was helped to my feet. Nursing a bloodied knee and inspecting the gash to my helmet, I stood upright and bashed my head on the jagged cave roof! No lasting damage was done, and in due course, the river delivered us to another opening, with more forest to be explored and data to be gathered.

Navigating the subterranean rapids

Three weeks into our stay, we were down to eating tinned sardines and dried bananas. Tim and Blaid offered to drive the seven-hour round trip to the nearest village to buy provisions. Tim volunteered to give our support guys a break and cook dinner. We had no refrigeration in camp, so the anticipation of a freshly cooked meal was a real treat and a one-off. Paul and I eagerly helped out washing, peeling and chopping as Tim's culinary creativity flourished over the kerosene burners. We were each served a large plate of chicken and vegetables in an enticing-looking sauce. We enthusiastically dug in and simultaneously spat out. Our bush kitchen store had two identical five-litre plastic bottles—one contained cooking oil and the other, washing up liquid!

Jim had been hard at work gathering shots of a multitude of wildlife. On the rare occasions we were moving and working together, I was amused to see him grab insects and lizards and pop them into plastic containers for future stardom (sometimes as prey). He told us of his footage of blind cave fish, shrimps, and amphibians, but wisely, he had not ventured alone into the below-ground waters known to be home to the world's only cave-dwelling crocodiles. These are of the same ancient lineage as the Nile Crocodile; they grow up to six metres and periodically come to the open to hunt, often feeding on domestic cattle. There had been many incidents of local people being dragged into the river and devoured, and myths of spirits inhabiting these caves. This was to be our next foray.

Michael was the team's local naturalist and the expert on crocs. Unfortunately, on the morning of the trip, a scorpion stung him on the bum through the groundsheet of his tent; the poor guy had a high fever and had to stay behind.

From our base camp, it was an off-road drive around the massif's periphery to a different entry point. Here we made camp. The plan was to go in light-handed and recce the situation. We inflated the canoes and dragged them to the river. They floated fine with the kit, but they went aground as soon as we boarded. The water level was too low, so we had to walk the canoes into the black chasm—was this wise? We were working on the assumption that crocodiles are 'solar powered' and would be apathetic in the dark—is that true? For a while, all we could see were areas of the stream at our feet, black rock picked out by our helmet lamps and the occasional bat briefly caught in the beam. All we could hear was the bats and our footsteps splashing through the water. It was eerie. The river deepened, and we boarded the canoes. Now, I felt a little less vulnerable. Then, I caught a glimpse of two fiery red points of light picked out by my beam. It was at water level and about eight metres away—our first crocodile encounter. It watched us for a few seconds and silently submerged without creating a ripple. We paddled on gently until we came to a large chamber. Scanning the water's surface, we could now see several individuals. Some were in the water, others lazing on rocks—all eyes on us. We were the intruders in their dark, silent world. It was unsettling in the extreme, though tempered with a sense of awe. Then came the thought of what to do if attacked. Oh, that's easy— poke out its eyes with your thumbs or jam its jaws open with a tripod. I think I'll just give in to the inevitable.

They seemed docile, so we carried on with the business of getting some shots. It was surprisingly straightforward. Roy was Sheila's caving number two, and he was extraordinarily blasé and reckless. He volunteered to be a human lamp stand for the SunGun and moved across the rocks to the various positions that I requested for the required angles of light. We set up the tripod on a convenient rocky ledge. I captured a selection of shots of somewhat bewildered crocs slithering into the water, eyes submerging, and some extreme close-ups. That was much easier than I had anticipated, and we returned to our temporary camp, satisfied. We now needed to tie in a subterranean canoeing sequence.

Early in the morning, we took all our lights and generators deep into the cave. As the water level was low, there was a saturated sand river bank along which we could carry our stuff. On returning for a second load, I noticed a slither mark and giant croc footprints, suggesting a much more substantial animal than the two-metre specimens we had filmed. It must have crossed my path in the previous few minutes. A shiver ran down my spine; it was a sharp reminder not to become complacent while we were preoccupied with filming. Roy, however, was undaunted as he waded chest-deep through the water, carrying lamps with stands above his head and running 16-amp power cables with connectors through the river. They are considered waterproof, but I don't think they are designed to be submersible. What the crocodiles made of all the commotion, bright lights and shouting, I can't imagine. Still, they kept it to themselves and looked on as we spent the day recreating the intrepid and chilling expeditionary components of the adventure.

Upon returning to base camp, we told Michael the details. Still nursing an inflamed backside, his reaction was one of utter disbelief. Had he been there, he would have forbidden us to take such risks.

16

Dark River

Carphones for the wealthy, followed by cumbersome hand-carried cellular phone units, had been around for a few years, but by 1987, the Motorola Dynatac 8500X, hand-portable 'Brick' was on the market in the UK. The cost of purchasing and using a personal mobile phone had decreased from exorbitant to very expensive. I convinced myself that one job I would have otherwise missed would justify it. A fine specimen of electronic engineering, it was eight inches high with a six-inch antenna on top and weighed one kilo. I bought a beautiful leather case with a belt loop that caused me to limp under the weight. I have a vivid memory of its first outing. It was a one-day shoot for the BBC at Alexander Palace. A beautiful summer's day; we sat on the grass for a break, and I was smugly showing off my new toy to the unit. "This," I said, "means work." As if on cue, the phone rang. I answered nonchalantly—it was a call cancelling tomorrow's shoot! Had the production not managed to make contact, they would have been obliged to pay me in full.

The other must-have item at the time was a Filofax ring-binder personal organiser. It was a British product that flourished in Thatcher's 'Yuppie' (young, **u**pwardly-mobile **p**rofessional) era. And, as well as the standard address book, diary, organiser pages, card slots and pen loops, there were hundreds of optional refills and accessories for every imaginable lifestyle and interest. They came in a variety of sizes and materials, and the fatter they were packed, the more important a person you were. It seemed that everybody had one, and they were very useful, BUT heavens forbid you should lose it; there was no backup.

Prior to the internet and inexpensive video, corporate promotional and training films were limited to the larger companies that could afford the healthy budgets and high production values that audiences expected. Some were dramatised and others documentary. One such film followed the building of an off-shore North Sea oil platform, shot as a cinema short over four years on 35mm film. On one of the shoots, we spent several days aboard a 'sheerleg' floating crane with a 20,000-tonne lifting capacity plus accommodation and facilities for hundreds of workers.

On another, the massive platform's jacket, lying on its side, had been towed out from Brittany. It had to be un-welded from the anchor points on its barge, positioned precisely and sunken onto the four sockets secured deep on the ocean floor. Not to say that the atmosphere was tense, but there was a story around that, on an earlier such operation, a jacket had failed to connect, toppled and sank—the chief engineer topped himself. There were days of waiting for the perfect conditions, and then the operation was completed within a couple of hours. We had a remotely triggered camera mounted on the barge. I was filming from the open door of a Chinook helicopter, and I had a couple of extra camera operators picking up other angles from an adjacent platform. It was a magnificent sight as the giant structure slid into the sea as if in slow motion, was righted by the flooding of massive chambers, and neatly settled into position.

Keep Safety First was a training film for British Rail, set up by its in-house production department and shot on Betacam video. As with anyone operating trackside, we, the crew, had to complete a two-day safety course culminating in an exam.

Similar in style to the BBC series *999* that I had been working on, the video was made up of dramatic recreations of nasty, sometimes fatal, accidents involving maintenance workers. Most filming was done on functioning tracks, so we had to shoot between scheduled trains using the systems of procedures and look-outs we had learnt. We had all the blood, gore and action of an XX-rated horror movie with convincing stunts, pyrotechnics and makeup. One after-dark scenario required 800 metres of track to be lit by numerous HMI lamps on cherry pickers. It was quite an operation involving a gaffer with many electricians and generator operators. We had a diesel-electric locomotive and rolling stock standing by in a siding, and our stuntman standing by to be 'hit' by it. On this occasion, the track was closed to scheduled traffic for the duration of the action.

Two years later, we were invited to shoot an updated version. Our safety qualifications had expired, so we had to take the course again. We sat down at our desks, and the instructor introduced himself and proceeded to show our film, *Keep Safety First*.

When talking to people about how I make my living, they sometimes have the impression that I have a jet-setting lifestyle of jollies. Sure, I have travelled a great deal, but as for jollies—certainly not. Though there was the occasional exception. Directed and produced by Ian Lewis, a colleague I had met when he was an editor at Visnews. *A Taste of O.S.L.* was a culinary tour of the Algarve, Dordogne, and Tuscany, produced for a tourism company. It was fronted by Roy Ackerman, a renowned restaurateur, chef and editor of the Egon Ronay restaurant guide. He was a bon viveur and a delight to work alongside. For the thirty-minute film, we had a week in each country. Roy didn't like to fly, so he and his companion drove in his vintage Jaguar between locations, giving us a few days at home between each of the three trips—very civilised. At every location, we would wander around the markets, tasting produce. Roy was an enthusiast, bursting with positive energy and excitement about everything around him, whether on camera or not. We would walk, unannounced, into a restaurant, straight through to the kitchen where he would lift lids off bubbling pots, inspecting and smelling what was on offer. He had an aura of the gourmet, and chefs would feel honoured. He would order and pay for a bottle of fine wine at dinner. On two occasions, He rejected them, though they tasted delicious to me—no quibble from the maître d'.

Malcolm Taylor is a talented writer and director. He had a successful production company specialising in high-end infomercials. I did several shoots for him, as varied as a rainforest awareness promo shot in Cameroon for the World Wildlife Fund and a comedy set in the office of a marriage guidance counsellor for computers: "Communication problems? The answer is Pirelli-Focon fibre optic cables."

Another featured a businessman being propelled through the streets of the City of London on a power-driven executive chair. This was promoting '*The Sunday Times*' classified ads.

What Malcolm really wanted to do was to write and produce arthouse movies. He wrote an excellent script called 'Dark River' (not to be confused with the 2017 movie of the same name). It was a period thriller set in a British colony on the banks of a river flowing through the lowlands of Africa. He had enthused a fantastic cast, with such actors as Siân Phillips, Kate Buffery, Michael Dennison and Freddie Jones. Each was the star of their own short but crucial scene, usually alongside the main protagonist, played by Tom Bell. Malcolm, who had his own Arriflex 16mm camera kit, achieved this economically by filming many of these scenes on the back of corporate shoots. For example, we would do an item or interview in London for one of his clients in the morning and, in the afternoon, move onto a set in a nearby location dressed as an African village bar. This way, the base rate for the crew was already paid, and he topped up the difference for overtime. Rather cheeky, I guess, but he took it a stage further. He employed me to film gold mines in South Africa for the renowned tycoon Tiny Roland, who had a far from 'tiny' bank account. That paid to fly crew and equipment out and back. Malcolm flew in Tom Bell and Ian McNeice to join us in Zimbabwe, where we filmed the river adventure on the Zambezi. This was the movie's backbone, stringing together the London-shot interior scenarios.

17
1989

'Nines' have always been consequential years for me. In 1949, I was born. I don't remember the experience, but I guess it was pretty momentous. 1969 was memorable for almost every Westerner of my generation as 'Flower Power' was at its peak, and, for me, it included the transformative travel experiences of the overland trip to India and becoming a cruise ship photographer. In 1979, I became a camera-owning, working freelance cameraman, and 1989 was the busiest and most financially rewarding year of my life so far... and since.

Along with the three-month High Arctic stint (Dan and Tali, now six and four years old, were still sceptical about my claim to have put in a good word for them when I met Santa at the North Pole) and Malcolm's Africa shoot, I was getting work from the BBC Bristol documentary unit. Life was good. I paid off the mortgage and had a fancy new kitchen installed (it still looks good after thirty-five years). I bought a second-hand cabin cruiser on the Thames— a long-standing dream

Yaffa, Dan and Tali, 1989

realised, and Yaffa and the kids delighted in our boating holidays.

I also invested in the latest Aaton XTR. It had many upgrades, but the significant difference was that it had a Super16 film gate. With the right lenses and some nimble mini-screwdriver work to re-centre them, it could be switched between Standard 16mm and the new widescreen Super16mm format.

Since TV began, the traditional, almost square, cinema 'academy' aspect ratio of 4x3 or 1.33:1 was universal for the small screen. In fact, widescreen movie formats for cinema had been developed to compete with television's ever-increasing popularity. A decade before the first flatscreen TVs were available, 16:9 ratio widescreen tube TVs came onto the market, and many drama and factual programmes started producing content accordingly, especially those that anticipated a long shelf-life.

For film cameras, the redundant sprocket holes on the right-hand side were gone, and the extra emulsion area was used for the picture. This increased resolution and decreased grain, producing excellent results. The image quality improved further with the growing refinement of film stocks. EFP video camcorders were progressing similarly.

It was a much more gratifying frame shape in which to compose an image. Still, the problem was that you had to compromise your composition to satisfy both the widescreen and traditional viewers. Beyond that, you would receive framing information on the daily call sheets. It may say, "Shoot Academy 1.33:1, protected for 16:9", i.e. all vital information within 4x3, but the rest of the 16:9 image must be clear of distractions such as the edge of the set, light stands or microphones. Sometimes, they would request 14:9 or 15:9 as compromises; the 3x4 viewer would watch with a thin black band at the top and bottom of the picture. This continued for years until the old tellies became obsolete.

Back to '89. Things were changing in the industry; Maggie Thatcher, the Tory Prime Minister, was, at last, losing public support, but not before decimating the trade unions. OK, it was much tougher on the coal miners than on us; nevertheless, the ACTT lost its sway in controlling rates and working practices. Now, freelance film and TV technicians were in the business of negotiating rates, and the line producers, who controlled production budgets, had new powers.

Around the same time, things were changing at the BBC. Under the new director general, John Birt, Ealing Studios began winding down operations, and a new system emerged. 'Director's Choice' meant that productions had no obligations towards staff film crews. This move was good for freelancers and bewildering for many staffers, who had always been cosseted by 'Auntie'. Over the space of a few years, the BBC was making Ealing crews redundant, albeit with generous severance deals that included camera kits for camera people and audio kits for sound recordists, thus boosting the freelance market with some excellent talent. Some flourished; others fell by the wayside, unable to adapt to the freelance working practices and lifestyle. Fifty-six staff crews were reduced to zero. The studio complex was eventually sold off in 1995.

My assignments were starting to follow a different path. I was working with more established directors on documentaries and shorts with more thought-provoking content and creative possibilities. They would encompass the arts, culture, history, science, politics, and more. Productions were well researched and involved expert contributors as well as the 'man in the street'. Television is a visual medium, and sometimes, the more academic subjects are at risk of becoming rather dry. This generated more motivation to think outside of the box and create meaningful and aesthetic imagery.

British terrestrial channels (e.g. BBC, ITV, Ch4, Sky) are often accused of having a political stance. In my experience of documentary and current affairs, I have been unaware of any entrenched biases. Invariably, side 'A' holds the viewpoint that it is in favour of side 'B', while side 'B' believes it to be in favour of side 'A'. That said, the reality is that a director, producer, or journalist inherently has a personal perspective, making it challenging to maintain the story's impartiality despite their efforts. In factual TV, every time a camera is switched on or off, every choice of shooting angle and crop, every lighting style decision, every selection of shot and edit point in the cutting room, every choice of words or, indeed, music, even the positioning in the broadcast schedule, affects the impact on the viewer. However hard a production strives to be neutral, the very essence of the process makes it not one hundred per cent achievable. Every decision shapes how the audience experiences the story.

18

This Land is Ours

I have worked on many documentaries in Israel. The first was for BBC's long-running series *Everyman*, which focused on moral and religious issues. *This Land is Ours* was about Jewish communities building settlements on the West Bank, organised and funded by the Gush Emunim. This minority, orthodox, fundamentalist movement claims that secular Zionists, through their conquests of Israel, had unwittingly brought about the beginning of the Messianic Age. This would culminate in the coming of the Messiah, which could be hastened by settling on land they believe God had allotted to the Jewish people.

My crew were Mike and Dave, as per *Icewalk,* and the assistant producer was Romaine Lancaster; we had a different fixer when working with the Jews than when working with the Palestinians. It was a good team, the logistics were well-organised, and the shoot had a positive vibe. Within BBC factual programming, the producer and director were invariably the same person; for this film, it was Jane Treays, who was already established at the cutting edge of quality documentary.

In today's Middle East, all Western media are regarded with suspicion, but this was an era when the BBC was looked up to as the exemplar of ethical and impartial broadcasting, and the phrase "We are from the BBC" still opened doors worldwide. Regardless, different Israeli factions were involved in this story—the Gush Emunim, the Haredim, the Israeli centre and the left (represented by renowned author Amos Oz), and the Palestinians. Each was wary of being misrepresented. Jane did an exemplary job of gaining their trust and obtaining access. She had a calm presence that put everyone at ease. Interviewees would open up to her because she listened to what they had to say rather than confronting them with hard-hitting questions. After all, these contributors were intelligent and articulate—their fundamentalist beliefs were heartfelt and driven by strong faith. There was no need for the film to spell out a viewpoint.

The settlements we visited were situated on hills in arid areas of barren desert, clear of the large towns. They were at different stages of development. Some were well-established and expanding; others comprised a handful of caravans and prefabs. All were fenced and patrolled by community volunteers sporting sub-machine guns and pistols. Day-to-day relations with neighbouring Arab villages appeared civil, but underlying tensions were tangible.

We filmed in one settlement where its first-anniversary party was being held. It was after dark, and there was a howling desert wind buffeting the awnings and Star of David flags. But the celebrations continued with speeches and homegrown entertainments on a rostrum in the 'town centre' as their armed guards patrolled the perimeter fence.

Our most vociferous protagonist was Daniella Weiss, a housewife, mother, campaigner, and activist with a look of fire in her eyes. While her children were playing in the living room and watching cartoons on TV, we filmed her sitting in her kitchen and 'operations centre', telephoning around the community, whipping up support for upcoming rallies and actions.

At the time, the majority of West Bank settlers were driven by religious and ideological fervour, but some were there for cheap housing. We interviewed a Jewish Russian immigrant family who, funded by the Gush Emunim, had been given a caravan in West Jerusalem. Along with many others, they had been instructed to gather their belongings and to join a convoy on a particular evening. By the next day, they had established a new settlement on the West Bank.

Back in Jerusalem, we stayed at the King David Hotel, which had the finest breakfast buffet on the planet. One day, we had an early start, allowing only five minutes for breakfast, so I grabbed a plate and loaded it with a fried egg, smoked salmon, rollmop herring and chocolate-coated halva. This combination caused much amusement and teasing that periodically came back to bite me for years to come.

Mea Shearim is an insular neighbourhood in the heart of Jerusalem. It has the appearance of an Eastern European shtetl. It is populated by ultra-orthodox Haredim, the most extreme faction being the Neturei Karta. At the time, they were not open to outsider intrusion, especially TV crews. But Jane and Romaine had managed to negotiate access to one of the most revered rabbis. They are also Jewish fundamentalists but with very different fundamentals. For one thing, they are not Zionists. They believe that Israel will come into being when the Messiah appears, and that can only be achieved through prayer. He told us, *"Though the Gush Emunim are devout, they are impatient."* We needed context for the interview, so we set up in a secluded corner and grabbed shots of street life until we were confronted and politely but firmly evicted.

Back to the West Bank, we boarded an Israeli public transport bus for the 30-kilometre drive to Hebron, the largest town in the territory and the main centre for Palestinian nationalism. Situated there is the burial place of Abraham, the founder of both Judaism and Islam.

En route, the bus was attacked by stone-throwing Palestinian youngsters, and a window was smashed. There was always an Israeli soldier on board for security. He got out, had words and chased them away. Since 1977 (it was now 1991), the Gush Emunim had moved in 500 settlers to establish a presence in the town.

We filmed our protagonists talking in their homes and wandering the streets. This had been the visual style throughout. These were committed hardliners. Many were American Jews, bringing up large families in a highly contentious environment. Their small children were bussed to school, protected by heavily armed guards. I was being guided around obstacles by Mike holding my belt as I walked backwards, my right eye to the viewfinder, filming an on-the-move interview. All the while, we were being protected by their community guards and by Israeli soldiers—the military was committed to a presence on the streets. At one point, our interviewee was taken aside by a friend and whispered to. His friend was concerned that he was using the word 'fundamentalist', which could "… liken us to Ayatollah Khomeini" (the Supreme Leader of Iran and instigator of the revolution). Contributors invariably forget that they are wearing a personal radio mic.

We also interviewed a Gush Emunim rabbi in their head office. He had a relaxed demeanour as he eloquently explained their reasoning and philosophy. Orthodox Jewish practice thrives on the discussion of religious texts. The men spend all day in yeshivas (religious study centres) in animated arguments over interpretations of the sacred teachings, so I guess one can justify any point of view to suit any agenda. These are people whose values contribute to the crises that plague the region today.

Back in 1981, when I first visited Yaffa, we made a day trip to the northwest corner of the Sinai Peninsula, a buffer zone bordering the Gaza Strip. The Strip was due to be handed back to Egypt in a couple of months as part of the 1979 peace treaty agreement. There were miles of beautiful white dunes with untouched desert beaches, where we swam in the turquoise Mediterranean water and had a glorious time. We drove to Yamit, a recently evacuated ghost town, where settlers had arrived just six years earlier, encouraged by the government offering affordable housing. They had toiled to build homes and create an infrastructure. They made the desert flourish with lush agriculture and exquisite gardens. When it became clear to residents that Yamit's future was threatened, many accepted government compensation and left; those who chose to stay were joined by Gush Emunim, who flooded in to boost their numbers. When the time came for eviction by the Israeli authorities in readiness for the handover, there was a great deal of resistance and violent confrontation by the settlers and their supporters, but to no avail. Since then, the battle cry of the activists has been, *"Yamit—Never again!"* Here I was, ten years later, shooting this documentary. For the final sequence, we drove across the Egyptian border into Sinai. The town had been bulldozed by the departing army and was being reclaimed by the desert. From our vehicle, we filmed a series of slow tracking shots along the rubble that had been Yamit. Jane used these for the concluding end-credit sequence.

19

Words on Film

Words on Film was a BBC 2 series out of Bristol, produced by Peter Symes. Each episode featured a purpose-written poem to be illustrated visually. Kim Flitcroft was the director for this one, and having recently worked together on *Them & Us*, a quirky consumer series, he asked me to shoot for him.

Simon Armitage was a fast-rising star (now, thirty years later, he is Poet Laureate and the UK's number one). The film was set on the Ashfield Valley Estate in Rochdale, Lancashire, which was due for demolition. It consisted of twenty-six alphabetically named blocks of flats; the ironic title of the poem and film was *Xanadu*, the name of the twenty-fourth block. There were well over one thousand flats and just a handful of remaining tenants; a few years earlier, it had been a fully occupied and austere council estate. Armitage had worked as a probation officer, and on his first posting, the estate had been included in his patch. His long poem was an innovative and unsettling piece, written with TV imagery in mind.

Having studied the text and discussed the content, this was a great chance to get the creative juices flowing and to optimise the visual potential of this derelict, brutalist, 1960s-built site. The poor weather that would blight most shoots was a blessing for this one. The sky was a deep grey, the ground was peppered with dirty snow-slush and puddles, and a fine drizzle was ever-present. We shot handheld tracking shots along endless walkways and corridors, dodging sodden mattresses and remnants of furniture discarded by departed squatters. We carried on through splintered doors into trash-filled rooms with broken windows, collapsed ceilings and fire burn marks on the patterned papered walls. We over-cranked and under-cranked the camera to mix slo-mo and fast-mo. Some shots included Simon moving from shadow into pools of light, sometimes reciting, sometimes not. For this section of the poem, every second line was *"...and the smell of the cabbage,"* bringing to mind the opening passage of George Orwell's *1984*. There was no shortage of material for imagery as we wandered around the location.

We then moved on to a film portrait of the bachelor caretaker. We photographed him in his armchair, listening to a music cassette of a Hungarian-language version of his favourite pop song, "Itsy Bitsy Teenie Weenie Yellow Polkadot Bikini", as he tells of his devotion to the estate. Then we follow him on his rounds, clearing snow, securing the front door of a newly vacated flat, and later to the Hungarian Club in town. There was drinking, merriment and a folk dancing event with girls in traditional dress balancing wine-filled bottles on their heads.

We filmed a few vaguely eccentric residents, including a man whose flat was home to dozens of stray cats. Another young man's flat was akin to the Kew Gardens' Temperate house, every spare inch filled with plants. They spilt out of the windows, all flooded with green-gelled light that he believed would encourage growth.

Moving on to Rochdale's magnificent Victorian town hall, we hired a 100ft cherry picker to crane down the ornate windows and a dolly to track along the highly polished, walnut conference table. With closeups of details and gavel-banging, it would be cut to Simon reciting his imagined conversation of pompous councillors discussing the naming of the twenty-six blocks.

Kim gave the footage his magic touch in the edit suite, and the film was well received.

In a similar vein, Peter Symes instigated another series that he directed himself, *Poet's News*. It was such a great idea, a five-minute slot following the main evening news, in which different poets wrote and performed verses on a topical issue. There were two or three per programme. The one that has stuck in my memory was with Benjamin Zephaniah. The two dominant stories of the day were a referendum on ending apartheid that was limited to white South African voters and UK immigration problems for Caribbeans. Zephaniah chose to do this by employing a newsroom format. Using their lighting, we shot him in the Television Centre news studio.

We find him briefly caught unaware, with his feet up on the desk. He composes himself, introduces an item on immigration, and hands over to *"...our roving poet out on the street."* Cut to him strolling through the graffiti-filled walkways under London's Westway flyover, microphone in hand, delivering his verse to camera in his inimitable Patwa-infused style. Then... *"Handing you back to the studio,"* where anchorman Zephaniah leans towards the camera, dreadlocks swaying. With his most earnest expression and voice, he announces, *"In South Africa today,"* his face morphs into a beaming smile and with immaculate timing, he concludes, *"...the sun shone on everyone."*

20
The New Europeans

In 1992, the UK signed the Maastricht Treaty to become a member of the European Community, a forerunner to, but not to be confused with, the European Union. I had a call from an English producer—let's call him 'James'. He told me he had a ten-week shoot. The working title was *Europe, Road to Unity,* but it was duly broadcast as *The New Europeans*, a co-production between Maryland Public Television (MPT), Washington, and RIAS TV, Berlin.

"Would I like to meet in his Soho office to discuss it?" On my underground journey into town, the dollar signs were spinning in my eyes as I calculated my quote. After exchanging cordial greetings, he opened with, "This is a resources-rich, cash-poor production." No, I didn't understand either. It turns out he meant they had sponsors supplying free flights, hotels and such. Having a comfortable room in a Sheraton hotel after a long day is lovely, but the budget wouldn't stretch to having breakfast there! The 'cash-poor' bit is self-explanatory, but, in retrospect, I feel that his own financial interests may have had a part to play.

The series was for public broadcast in the USA and was to be made up of many ten to fifteen-minute cultural stories shot throughout Europe. MPT sent along an overseer. It was her first time out of America; a cheerful, almost spherical young woman whose biggest thrill was to discover that, in Italy, Wendy's had spaghetti on the menu.

During the Cold War, West Berlin-based Radio in the American Sector (RIAS) created a successful multimedia network broadcasting Western propaganda to the Eastern Block. It was now (1991) operating as an independent TV station. They provided some facilities and four crew members: Maria, an assistant producer; Migo, a sound recordist; and two camera assistants, Lottie and Ulrika, who would also shoot second camera when required. I brought along my friend and colleague, Nick Merry, a jack of all trades and a master of many. Nominally, he was my gaffer and grip, but I knew him to be an effective coordinator, and I had a feeling that we would need an unofficial first AD to oversee the on-location logistics. I was right.

We shot on Betacam, of which I was not a fan, and worse, it was on the American format, NTSC, which was noticeably lower resolution than the UK PAL system. In addition to the two camera and sound channels, we carried a portable dolly and a substantial lighting package. We travelled by air, train, minibus and, for one section, a rock and roll tour bus from Berlin.

The German crew were *Fawlty Towers* fans, and they brought the complete VHS collection for on-the-road entertainment. All eleven episodes; hang on—eleven? Surely, there were twelve. Any reader familiar with the classic TV comedy series can guess which one German television had chosen not to broadcast. A clue—Basil Fawlty: "Don't mention the war (I mentioned it once, but I think I got away with it)." I later sent them a copy. They found it hilarious.

The stories we shot were diverse, varying from the trivial to the historical. The schedule was unrealistic. At least I had a good-sized crew, or so I thought. As soon as James sussed that Ulrika was a competent cameraperson and that Lottie could swing a microphone, he started sending them off to shoot some of the more basic stories, often hundreds of miles away. This left Nick, Migo, and I understaffed to rig and shoot much of the heavy-duty stuff involving sizeable lighting and dollying setups.

Meanwhile, James would be stressing himself out, flying backwards and forwards between crews. To make things worse, he would insist on overshooting, treating every clip like a half-hour film. Occasionally, I managed to dig my heels in and say, "That's it. We have the story." We were all exhausted and running on empty much of the time. Getting the agreed interim payments into our bank accounts was a struggle.

All in all, there was much tension between the crew and James. As HoD (head of the camera dept.), I was responsible for handling any discord, which was tough. Fortunately, they were a good-natured, supportive crew, and we survived the ordeal.

Around mid-shoot, a UK story was followed by a desperately needed and prescheduled week-long break. The second half started with segments in Italy. James, Nick, Migo and I set off from Victoria Station on board the Orient Express. It was actually two trains, a historic British Pullman train from London to Folkestone and a French locomotive pulling classic 1920s sleeping cars from Calais to Venice. Along with the fare-paying passengers, we were greeted like royalty by an abundance of attendants ensuring everyone would be treated to the best in five-star luxury railway travel. We were directed towards a carriage where our steward, impeccably dressed in his sky blue uniform, escorted me to my sleeper compartment. It was exquisite. The hard surfaces were high-polished walnut veneer. Twin curved doors opened to reveal a sumptuous wash station with chrome fittings and mirrors, all in art-deco styling. On the cabin table was a bottle of fine champagne chilling in an ice bucket. "Things are looking up on this shoot," I was thinking when the chief steward turned up.

"Monsieur Colin Clarke?"

"Oui."

"Pardonnez-moi monsieur; ze wrong Colin Clarke." At this point, he disappeared down the corridor with my bottle of bubbly. If they were really that classy, he should have swallowed his mistake and left me the bottle.

Our story was about the passenger experience and some behind-the-scenes workings. As the train sped through the countryside, we filmed travellers in the sumptuous bars, lounges, and dining coaches. We shot stewards and other staff going about their business. We filmed, and we filmed, and we filmed. Dinner time at last. Our call sheet had said 'black tie'. For Migo, it got a bit lost in translation, and he had literally bought along a black tie to go with his jeans and crumpled shirt. Fine dining was a fundamental feature of the Orient Express experience; we were famished and eager. The hors d'oeuvres arrived. More beautiful scenery. "Let's go shoot through the window."—Main course. "Quick, into the galley." Film the chefs and waiters at work.

The following day, upon arrival at Santa Lucia station, Venice, we offloaded our kit onto large trolleys and went straight to waiting water taxis to take us on to the next story on the lagoon. Then, back to the mainland and onto Treviso to film a fashion show at Benetton's futuristic headquarters. There followed a six-hour train ride to Naples to film the Feast of San Gennaro.

The highlight is the miracle of St. Januarius' congealed blood liquifying, induced by intense prayer. On the rare occasions when this miracle failed, disasters followed, such as the outbreak of the Second World War and a devastating earthquake in 1980. The story is of particular interest in the US, as the feast also takes place in Little Italy, New York.

Nick points out that wherever we go, the same black Fiat with two black-suited men inside is parked at a discreet distance. It's unnerving, but we are too busy to get distracted.

In the cathedral, we set up our two camera positions on rostra. Crowds of the faithful occupy every corner. The excitement is palpable as the time draws near. The clergy appear in their finery, the smell of incense fills the air, the organ bellows, and the choir sings praises. Latin words of prayer resonate through the speakers. Dominating the frame on my longest lens is the round vial containing the blood of the fourth-century martyr. It is suspended in an ornate gold and silver encasement and held high by a senior clergyman. I hold the shot for about ten minutes. Eventually, he turns it through ninety degrees, and the contents self-level, suggesting it is now liquid. A roar of ethereal Catholic joy fills the cathedral. I've seen nothing in my viewfinder that actually tells me that it was not already liquid, but I am an atheist Jew (or is that a Jewish atheist?), so what do I know?

After shooting some additional footage on the city's streets, we head back to our vehicle, resisting the temptation to wave to the black Fiat. Our driver is distraught and tells us the minibus had been broken into and flight cases with some of our peripheral equipment had been stolen. This is a hassle we do not need. Details are reported to the police, and we return to our hotel. The following morning, we are driven 50 kilometres to Sorrento, our next location. We check into the hotel. I open my room door to find all the missing kit neatly stacked in the corner. The boys in black had obviously 'convinced' the culprits to return their ill-gotten gains. The Mafia does have its uses.

21

State of the Ark

It was not unusual for a small crew to fly with twenty pieces of baggage, considering the camera, lighting, grip equipment, sound kit, film and audio stock, plus personals; so how come we had nearly twice that for shooting a documentary in a European capital? It was December 1993, and we were heading for Yerevan in Armenia. We had been forewarned of a lack of infrastructure, food, heating, electricity and bath plugs. We took a 2.2kW generator to power some filming lights. Usually, such a cumbersome, inexpensive item would be hired or bought locally, but all attempts by Alexei, our Muscovite fixer, had failed.

Nick Merry was with us, and he brought an electric thermostatic power shower. David Jones, the camera assistant, volunteered to shop for provisions and provided six large cartons of goodies; he also packed a hi-fi system and speakers? And Paul Nathan, on sound, brought a couple of electronic keyboards for evening entertainment—stranger by the minute. I have to admit that I was feeling somewhat embarrassed by the excesses as we offloaded the Heathrow porters' trolleys, but it didn't seem to bother Kate Broome, the producer, so all was well.

In the evening, we made our connection at Charles de Gaulle Airport, Paris, for the four-and-a-half-hour flight in a Russian-built, Armenian Airlines wide-bodied jet. On boarding, we were ushered through the cargo hold, past shelves of baggage and goods and up a staircase to the passenger deck. It felt more like a cross-channel ferry than a long-haul aircraft. Our seats could tip all the way back, and as the plane was half empty, we could put our feet up on the tilted back seat in front and lie flat, which we did—even for take-off!

I was rudely awoken at 2:30am by the jolt of touchdown at our destination, still lying flat, without a seat belt and without an announcement. It took another five hours to retrieve the baggage even though ours was the only plane at the airport—apparently, an equipment malfunction.

We were met by Alexei and a driver and taken to our accommodation. It was not a hotel but a monumental 1920s Soviet-style government building that, in its heyday, housed diplomatic facilities. My suite had been the Egyptian embassy. This building was the best place to be, as it had generators providing electricity but neither heating nor hot water—thank goodness Nick had brought the power shower.

The only nearby public facility, for the few who could afford it, was a traditional Russian bathhouse. We all enjoyed it as a place to relax and warm our bones from the icy weather outdoors and the cold conditions indoors. It was a great environment for a production meeting and to discuss filming plans while our perspiration merged with the herb-infused steam. A pressured hose-down followed.

We would be having one proper meal a day (hence the goodies cartons), and we headed to the only suitable restaurant in the vicinity. It was costly but had been budgeted for. A great meal with some of my favourite dishes: black and red caviar, blintzes and shish kebabs, all garnished with fresh coriander and washed down with shots of vodka. It was delicious and was to be our menu most days for the following two weeks.

So much for our story; how about the story we were here to film? *State of the Ark* was a five-part BBC series—four films followed by a televised debate examining zoos' past, present and future roles. Crisis was bedevilling those of the Eastern Bloc, and we were looking at the plight of two.

Armenia had been absorbed into the United Socialist Soviet Republic (USSR) in 1920 and transformed from a predominantly agricultural hinterland to an important industrial centre. Yerevan, the capital, flourished as a hub for culture and education. The now-struggling zoo, the focus for half of the film, had been a Soviet showpiece. But Armenia suffered a series of crippling events. In 1988, the Spitak earthquake devastated the country. Over 50,000 died; 58 towns and villages were reduced to rubble, and the nuclear power plant, 35 kilometres from the capital, was severely damaged and closed down (fortunately, there was no radioactive fallout.) At the same time, an ongoing ethnic and territorial conflict between Armenia and Azerbaijan had escalated into a full-scale war. Three years later, in 1991, saw the dissolution of the Soviet Union and the consequential ousting of the communist party government. All these factors contributed to the harsh conditions we observed and filmed.

Doubtless, there was an elite somewhere enjoying the finer

things, but what we saw was severe hardship all around. Nine out of ten of Yeravan's 1.2 million population lived below the country's official poverty line. The few with a regular job were lucky to earn the equivalent of $3 a month. More than once, I asked individuals how they could live on such a pittance, and the answer was that they couldn't. But, somehow, they did, and beyond that, they seemed to remain cheerful and optimistic about the future.

On the streets, people huddled around improvised firebins containing minimal fuel as there was so little combustible material left. The temperature was way below zero, and I was thankful for the Arctic cold-weather gear I had kept hold of from *Icewalk*. The daylight was sombre and oppressive, and persistent fog gave our shots a bleak atmosphere; the more distant people and buildings blended ghost-like into the grey nothingness. I recall a tinge of guilt as I thought, "These are perfect shots to convey the dismal reality." Nevertheless, the people we met were warm towards us and generous with what little they had.

All twentieth-century infrastructure was on hold. Fuel, such as paraffin, was scarce, so indoor socialising and interaction took place huddled around wood-burning stoves. Most urban trees had been cut down, and people were now burning their furniture and any wood they could lay their hands on. Someone had a good business model forging rudimentary metal stoves with flues that channelled smoke and fumes out of the windows. There was one in every home and office.

The documentary nominally concerned the appalling suffering of animals, but what made it powerful was the intertwining of the parallel lives of our human protagonists and, indeed, the whole nation.

The working script opened the film with the grand metaphor of Mount Ararat, the resting place of Noah's biblical ark, towering over the world's first Christian nation. It did not look promising as the weather worsened, and visibility was too poor to see it at all. We kept a close eye on the meteorological forecast, hoping it would clear.

We went to the zoo, met with the small staff and were given the tour. We saw dilapidated buildings and cages that hinted at its glorious past. We started doing general shots around the site. Every film crew knows that captive or domestic animals are indifferent to cameras, but if you want a guaranteed reaction, get the recordist to swing in his boom microphone with its furry wind-dissipating muff. It is instantly perceived as prey, predator or plaything. We shot extended tracking moves past the outdated cages and enclosures, in which a variety of under-fed mammals were pacing back and forth in the snow and slush. We shot close-ups of listless animals suffering from the cold and lack of any semblance of their natural environment. We quickly learned their plight was in no way due to ignorance or complacency. The staff and management were knowledgeable and committed professionals constrained by circumstances. Their dedication, love for the animals and personal sacrifices drove the zoo's survival. An aid package had seen them through the previous winter, but only an economic miracle could keep the animals alive this year.

A new sequence opens with a black screen. The striking of a match reveals a closeup of a windup alarm clock as Roland Sergeevich, the headkeeper, leaves the warmth of his bed. Three generations of his family remain asleep in the room, swathed in numerous layers to fend off the cold. Wearing a heavy jumper and thick scarf, he stokes the wood-burning stove in the kitchen to heat some coffee. It is a spacious mansion flat with plenty of accommodation, but they all spend the long winters in two small rooms as there is no way to heat or light the rest. The living room has some fine furniture. Under the large, ornate windows are cast iron radiators that no longer have an operational boiler to fill them. There are framed family photos where the proud, well-built, full-faced patriarch is barely recognisable as the skinny, gaunt man we are now filming.

On a good day, mains power will come on for a couple of hours at random times. When it does, households burst into life, the occupants busy themselves, optimising the situation, even if it's at three in the morning. A capable handyman, Roland, has built an accumulator that charges a line of lead-acid batteries during the occasional bursts of mains electricity. The family can use this to power a lightbulb, to read by, or to watch TV. It is insufficient to heat or cook with but is enough for a 100W Dedolight, which we wire into it to light an interview.

He tells Kate that before the earthquake and war, the zoo had 240 species; today, there are only 150. Desperate people have broken in and stolen deer for meat. They now have police patrols to protect the remaining few. Many animals had died from cold the previous winter. The Temperatures drop to -25ºC. There is minimal food and hay, little fuel for heating or light and insufficient wages for workers. He earns $1.50 a month. The zoo is state-funded, but the state is virtually bankrupt.

Banuk the hippo had been a regular feature on a children's TV programme. His den had central heating and a heated pool, but now the pool is 8ºC and too cold for him to wallow or bathe. He is unwell, and his skin is drying and cracking. Puss appears, and infection can spread. We film Roland and a colleague oiling his skin. The oil costs $25 a time—more than eight months' wages for his keepers, and it is just staving off the inevitable as he is unlikely to survive another winter.

We meet Haik, who runs the reptile house. He has the same problems as the other departments. Most of the time, it is very dark inside. There are no torches in use as they cannot get batteries. Even simple paraffin lamps are at a premium, so bottles with an improvised wick are the primary artificial light source. A local factory has donated a small generator to heat and light a corner of the reptile house, home to the most dangerous inhabitant, the Spotted Jararaca. It has a lethal venom for which there is no antidote. When the energy crisis arose after the earthquake, Haik started evacuating the snakes to his two-room apartment, a situation he kept secret from the neighbours. Early one morning, we film him

Roland with Banuk, the TV star

manhandling a five-metre python from its vivarium into a sack using a long-handled hook. He transfers it to a large cardboard box and trollies it through the dark, snow-covered streets to his home. He places it close to the others around the stove. All this while his parents, wife and two school-age kids sleep peacefully just a few feet away. Occasionally, there's an escape, and his wife calls him at work to come home and reconfine the culprit.

Zak Aruvian, the zoo's director, takes us to his hometown, which had been badly affected by the earthquake. I have never encountered anything like this. It is deeply disturbing. The whole place is still strewn with rubble. There are apartment blocks where, at one end, walls and floors have collapsed, exposing rooms that still have furniture and fittings in place and the other end is occupied by families going about their lives. There are lines of shipping containers and old railway carriages, now home to people who had lived comfortable lives five years earlier.

Back in Yeravan, we film the daily routine that starts with Zak overseeing the distribution of the paraffin rations. At $1 per litre, it is stored under lock and key. Keepers carry the meagre meat and grain animal feed quota on their backs to conserve tractor fuel. How they maintain their high spirits and positivity amazes and humbles me. Dave, our 'head of snacks', is something of a foodie. At lunchtime, we open one of his boxes and find it brimming with fine cheeses, tinned pâté, choc bars, and sweets. I feel uneasy under the circumstances, but the touch of luxury is much appreciated when shared with our hosts.

By this time, Nick, the spark, has again assumed the role of AD. Kate is happy, as the young researcher, whose primary job is to organise and anticipate, is not up to the job.

We had a day off, and Kate, Nick and I took a trip with Alexie as our guide. Our driver picked us up in a Lada Niva, Russia's answer to the Land Rover, and we headed towards the Azat River gorge. As usual, visibility was close to zero as we were driven up winding snow-covered tracks. At the height of 1,700 metres, a vision of a medieval church loomed through the mist. It belonged to the Geghard Monastery. This complex was completed in the twelfth century, but we soon learned that this was merely the comparatively modern front to a system of historic chapels that penetrated deep into the mountain. Some were cavernous in scale and magnificent with intricately carved detail. They had been hewn out of the solid rock. The oldest dates back to the fourth century A.D. There was an English-speaking, hooded monk who showed us around. He led us from chapel to chapel, pointing out the beautifully crafted inscriptions, crosses, tombs and artefacts. He took us up stone steps to a second-level chamber where impressive columns carved out of the rock supported a spherical dome with an opening for daylight at its zenith. A hole in one corner gave a view of a tomb down below. Our guide offered up a devotional chant in a rich baritone voice to demonstrate the extraordinary acoustics of this chamber. The setting for the monastery was sublime, and the atmosphere so ethereal and peaceful that I could relate to the concept of a life of spiritual contemplation.

I am not a practising Jew, but at home, we do mark the main holidays (especially the fun ones). They are entrenched in Yaffa's family tradition, and it is important for Dan and Tali to have a sense of their heritage. This was the third day of Chanukah, the Festival of Lights, so I thought it pertinent to light three candles to send vibrations of my love. Maybe it was also to ease my conscience for not being there to celebrate with them. Some may think it inappropriate in a Christian monastery, but that's their problem.

Back at base, I managed, against all odds, to phone home and tell Yaffa about the candles—she was delighted. I then had a couple of shots of Boris Yeltsin Vodka (produced in France) and wound up the lovely day with a visit to the bathhouse, followed by dinner and more shots of Yeltsin.

Meeting the big cats is on another level of bizarre. To protect them from the worst ravages of midwinter, they are confined to what I can only describe as a large, lightless dungeon with a crescent of cages. I descend a ramp into the dank cavern and hear the growls and roars of dangerous and hungry lions, tigers, leopards and jaguars. As my eyes adjust to the dark, I see many pairs of eyes looking back at me. Like the crocs in Madagascar, cats have eye shine and much superior night vision to us. Now, I see vague outlines of these mighty beasts pacing up and down behind the bars, anticipating lunch. It is eerie and unnerving. But lunch will have to wait. It is going to take a while to set up for filming.

Once again, I have the task of lighting a dark space to look dark but still see what is happening. Tricky—but I guess that's what I'm paid for. We only have our minimal generator power. I position the two Redheads out of doors, shining through a grid in the roof of the 'den', casting shadows of the grate across the entire area and doubling up as subtle backlight on the cats and the working keepers. Down below, I use the Dedolights as floating lamps to pick up the action. The level is very low, making filming difficult. The upside is that the glow from keepers' bottle-wicked lamps registers as light sources, helping the low-key mood of the images. Unlike video, where you see what you are getting on a monitor, in a film camera, you only see a through-the-lens image that has

been reflected by two mirrors and then flipped via a prism onto a ground glass in the viewfinder. Hence, a dim image to the eye is considerably dimmer in the viewfinder.

There may be no power running through the mains' cables, but there's electricity in the air as the big cats smell the approach of a wheelbarrow laden with raw meat coming down the ramp—I can feel it down my spine. The meat had been supplied by soldiers bringing carcasses of farm animals killed by bombs and missiles at the battlefront and considered unfit for human consumption. The zoo's only elephant had recently been put down after a nasty fall, slipping on ice in her enclosure; she is added to the menu. The cats know the drill. They are in double cages. While enclosed in one, the meat is shovelled into the other, and when the keeper is clear, his colleague winds open the heavy portcullis, and the cat rushes to claim its prey. It is a miserable life for the animals, and the keepers fear that the darkness is driving them mad.

We visited the home of Julieta Stepenyan, a characterful old lady who had been in charge of the zoo in Soviet times. Kate interviewed her sat by the stove. She reminisced about its heyday when people travelled from all over the vast USSR to see the collection of 1,000 animals. Stepenyan lost her job when Armenia became independent because she had been a member of the communist party. Kate asked whether we could film her at the zoo, but she responded, "Never return to where you were once happy." Nonetheless, she agreed to talk to us standing outside with the gates and sign in the background. At the end of the piece, she expressed her sadness at its decline, turned away and walked off into the mist—a poignant image.

Filming was completed, and we said our farewells and heartfelt thanks. We distributed the remains of our snacks collection and were toasted with local Armagnac and a homemade tipple distilled from fermented cherries.

Our long flight to Paris was scheduled for the late evening (it actually took off at about 5:00am because a road tanker had to drive to another airfield in search of aviation fuel). While Paul, Dave, and Nick finished packing and Dave prepared 50 or so rolls of unprocessed, exposed film for safe travel, Kate, Alexie, and I set off for a final attempt at getting some shots of Mount Ararat. It is not in Armenia but situated across the border in modern-day Turkey. Our driver picked us up, and we drove, through heavy snow and mist, to a suitable viewpoint—nothing but whiteout. We hung around for an hour. It was 5:00pm, shortly before sunset, when an orange glow penetrated the clouds to the southwest. As if by magic, the magnificent sight of Ararat's two volcanic peaks appeared shrouded in a blanket of warm, diffused sunlight. The camera was standing by, and I milked the opportunity, shooting different speed pans and alternative framings. "It's in the can," I proclaimed. With a beaming smile and a hug, Kate announced, "It's a WRAP."

22

The Land of all Impossibilities

The second trip was to Bucharest Zoo in Romania. It looked like a zoo from another time because it was a zoo from another time; nothing had changed since it opened in 1959, and even then, it was outdated, styled like a Victorian menagerie—all iron bars and stone floors. Now, it was severely underfunded and dilapidated, and the animals were hungry and sickly. That is where the similarity to Yerevan ended. There appeared to be little commitment to animal welfare. Any potential improvements were strangled by red tape. They needed a state licence to dig turf, put down a suffering animal, raise entry fees to the cost of a cigarette, or cut a branch for feed, even though the zoo was surrounded by forest. The communist dictator, Nicolae Ceaușescu, had been deposed and executed on Christmas Day four years earlier, and the Socialist Democratic Party had taken over, apparently inheriting the constrictive bureaucracy. Much of the population referred to their home as 'the land of all impossibilities'.

The Land of all Impossibilities

Stefan Ormrod, a leading zoo consultant from the UK-based Born Free Foundation, talked to us as we filmed him driving to the capital on a mission to convince the management to update their practices and source more funds. He had visited six months earlier and was heartbroken and frustrated by the sheer incompetence and indifference displayed towards animal care.

Dr. Koču, the zoo's director, was a man of importance—a scholar and a senior figure in the field of biology. He had the profile of a bad-tempered eagle, which echoed his temperament and, out of doors, he wore a severe-looking trilby hat, further exaggerating these features. No love was lost between the two men. Stefan did his best to suppress the expression of his disdain, and Koču, always on the back foot, resented the imposition of this foreigner threatening his authority on his patch. Communicating via an interpreter made it even more awkward. I almost felt sorry for the man as the camera and microphone were ever-present to record his vulnerability.

Touring the zoo was a depressing experience, as all around were classic signs of 'zoochosis' (mental anguish in animals made visible by abnormal behaviour.) A common indicator of poor welfare. At every stage, Stefan would point out wrong practices and suggest simple strategies to make improvements. When on display in the open, Gaia, Romania's only elephant, was always restricted by a heavy chain tether around her foot. Stefan explained that an elephant needs 'browse'. "It is easily accessed—there is forest all around." Koču shrugs and says that you need to apply for government permission each time. Stefan responds angrily, "*If the city of Budapest wants an elephant, they are obliged to give it browse every day.*"

The animals had nothing to occupy themselves. He pointed out that monkeys enjoy searching for food. You have to scatter it among the straw. We filmed Koču displaying great authority as he instructed the keepers how to do it. There were similar scenarios with several animals. Stefan demonstrated simple behaviour enrichment practices; maybe he inspired a few keepers, but Koču viewed him with suspicion and responded to all constructive critique with rhetoric relating to state inertia.

Probably thanks to the fact that the BBC was in town, a meeting was set up between Stefan and a senior state environment official. We opened the sequence with a wide shot of the world's biggest and most extravagant government building, Ceaușescu's folly, the notorious Romanian Palace of the Parliament. Dressed in a suit and tie, Stefan walked into the shot, and we panned with him as he entered a somewhat less imposing complex on the opposite side of the road.

A diplomatic but disheartening discussion ensued with responses from the senior bureaucrat such as, *"The zoo management need to take the initiative…"* and *"…resolve their own problems"* and *"…reluctant to help themselves.."* Nothing was achieved.

The next day, we were back at the zoo to find that no effort had been made to continue any of the practices that Stefan had been promoting. However, among the 155 staff, he had found one kindred spirit. Dragoš was an assistant vet. A young man with long matted hair and the furrowed brow of a person struggling against the system. We first filmed him playing with and exercising a young lion and a black panther in the corridors of the monkey house. I started with a low-angle, long-lens shot as they scurried towards us. For some reason, all the non-vital crew had taken shelter in a different room. I quickly made the 'creative' decision that the rest of the sequence should be from a high-angle viewpoint—i.e. out of claw and jaw reach of the cats! So Paul and I climbed onto a handy ledge above a double door as the unlikely and potentially dangerous ritual played out below.

We interviewed Dragoš as he sat in the ill-equipped veterinary clinic. He said that the zoo was "Romania in miniature." To get anything done, you had to do a favour for someone else, even if your motives were honest. Management was not concerned with animal welfare; people were living off the backs of the animals, and money was getting diverted along the way. He suggested we take a look at the foxes' compound.

After some searching, we found it tucked away in a remote corner of the zoo complex. Stefan immediately recognised the style of cages as those used for commercial fur factory farming. He had no doubts these were for that purpose and served no role in conservation or education.

It is time for the final confrontation. We are in the 'conference room' with Koču sitting at the head of the table, Stefan to his right and Andrei, the translator, to his left. I shoot handheld for maximum flexibility, and Paul swings his boom mic as well as radio mics on the two main protagonists.

You can cut the atmosphere with a knife. Though Koču denies any suggestion of a fur trade connection, he does say that they are expected to be financially productive. All income must be handed to the city council, from where it is reallocated to various departments, with a small percentage returning to the zoo. Stefan expresses his outrage at the ugliness of the system. He expounds that they have to work hard to shake off thirty years of inertia, and he questions why all simple enrichment ceased as soon as he turned his back.

Stefan: *"For thirty-four years, there was not a branch in the monkey cage—that's the baseline."*

Koču's retort: *"I know well what we have achieved, and all your prejudicial comments lead me to conclude that you don't want to help Bucharest Zoo; you just want to show us in a negative light and rubbish our efforts. You are distorting everything—this interview is terminated!"*

Fuming, he stands up and steps away from the chair. His back is against the wall—literally, as there is very little space in the room.

The question enters my mind as to how much the crew presence is affecting this scenario—the eternal dilemma of documentarians.

I have got to know Stefan a little and empathise with his passion for this crusade. He is exasperated but displays an outward calm as he talks Koču back to his seat.

Koču: *"You want to shut down the zoo—it would be another present from Great Britain after Churchill swapped us for Greece, with Stalin at Yalta in 1944!"* (factually dubious).

Stefan: *"That's a cheap trick. Enough of the: 'I'm a pained Romanian, and what a load of shits you English are!' My recommendation to the State would be to close it down. But the State wants a zoo; therefore, it must define it without false delusions about education and conservation."*

Koču: *"This is futile—we could go on forever."*

There was no meeting of minds. From Stefan's viewpoint, the only way forward was to close the zoo or sack the director, neither of which was likely to happen. For him, Romania had indeed proved to be 'The land of all impossibilities'.

A sad coda to the tale is that Stefan Ormrod took his own life a few months later. Who knows why? But I have little doubt that this, and similar frustrations with other failing zoos, played a part. RIP.

23

Congo

As our minibus left Brazzaville Airport with a police escort, we were the only motor vehicles on the road—strange and a little eerie. It turns out that it was one of a series of polling days in the Republic of Congo's first democratic election, and a traffic ban was in place to ensure that no one could travel to vote in more than one area. Happily, Brazzaville is on the north bank of the Congo River; on the other side was Kinshasa, the capital of Zaire (today the Democratic Republic of Congo), where a horrific and bloody drawn-out war was underway.

We were here to make a documentary produced by Yorkshire Television for Channel 4 and the Discovery Channel about anti-poaching patrols and enforcing conservation measures in the jungle. It was titled *Defenders of the Wild—Keepers of the Congo*. Katrina Murray was the director, and my assistant, Mark Smeaton, and soundman, Chris Barker, were YTV staffers. Our local fixer was Peter Moss.

After a couple of days of travel by light aircraft and Land

Rovers, we arrived at the newly built Camp Caravati. A British couple had set it up as part of an EC project promoting conservation and protection of the national park. Though yet to have a generator for power or running water, it was spotless, spacious and comfortable. They employed many locals, thereby promoting awareness that there were worthier ways to earn a living than supporting the poaching industry. The service and food were terrific, and it offered the finest jungle accommodation I had experienced. When you wanted a shower, which was often, you would call out, "Douche." By the time you arrived there, the hot water staff would have filled the overhead tank, and you had just to pull the 'chain' to operate. Our laundry was done daily and awaited us each morning, beautifully ironed to kill off any number of bugs or their eggs that could otherwise burrow into you for a feed or gestation.

The surrounding area had an unusual terrain; within a few kilometres, you would move from rainforest to savannah, to grassland and back to rainforest. No one knew how this had come about, but theories suggested that, historically, vast herds of elephants had created clearings or maybe indigenous tribes had burnt down large tracts of forest. We were on the equator, and the blistering heat and humidity were relentless, as were the mosquitos and numerous other flying insects. I now understood why ponies have tails, and my own ponytail finally found a use—to swish away airborne beasties from my face, at least momentarily.

We trekked eight kilometres to the Grande Saline ('salt lick' sounds so much more evocative in French, Congo's official national language). This marshy area is where all the animals come from near and far to obtain their mineral needs, so it is the best hunting ground for elephant poachers. They were only interested in the valuable tusks. There was, and still is, a multi-billion dollar worldwide trade in illicit ivory, with international villains at the top of the chain. I knew we had come to film a killing field, but I had no idea of the scale. I was horror-struck. There were hundreds of elephant skeletons and tusk-less skulls with bones picked clean by scavengers and as many rotting carcasses in various stages of decomposition. Scavenging birds took to the sky as we squelched through the marsh to get our shots, and the stench was foul; thousands of flies and bugs were busy devouring the rotting remains. Hundreds of fish were gorging on chunks of flesh in the small river that flowed through the saline. The images were very disturbing and have stayed with me to this day.

The poachers were outlaws—well-organised, cunning, armed, and ruthless. When not on raids, they melded into village life. Our principal protagonist was Dr Oko, a highly educated man who had achieved his PhD in Moscow and a 'Rambo' streak from I know not where. His task was to create and train a para-military wildlife protection force. He set up a role-playing exercise for his troop. A local young man volunteered to play the part of a poacher, most probably seduced by the presence of a TV crew. Guards hammered on the flimsy door of his mud and thatch rondavel. He was dragged out, fiercely protesting his innocence. It was a masterly performance. I panned with the action as he was frogmarched to the waiting Toyota pickup truck, which then drove out of shot to reveal a grinning Mark sitting on a kit box with his hands in the film-changing bag. For another exercise, Oko led his men through the forest. Their poorly maintained Kalashnikov rifles were being waved around in all directions as we followed them, slashing their way through the jungle growth in search of the 'baddies'.

No guns were fired in anger, but we were forever ducking as barrels swung in our direction—of all the potentially life-threatening animals in the jungle, these guards were the most dangerous! Oko arranged an obstacle-vaulting exercise. I aligned the camera, looking along a horizontal liana. The men were all to follow his lead. He ran up to it and vaulted over with the ease and the grace of a commando. The next man snagged his foot, falling flat on his face; the next did some sort of somersault and landed upside-down; another got stuck on the top, causing a collision with the one who followed, and the chaos escalated. With limbs and bodies flailing in every direction, it was all I could do to hold the camera steady while trying to contain my laughter as this Monty Pythonesque scenario played out in my viewfinder.

Production had organised contact with a remote Pygmy village. The Mbuti tribe are one of the oldest and most primitive tribes in the world, with a culture and way of life that has changed little for thousands of years. They are expert hunters and gatherers, relying on the forest for everything from food and medicine to shelter and tools. We were driven for many hours to the end of a very rough track that the French colonialists had cleared in the 1950s. We arrived at the village of Mbaza, where we had to register with the chief of police, a middle-aged man wearing sports shorts and a once-white tee shirt with more holes than cloth. We employed some porters, drove on to the furthermost point and trekked the last few miles to our rendezvous.

The chief greeted us enthusiastically. I was surprised by how youthful he was until I observed that no elders were to be seen. Not only are they of short stature, but they also have short lives. I was dumbstruck; with an average life expectancy of 15 years, few reach their 30s, and they reach sexual maturity early. He was eager for us to go to his hut to eat, drink and meet the family, but we were running late. Good filming light is a rare commodity in equatorial climbs as the sun, when out, is overhead for most of the day, casting hard, ugly shadows and burnt-out highlights. It is low and soft just briefly after sunrise and before sunset. It was a beautiful evening, and I was eager to capitalise on it to film some tribal and fetish dancing that Peter had prearranged to take place. The chief was a bit put out by our insistence, but he complied.

Dancing is a celebration of life and nature. They use their bodies to convey a deep connection to the world around them. The movements are precise and deliberate, each step and gesture imbued with meaning. Dressed in colourful robes and adorned with feathers, beads, and face paint, they moved with fluid grace, swaying to the rhythm of drums and melodic chants, each individual playing a vital role in the performance. Men and women took turns leading the dance, their movements becoming more trancelike as the music built to a crescendo.

What we had not expected or wanted was the hundreds of guests from nearby villages that the chief had invited—and they all wanted to participate in the shindig and perform. We had brought a generator and lights as we had planned a 'dancing into the night' sequence; we carried on filming until we had the footage we needed. But every group wanted their moment in the spotlight. The average adult male may be only four foot ten inches tall, but you didn't want to get on the wrong side of these guys, so out came the strawberry filter. 'Strawberry Filter' is the term used when, not wanting to upset the status quo, you go through the motions of filming but don't actually run the camera or sound.

After the day's filming was completed, we were invited to

a grand feast in the community hut. This was a large structure built from what the forest had to offer, with a long and low anchored table with fixed benches where all the senior tribe members sat. We were esteemed guests; I don't know how Katrina felt, possibly having been the only woman to have ever graced this table. I was seated with my knees scraping the underside of the tabletop next to a vivacious young man who laughed a lot and was extremely talkative. I didn't understand a word he said in his Bantu language, and he didn't understand any of my schoolboy French, but it didn't seem to quash his fervour. The spread was something else. Of course, there was Africa's ubiquitous staple, manioc or cassava, in the form of a tasteless gluey slime, and there was a large selection of mostly unrecognisable chunks of bushmeat body parts. I consider myself an adventurous eater and am blessed with a strong constitution, but I was not eager to partake. Our enthusiastic hosts encouraged us to try everything. Fortunately, dogs were sniffing around our ankles in search of scraps—they must have thought all their Christmases had come at once! I felt like Mr Bean in his hilarious solo birthday party sketch, trying to hide his unwanted steak tartare. When everyone, except for us, was sated, the chief handed the bill to Peter!

The following day, we went on a hunt. There were about 30 men and boys. They had a long rolled-up net that they took to a clearing and opened into a large horseshoe shape. They yelled and beat the undergrowth and, with help from the dogs, drove all animals in their path into the net, which they then closed around them—a similar concept to purse fishing. On this occasion, they trapped a few blue duikers and porcupines. There followed gruesome sights and sounds as the men wrung the necks of the duikers, and the boys hacked the spines off the still struggling porcupines. We filmed Dr Oko lecturing on sparing females to help the wildlife populations flourish in this ever-diminishing forest.

Back at Caravati, the travel alarm wakes me at 6:00am. I get out of bed from under the mosquito net, splash my face from the basin of water, and don my freshly ironed long-sleeved shirt and Rohan bush trousers. I check my boots for scorpions and spray any still-exposed flesh with Deet—jungle formula insect repellent that could double as paint stripper! I wash any residue from my palms as anything non-organic I touch will likely dissolve. Lastly, on goes my Tilley Hat, which is guaranteed to last a lifetime. In my 'lifetime' I have got through three (and only paid for the one). Today is going to be special. As an exercise in conservation awareness, Dr Oko has organised for villagers from miles around to be transported by pick-up trucks and then on foot to the Grande Saline. Their expressions of shock and bewilderment need neither narration nor interviews to enhance the story. Oko and his rangers instruct the people to gather bones and bring them to a certain dry spot where one of the guards, selected for his creative flair, directs them in arranging the bones of fifty-eight elephants into a large 3D artwork. We have all seen images of African women carrying heavy water containers on their heads—here was a line carrying forest elephant skulls. This surreal scenario playing out in front of the camera will make a unique sequence for Katrina's film.

Most wild animals keep well away from humans, and with good reason. In the Congo, anything that moves is hunted for the dinner table. Apart from snakes, scorpions, and insects, we only saw a few buffalo and bushbucks in the flesh, but there were plenty of lion, leopard, elephant, and chimp tracks. But it was not my job. Wildlife cameraman David Wright joined us for a couple of weeks. Operating independently, he went out with some trackers deep into the forest, but he had little success. Giuseppe, an anthropologist studying Pygmies, and his travelling companion, a young woman doing a thesis in primatology, overnighted at Caravati, and David cadged a lift to Mbaza to try his luck in that area. En route, their car came off the track and hit a tree. David and Giuseppe were OK, but the girl hit her head and was in a bad way. David ran to Mbaza to get help. I don't know the outcome for her, apart from the fact that it was not fatal, but David's camera was trashed, putting an end to his shoot.

We returned to Brazzaville to pick up some sequences. The empty streets we had experienced on our arrival were now full of cars and trucks with colourful banners and bands playing. Horns were blasting, people were dancing and cheering, and kids were running around excitedly. There had been 168 presidential candidates, and it had been more like a knockout competition than an election, with four days of voting spread over a few weeks. Now, the results were out; the Marxist-Leninist state was ousted, and Pascal Lissouba was the Republic of Congo's first elected president (though the democracy would last for only five years).

We had an enchanted morning's filming at The Jane Goodall Institute Chimpanzee Orphanage. A wonderful group of staff were caring for traumatised infant and juvenile chimps whose parents had been taken or killed by poachers. It was very touching to see the close bonds they had created. We wanted to film a group of youngsters, with a couple of carers, going to a nearby patch of forest for their daily outing. I naively suggested we set up the camera with a long lens on the baby legs (low tripod) concealed in the undergrowth at a distance from the clearing so as not to become a curiosity.

Naturally, they sussed us within a millisecond and came bounding our way, charging and challenging us until they were satisfied that we posed no threat. We gave up being 'invisible' and joined the party. We were the centre of attention, and they were all over us.

One mischievous individual grabbed my beloved 300mm lens and swung his way to the top of a tree. When he got bored, he handed it back. I made a particular friend. She was two, maybe three years old. The instant you hold a baby chimp, you can feel how immensely physical and powerful even an infant is. She could have easily broken my arm if she had chosen to. She took a genuine interest in my camera. I took her over, and she put one eye straight to the eyepiece. She was not mimicking me; I could tell she was looking at the reflex image—a sophisticated concept. Chris took a photo I later used as a showreel sleeve with a speech bubble saying, "Not just anyone can do it, you know!"

"Not just anyone can do it, you know!"

Later, we filmed in an ivory carver's studio. There were some exquisite pieces. Then, a street market where several booths were selling fetish items such as gorilla hands and monkey skulls. There was no culture of livestock farming, so stalls were displaying an enormous variety of bush meat. We saw elephant and hippo meat; there were snakes, monkeys, cats, armadillos and numerous unfamiliar creatures. Though to my Western sensibilities, they were disturbing sights, I have no problem with the concept of subsistence foraging, but the diminishing forest could not sustain such commercial hunting.

Powerful visuals and compelling content are key to this sort of documentary, but the most crucial element is a strong story. We were missing two vital things: the wildlife footage, through ill-fated circumstances, and the visible presence of, or confrontation with, poachers. We had fascinating experiences, though sadly, a mediocre documentary.

Today, the illegal trade in ivory and endangered animals, alive and dead, is still massive, and there are more wide-ranging, better-funded anti-poaching initiatives in place. There has been a great deal of violence involving shoot-outs and hundreds of human deaths on both sides. The mighty dollar still reigns.

24

First Taste of Japan

I did a two-day shoot for an arts documentary about the French composer Erik Satie. It was the first time I worked with Chris Hale, the director, and it went well. Later, he invited me to film an interview with Renzo Piano, the renowned architect responsible for designing several of the world's finest buildings. It marked the beginning of Chris' four-year-long, sporadic shoot tracking the construction of Kansai Airport in Osaka, Japan, produced by Skyscraper Productions for Channel 4. Such long-term projects were rare then and are much rarer today, as commissioning editors seldom remain in the same position for that length of time time.

Piano's studio is a stunning building. Nestled between the mountains and the coast west of his native Genoa, Italy, it is built on several terraced levels that hug the hillside. Constructed from glass, wood and minimal steel, it blends into the shape of its surroundings and stands out as an ultramodern piece of environmental art. We load our equipment into the glass cube cablecar that whisks us vertically up the steepest section and changes orientation to follow the profile of the mountainside towards his studio. The interior is equally intriguing, with nature-inspired beauty everywhere you look and a hive of activity from the employees and students engrossed in their work. He is a delightful man to interview—gentle, articulate and brimming with inspirational ideas for the project.

It was on these shoots that I met Andy Cottom, a sound recordist with whom I would collaborate sporadically for many years. (He has an exceptional memory, and when I met him recently while prepping this book, he reminded me of several details I had completely forgotten and some I still have no recollections of. He also remarked that I was invariably concerned that, after every job, no further work would come my way. I asked whether that wasn't common for most freelancers—apparently not.)

A couple of weeks later, I received a call from Skyscraper checking my availability for filming in Osaka. I was very excited as I had long been eager to visit Japan. Perchance, I also had a call from Tim Copestake, a director I had last worked with ten years earlier on BBC's *Panorama*. His regular cameraman was unavailable, and I guess he was working through the list. He was after a shooter for the final episode of *Locomotion*, a BBC series on the history of railways. Titled *Track to the Future*, it was about the Shinkansen, the Japanese bullet train, and the experimental 'Maglev', which hovered above its track using powerful opposing magnetic fields. What was the chance of the two such opportunities coinciding?

After a few days, I received the dreaded calls from both productions, offering apologies and saying that the budgets were tight and they would have to hire local crews. Somehow, I managed to get the BBC and Skyscraper Productions for Channel 4 to speak to each other and agree to share my travel expenses—serendipity.

Japan is a technically advanced, developed country. Although I was well aware of cultural differences, I was taken aback by their extent. Was I on another planet?

My first faux pas was bowing back to the line of waiters who bowed to us as we entered a restaurant. The whole etiquette is complicated and steeped in tradition, encompassing variants on back angle, hand positions, eye positions, etc., all according to your social standing in relation to whom you are greeting. I was told of a petrol station chain whose new staff had to wear girdles to control their angle of inclination precisely.

More than 4,000 trains arrive and depart Tokyo Station daily, servicing over 500,000 passengers, and this was our first location. Tim's frustration was palpable as hours of valuable shooting time were absorbed by formalities, meetings and discussions with the railway's hierarchy. Also, they politely informed us where to set up our tripod in each area—this did not sit well. Eventually, with much diplomacy and help from our local fixer and translator, we won a modicum of autonomy. We filmed the rush-hour commuters as they streamed through the turnstiles. A line of guards synchronously bowed from the waist. The passengers formed orderly queues in the marked channels that aligned precisely with the arriving train's doors. Everyone looked forward, and no one interacted. As the doors opened, they started squeezing into the already-packed carriages. When it appeared to me that there was no room to fit in a pin, the smartly uniformed 'pushers' proceeded to do precisely what the term suggests.

They pushed the passengers, using all their body weight and their learnt skills. Business travellers stood on the threshold, awaiting a white-gloved pusher to manipulate their limbs and briefcases into the tiniest of gaps as the electric doors closed. Having completed the task, they would rush to the aid of a colleague at the next door along and hold it from closing as the other made his final shove. There was no display of discomfort or emotion on anyone's face.

The railway system is super-efficient and has a pristine safety record. Delays are measured in seconds, not minutes, and drivers may be docked wages for lapses in punctuality. At the time, there was a top-rated cop show on Japanese TV in which meticulously scrutinised railway timetables were used to solve complex crimes.

Liz Dobson was Tim's AP (assistant producer). I would work with her two years later when she started directing. On sound, we had BBC Bristol staffer Dickie Bird (his real first name was Lyndon, so why Dickie? I don't know; maybe it was because he was the Natural History Unit's first-choice recordist). We picked up the rest of the crew locally; they were a friendly, efficient bunch and always eager to please. I had requested a crew minibus with an opening roof through which I could shoot tracking shots of the city. Checking it out while parked at the kerb, I stood on a flight case secured to a seat, my head and chest protruding from the roof, steadying myself with my hands. The camera assistant slid the door closed, crushing my fingers. It was excruciatingly painful, and I yelped. He was mortified. The look of horror on his face concerned me more than my wounds—I worried that he would commit Hara-kiri! I played down my suffering. Fortunately, no bones were broken, and an ice compress, local medicine and a couple of days of healing worked nature's magic.

Launched in the mid-'60s, the Shinkansen was the world's first high-speed railway system. With their distinctive aerodynamic styling, the trains reached operating speeds of 320 km/h, silently and smoothly transporting 1,300 passengers at a time. They had dedicated tracks to be unimpeded by slow local traffic. It struck me that, within the carriages, people didn't chat—not even those who were travelling together. But what I found most fascinating was filming in the operator's cab. The driver was a senior employee. He wore an immaculate uniform—charcoal with gold trim, 'scrambled egg' gold braid on his cap, insignia on his epaulettes displaying his rank and the ubiquitous white gloves. He sat straight-backed at the controls, assertively gesturing and announcing his technical observations aloud as he reacted to various trackside signals—an industrial safety method known as pointing-and-calling, a compulsory scheme to reduce errors.

We stopped at a station, and there was a staff changeover. With the precision of a military parade-ground ceremony, the driver released his personal highly-polished power handle lever and carefully placed it in a padded cut-out in his briefcase. He then removed his traditionally styled pocket watch from a cut-out in the cab's dashboard and put that in an identical cut-out in the case. The replacement driver entered the cab, they bowed, and verbal formalities were exchanged. He performed the same procedure in reverse, and with a push of the handle, we smoothly accelerated towards our next destination.

It was great to shoot for Tim again. He is an excellent director and a lovely man. Unlike some documentary directors, he has a good understanding of what the camera can do, and we have similar aesthetic tastes. I soon learnt what he liked, and we developed a close working relationship that lasted until his retirement fourteen years later.

My film camera kit went back to the UK with Liz, Dickie and Tim as the Kansai shoot was to be shot on locally hired Betacam equipment with the help of Tokyo-based assistants and sound recordist. It would be a couple of days before Chris's arrival, so I was happy to be a tourist. I love Japanese food, and I found an area where locals gather to eat. There were lines of rotation sushi shacks where enthusiastic diners were spilling onto the streets. Conveyor belts packed with delights—I was in heaven. The only foreigner around, I was something of a curiosity. I had learnt that outward signs of aggression and street crime were virtually non-existent in this culture where everyone follows the rules, so I felt no threat. Tokyo's criminality was apparently limited to the privileged, wealthy, and powerful gangsters.

It was a Sunday afternoon, so I visited Yoyogi Park, famed for its rock 'n' roll performances. Western influences are a bit more prominent now; but then, it was different. In a country where conformity is embedded, youth culture emerged, but rebellion took on a different form. There were rockabillies, punks, hippies, folkies and techno-lovers, and their allotted performance and dance spaces were organised in a neat line. Within each genre, the fans were dressed virtually identically, and their dance moves were equally uniform. To a Westerner's eyes, the idea of punks all looking the same doesn't quite cut it—individuality was limited to the colour of your Mohican. The rockabillies all wore white T-shirts, tight denims and winkle-picker shoes; maybe the length of your heavily greased quiff could give you an edge.

Three mountains had been flattened to provide the 21 million cubic metres of earth needed to construct a four-kilometre-long artificial island in Osaka Bay, which was to become home to the Kansai International Airport—an unprecedented engineering feat. To connect to the mainland, they had built a $1 billion, four-kilometre-long double-decked bridge to carry six lanes of traffic with two rail lines below. If you like impressive statistics and big numbers, Google it.

But our three one-hour programmes were about the design and construction of the world's longest airport terminal, and our central Character was Renzo Piano. We donned yellow hard hats and hi-vis jackets to follow him around the skeleton of the extraordinary one-point-seven-kilometre-long building as he briefed his mainly Japanese team of design collaborators and engineers.

Shooting observational footage of dialogue on the move is a craft based on experience. The knack is to cover the whole conversation in such a way that, in the edit suite, the director can pick and choose what bits he wants. It's a dance. Invariably, the subjects are not standing in a straight line, so you have to move around to get their close-ups—sometimes making useable camera moves and other times rushing to get into position. At times, it is best to hold the shot after they stop speaking so you see them listening, making it easier for the editor to get the 'scissors' in. While you operate using your right eye, your left eye is used to anticipate your next move. When there is dialogue that is unlikely to be used, you shoot cutaways of characters listening—maybe including an over-the-shoulder shot where you can see that the de-focussed foreground character is speaking but can't see their lips. Then, you can rush back to get a wide-angle perspective that can be used over any audio. With luck, they may walk out of shot to neatly tie up the sequence or segue into the following shot. All the while, you are attempting to keep the images interestingly composed, in sharp focus and correctly exposed. It's fun to glimpse the rest of the crew rushing around, trying to keep out of your shot!

In such scenarios, high-quality sound is key, and the skills of the often under-appreciated one-person sound department are vital. Audio runs the whole time, so no dialogue is missed. The usual set-up is radio mics on the main two protagonists, and a handheld, telescopic overhead boom covers the rest. As well as controlling the levels of three audio channels on their SQN mixer (Nagra quarter-inch tape machine or DAT recorder, if on film), the recordist miraculously hovers the boom mic just clear of the frame without casting distracting shadows.

The architect, Piano, would break off to explain the plans to us. It was anticipated that the island would sink as it settled, so the terminal was built on computer-controlled adjustable columns. 'Computer-controlled' was, then, a cutting-edge concept. They would compensate for the movement and, when necessary, could be extended by inserting metal plates at their base. The island was supposed to keep the airport four metres above sea level for fifty years. It had been calculated to settle by approximately six metres by 1990, but it had already sunk more than eight—an engineering headache for the future.

Chris filmed on a few other occasions, working with a Japanese crew. I revisited the site with him twice, including the final shoot that encompassed the grand opening in September 1994.

The exquisite building now resembles a giant glider. Numerous boarding gates run along its wingspan, with the terminal's main body placed behind it like a fuselage. It gently curves, lifting in the middle and decreasing at either end so as not to interfere with lines of sight from the control tower. The roof is clad with tens of thousands of steel panels supported by a steel structure integral to the interior. In place of traditional power-hungry air conditioning units, elegantly styled giant ducts circulate air via the aerofoil-shaped ceiling. Mobile sculptures by Susumu Shingu, an Osaka-based kinetic sculptor, hang from the roof—their constant mobility makes a feature of the airflow. Blade-shaped deflectors help channel the air and reflect sunlight from the skylights.

They have managed to stabilise the sinking rate from fifty centimetres a year to just six, but climate change and more powerful storms will pose an additional threat. Today, the terminal is just a metre or two above sea level, and in 2014, it was swamped by a typhoon.

Goodbye to Japan for now—I'll be back.

25

Lost Tribes

The car kicked up a plume of dust as it sped towards Armageddon, where, according to the Bible, the dead will rise, and the faithful gather. At the wheel was Professor Steve Jones—a biologist, geneticist and broadcaster. As I braced against the dashboard in the front passenger seat in an attempt to absorb the bumps, he explained we were in the land of the Tribes of Israel and heading for the ancient city of Megiddo, from which the term Armageddon is coined.

In the back, almost as uncomfortable as I, were squeezed Chris, trying to keep out of shot, and Andy Cottom, with his Nagra recorder on his knees and his short boom mic positioned just below my frame.

Megiddo, in Israel, is a fascinating site where over twenty cities were built on top of one another and were inhabited continuously from 7,000 BC to 300 BC. The hill on which the Biblical-era fortifications stood rises twenty-two metres above the valley floor. Because of the location, it had great strategic value; whoever had control of the city had control of one of the major trade routes of antiquity—Egypt to the south and Mesopotamia (modern-day Iran and Iraq) and Anatolia (modern-day Turkey) to the north. For thousands of years, every invading army fought battles over it. We were interested in the Assyrian attack in the seventh century BC. As Steve clambered over the excavated ruins, he explained to camera how the defeated fled, scattered and became exiles—ten of the Twelve Tribes of Israel are lost to history.

Some believe these mysterious 'Lost Tribes' are endowed with mystical power. The search has been going on for 2,000 years, and there are ethnic claims worldwide to be their descendants. This documentary investigated four of these claims. It was for a 1996 BBC series called *In the Blood*, which searched for answers using genetics, an area little explored in popular science programmes.

When Megiddo fell, the Samaritans remained close to their native land. After centuries of persecution and a certain number of conversions to Christianity and Judaism, only 600 descendants of the 300,000 survivors remained. They consider themselves pure Israelites and the last to follow the true teachings of Abraham and Moses. They regard Judaism as a closely related but altered religion.

Mount Gerizim, in Israel's West Bank, is their holiest site as it is believed to be where Adam and Eve set up home after being expelled from the Garden of Eden and from where Abraham surveyed the Promised Land. The majority live in close proximity.

One of the world's most inbred communities, the Samaritans have five distinct lineages and, where practical, marry within them. They have excellent ancestry records—at least on the male side—making them good subjects for genetic research. It was proven that they indeed had an unbroken link with the people of the Old Testament.

We filmed an extraordinary event. The community was celebrating Passover for the three thousandth time since their ancestors settled. The proportion of priests is very high for such a small community. They have eminent status, and the role is strictly hereditary. They were dressed in their colourful finery, and all the other men were dressed head-to-toe in white. Dozens of fire pits had been lit, and everyone gathered around them. An equal number of sheep were tethered nearby, probably bewildered by the buzz of excitement but unaware of their fate. I shot from the shoulder all that was going on.

Unlike the sheep, we knew what was planned, and set up the tripod at a suitable high viewpoint to maximise our selection of shots for the main event. Come sunset, there was to be a series of prayers, chants and songs, culminating in a simultaneous slaughter. What we didn't know was how long the prayers would continue, making it tricky to anticipate the rather gruesome 'money shot'. This was one situation where a video camera would have come up trumps—I could have just kept it running. We were on film, which was expensive to waste, and each roll only lasted ten minutes. I kept starting and stopping the camera in the hope we would catch the moment and not be caught out during a magazine change. More by luck than judgment, we got it. In a single instant, dozens of sheep's throats were expertly cut; a sea of white clothing was splattered with red, and a cheer rose from the crowd. The shot didn't make the final edit—probably too morbid. The sacrificed were roasted over the fire pits, and the celebrations continued throughout the evening.

We took more driving shots through location-specific scenery, which were to become a regular transition device throughout the series. Our next stop was Rosh Ha'Ayin, inland from Tel Aviv.

Small groups of Yemenite Jews had been returning to areas like Jerusalem and Jaffa since the late 19th century. The biggest influx was in 1949 when 20,000 were flown to an old British air base here as part of the newly formed Land of Israel's 'Operation Magic Carpet'. They had kept their faith through three thousand years of exile.

Markets are often the ideal place to get a feel for the population and a good choice of shots of daily life. We filmed Steve walking around and interacting with locals, a handy device to insert voiceover commentary at a later stage. There was an amazing variety of interesting and characterful faces to photograph. They are largely devout people, but their features were more Arabic than Jewish, though the men all wore kippot (skull caps), and many had payot (orthodox curled side locks).

In most parts of the world, Jews are genetically distant from their neighbours and similar to Jews elsewhere. This community had more genes in common with non-Jewish Yemenites and other Arabs. This is because of mixed marriages and conversions over the years. It doesn't make them any less Jewish, but in genetic terms, it turned out that their 'Lost Tribe' credentials were not good.

Our next trip was to southern Africa. More shinnying over the ancient ruins for Steve and us. This time, it was Great Zimbabwe, a medieval city in the southeast of the country now named after it. Little is known about the site, but experts believe it to be the Iron Age capital of a great nation and to have been built by the ancestors of the Shona people. Professor M.E.R. Mathiva, a Lemba tribesman, wore a western style suit, kippa skull cap and a tallit (Jewish prayer shawl) and held a highly polished wooden staff with a beautifully carved elephant on the top. He briefly prayed facing the wall and then proudly stood before the ruin's tower, explaining their version of the history. The Lemba believe that it was constructed by the builders of Solomon's Temple in Jerusalem and, as such, has always been linked with the story of the ten lost tribes.

We then travelled across the border into Vendaland, an 'independent' homeland within the Republic of South Africa (later known as the Province of Limpopo), where we had arranged to visit a Lemba village. We were greeted by the gathered villagers with a slow hand clap. It was similar to many traditional African villages—lines of round huts with thatched roofs and leaf-covered mud floors with hearths in the middle where women wearing 'kanga' skirts and 'doek' headwraps prepared cassava-based meals while their children played noisily.

Our host was Chief Mposi of Berengue, a portly, jolly man, the latest in a long line of chiefs. He wore a deep red robe. He explained their presumed heritage to Steve and told him that they eat kosher. *"Don't eat pig meat—very dirty and smelly. And not the meat like everybody else; we cut here,"* he said, pointing at his throat. *"We also have what is known as circumcision."* Steve asked how they go about it. *"Great secret—comes from Israel —centuries old."*

It is Saturday morning, and everyone is dressed in their Sabbath finery. Drums beat out a rhythm as hundreds of Lemba climb a hill to their own 'Dome of the Rock', a holy mountain on top of which they are building a grand synagogue that faces North to Great Zimbabwe—their Temple of Zion—and Beyond, in the same direction, to Jerusalem, their spiritual and perhaps ancestral home.

The people gather in the shelter of the roofed skeleton of the synagogue, the men to one side and the women to the other—I am curious as to whether that is the influence of Jewish or African tradition. Professor Mathiva is back in the picture, this time as the rabbi. Beneath his tallit, he wears a blue velvet robe. On the back is a gold embroidered Star of David with an elephant in the centre. He sees himself as the keeper of their ancestral conscience and guardian of their biblical routes. He preaches to the gathered crowd in the Bantu language, informing them of their heritage. Standing beside him, an interpreter translates into English, displaying equal fervour. This is rather strange as few of the tribespeople speak English—I feel this is a show for our benefit.

"Your great grandfather Abraham said you should never forget about this. He said you should preserve all your cultures and all the rules that we say. Our history starts from here, back to Yemen, from Yemen to Judea; that's where we originated. Whether you like it or not, we are telling you that."

The congregation dutifully sits through the sermon but seems happy when it is over, and they can get on with partying. There's music from Mbira's—finger harps with gourd sound boxes. The Djembe drums join in, and the dancing begins. Most impressive are the large, athletic women, wearing queen-size bras and colourful Kangas, losing themselves in the rhythm.

We film at the graveyard. Women chant high-pitched trills and ululations as they approach the graves of past leaders. People encircle them, singing and slow hand-clapping. Mathiva explains how the dead were buried facing Jerusalem and how water had been poured into the coffins to represent the seas their ancestors had crossed in order to settle in Africa and so their souls could travel back to Israel.

Geneticist Professor Trefor Jenkins had built a close relationship with the Lemba Jews over the previous fifteen years and was using genetics to test their legends. He concluded that they were genetically distinct from their neighbours and had evidence that they had similarities to Jewish Arab groups as well as to white South African Ashkenazi Jews of Eastern European heritage. The link with the Middle East was only on the 'Y' chromosome, which exclusively comes from the male line. The men have a similar tie to the past, as do the Samaritan priests. However, their other chromosomes were more in line with the Venda people among whom they live.

Steve sat on a rock with a backdrop of beautiful savannah scenery and delivered his concluding piece to camera. *"Centuries ago, traders from the Yemen travelled down the African coast. Many had children by the local women, and over the generations, their genes spread. That's the message of genetics—history is made in bed, genes move across the world through sex and not within a wandering tribe of heroes."*

The fourth contender was the Mormon religion. Though not a tribe, worshipers are taught that they are Israelites and that they may learn of their individual tribal affiliation within the Lost Tribes. Their Articles of Faith say that in the last days, there will be a literal gathering of Israel and that Zion will be established on the American Continent in Independence, Missouri. Adam, Jesus Christ, and all the major players of the Old and New Testaments will be there.

It is a fascinating story, but unfortunately, I was committed to another shoot, so my involvement was finished. Generally speaking, it's in the director's and the production's interest to keep the same camera crew throughout a documentary to maintain a continuity of style and efficient working practices. However, logistically, financially, and in terms of availability, it is not always possible.

26

Meeting the Korowai Tribe

'Manop telobo'—the only words I know in the Korowai language. In fact, in November 1995, Tim White, John Beecroft, and I were probably the only English people who knew and used it as a greeting, a farewell, a thank you, and for just about anything that required a response. It literally means 'it's good'. At the time, the only person in the world who could speak both Korowai and English was a Dutch ex-missionary, and he was not on our radar.

Some months earlier, I had been invited for a meeting with Richard Wawman, a producer I had previously worked with. We sat in his office at Bray Studios, and he asked if I would like to direct and shoot three documentaries in Irian Jaya for a Discovery Channel series, *Warrior Island*. I reminded him that I was a cameraman, had not directed anything since film school and had no ambitions in that direction. Surely, it would be better to stick with what I am good at. He persisted, saying that he had every faith in me. I gave it some thought; after all, I have nothing to lose, and I had occasionally asserted—usually to myself—that I would make a better job of it than the director. Maybe this was the test.

Though I had shot in jungle environments, I had never worked on a specifically ethnographic film, a genre I had aspired to from the start. I was not going to commit to all three. Still, it would make a gratifying change to see a film through from conception to completion, and it would be wonderful to have some months of extended time at home with the family during the pre-production and post-production stages. After discussing it at length with Yaffa, I agreed to do just one.

New Guinea is the world's second-largest island after Greenland. It is a mountainous, sparsely populated tropical landmass divided between two countries, the independent nation of Papua New Guinea in the east and the Indonesian provinces of Papua, then known as Irian Jaya, in the west.

My brief was to film the buildup to and implementation of a 'Sago-Grub Festival' that the Nandup family clan had planned. This was the event around which I had the freedom to build the documentary based on my observations. What an exciting and daunting prospect.

The Korowai were one of several tribes living in southeastern Papua. They were believed to number about 3,000 and had first contact with Westerners in the mid-1970s. Until then, they thought that they and other nearby tribes were the only humans in existence. They lived in the rainforest in small clusters of tall tree houses which protected them from rising water levels, insects, wild animals, marauders and sorcerers. For crew, I engaged the talents of Tim on sound and John, a good friend who had shot his own ethnographic films in South America and was happy to work as my assistant. We flew to Bali, where I swam on an idyllic beach, followed by dinner and a relaxing seven-dollar massage. The following day, we took the nine-hour island-hopping flight to Jayapura, the capital of Irian Jaya. Richard travelled with us this far in order to help with logistics, which was fortunate as he had decided to save a few hundred pounds by freighting the bulk of our equipment rather than carrying it as excess baggage. An expensive and time-wasting decision as, unbeknown to us, it had been impounded by customs in Jakarta.

With the help of Jeed Yoku, our local fixer, we sourced a small generator for battery charging and the running of one 800W Redhead light, plus 12v car batteries to run three small 100W Dedolights for night-time filming. We lunched in the town's 'finest' restaurant, where we bumped into David Attenborough, whom I had filmed on a couple of occasions in the UK, and his crew, which included soundman Dicky Bird with whom I had worked on the *Locomotion* shoot in Tokyo—small world. They were making a documentary on Birds of Paradise.

It was time for Tim, Jeed, his wife Maria, who was to be our cook, and me to head into the bush. We left John behind in Jayapura to await the arrival of our kit that Richard flew back to Jakarta to retrieve, presumably with the aid of a suitable stash of cash. First, we flew in a Fokker cargo plane over the stunningly beautiful Balien Valley, home to the Dani tribe. We landed in Wamena, the last runway that could facilitate a medium-sized plane. Only recently, there had been some 'first world' (as it was then referred to) type development in the village, starkly contrasting the tribespeople's demeanour and lifestyle. Most men still sported their highly decorative face and body decorations, piercings, bones through their noses, elaborate headdresses, and penis gourds. Jeed hired a driver with a Land Rover and took us on the grand tour. Somewhat ironic as the few roads that they had petered out at the edge of town.

We met up with Rupert Stasch, a young American anthropologist researching his PhD on the Korowai. He had already spent a couple of weeks living with the Nandup clan and was set to join us in the field. He struck me as a dedicated and astute young man and was sure to be a great asset. While Jeed returned to Jayapura to finalize paperwork for our equipment transfer, Tim, Rupert, and I, plus our baggage and supplies, flew in two Cessna Caravan aircraft to the jungle outpost of Yaniruma, a line of stilt huts Dutch missionaries had established in 1979. I understand that they failed to have any converts to Christianity, so they decided to remain as guests rather than as conquerors, putting no further pressure on the Korowai to follow in the footsteps of Jesus. Here, we hired guides and porters for the trek to meet the Nandup clan.

Fenelun Molonggai was our key contact and mediator with the Nandups, arranging the construction of an accommodation hut for us on stilts and another for Maria and her helpers Importantly, he had convinced them to time their planned sago-grub festival to fit our five five-week filming window. I had no involvement in negotiations, but I understand that the settlement included steel axe heads, machetes, cooking pots, fishing line, tobacco, and some cash. Though they had no understanding of money in our terms, they had adopted it as a supplement to their traditional cowry shells and pig teeth for the trading of goods, dowries and the like. I guess it all comes down to the same thing. I feel we got the best end of the deal.

Still no positive news of our equipment, but it was time to head into the bush with a mass of baggage and kit, provisions, generator and fuel. We headed upstream in long dugout canoes to the closest access point. There followed a gruelling nine-hour trek through challenging terrain. Our guides hacked through dense undergrowth while we navigated a flooded forest floor filled with trip hazards such as submerged roots and decaying vegetation. Every so often, logs as long as ten metres had been laid on the mud where the jungle floor had particularly treacherous dips. The barefoot porters walked them with ease, but they were like greased tightropes for us clumsy, heavily shod Englishmen. The oppressive heat and humidity were relentless, and we were constantly on guard for snakes. Parrots shrieked from high in the canopy; mosquitoes and other insects buzzed around our faces. I foolishly insisted on handcarrying my Aaton film camera and Nikon stills camera, making the trek even more arduous. A sudden downpour attacked us through gaps in the sodden canopy. Though we didn't see anyone else en route, we heard the occasional exchange of distant whoops and melodic chants. I was forty-six years old, with jungle experience and considered myself reasonably fit, but I was struggling. We had brief rests, but there was no option to slow down as we needed to reach our destination in daylight.

Exhausted, I was on the verge of collapse when, as if in a vision, shafts of evening sunlight penetrated the canopy to reveal a clearing—a magnificent sight. In the middle was a banyan tree with an under-construction tree house about forty feet high. We soon discovered that this was a play hut for the kids to enjoy and to learn building skills. We nicknamed it the 'Wendy House'. Nearby was the substantial raised bivouac that the clanspeople had built for us.

I should have been relishing this extraordinary experience. I had envisioned a grand arrival and being greeted by the

Nandup family with an exchange of smiles, laughter, and whatever ceremony they deemed appropriate. But my only thought at that moment was to slump onto a dry surface. I did.

Next morning, we met with our hosts at the party 'bivac' (the local Indonesian name for a ground-level building). This had been built for the forthcoming Sago-Grub Festival. There were about twenty people—women and children on one side and men on the other. Small fires were burning, and everyone smoked tobacco from bamboo pipes or rolled in leaves. They looked at us inquisitively, proffering broad smiles and chattering among themselves. I approached the men offering my hand, which appeared to confuse them—so, handshakes are not a thing. I said a few English words as a greeting. There was no response, nor was there the feeling of an awkward silence. We soon learnt that this was the Korowai way; a visitor would turn up at your home and stand or sit around, maybe for several minutes, until someone had something to say.

The men were mainly small and wiry with very dark skin. They were naked; their penises pushed inside their scrotum with a leaf wrapped and tied around the protruding foreskin. They adorned themselves with anything available from their environment, such as cassowary quills or small bones through facial piercings, rattan hoops around the waist and strings of pigs' teeth or cowry shells as necklaces. Four weeks later, these would be supplemented with 16mm gash film stock, cable ties and gaffer tape.

The women, with similar decorations, wore grass skirts made of fibres from sago palm leaves. Many had circular scars running the length of their arms, around their stomachs, and across their breasts to make them more attractive; these had been scorched on by bark embers from the fire. One was breastfeeding a piglet whose trap-caught mother had been yesterday's lunch.

Skin disorders such as ringworm were common to almost everyone. They suffered from many diseases, largely due to a lack of awareness of infectiousness, poor balance in their diet and a minimal intake of liquid. There were no elderly people as no one had reached old age, and there was no expectation of longevity. From their perspective, all sickness and death itself is brought about by sorcery.

There appeared to be no hierarchy among the men. Each contributed according to his strengths. But apart from the macho stuff like hunting, fishing, tree felling, and building, the women seemed to do all the hard work.

I had participated in a few shoots involving interaction with tribal peoples—mainly in Africa, but this was completely different. Most of these folk had never seen a white man or knew anyone existed outside their jungle environment. The few who had, had only encountered the Dutch missionaries in Yaniruma. They had no concept of television or motorised transport or, indeed, any of the trappings of the 'developed' world. They were alien in our eyes; I can't begin to imagine what they thought of us.

In due course, we men gathered in a circle, and I thanked them for their hospitality. I introduced the team and attempted to explain our purpose and how we hoped to achieve it. This was a prolonged process as I spoke in English to Rupert, who translated into simple Indonesian to Fenelun, who, in turn, translated into Korowai. The response came back via the same route. Fortunately, there was plenty of tobacco, so no one was in a hurry, but I have no idea how they got their heads around the fact that we couldn't start filming because the bulk of our equipment and all our film stock was yet to arrive.

Clear skies and sunshine are rare in the New Guinea rainforest. Still, that afternoon it was blasting, creating beams of light through the ventilation holes in the party bivak roof, spotlighting selected areas of the activity, backlighting the plumes of smoke from fires and tobacco, offering up beautiful atmospheric silhouettes—a cinematographer's dream. If only he had some film stock. It was time for a tour of the clan's territory. We were led along a trail of felled sapling trees, which, as on our trek to the clearing, were easy for them but not for us. We would slip into the mud and groundwater that was everywhere. In due course, they kindly constructed more substantial walkways for us along our regular routes.

We came to another clearing where Bulowal, the senior member of the Nandup family, had his fine tree house, and about thirty metres to the left was the smaller and lower tree house belonging to his bachelor brother Yowo. We were invited into Bulowal's house. We had to climb the notched pole, which was incredibly difficult, not least because it was lashed at only one point at the top. This was so that it would swing from side to side, giving the occupants ample warning of any visitors, be they welcome or not.

Day-to-day social and family interaction takes place on the verandah, sat around the hearth, made from strips of clay-coated rattan suspended over a hole in the floor so that it can be quickly hacked loose should the fire get out of control. Men sit to one side, women and children to the other. The sexes remain similarly separated inside, with a divide down the centre. I am given to understand that intimacy and sex, though high on the agenda, are kept pretty discreet and generally take place in the forest. However, there is no shortage of bawdy talk and banter around the hearth. Smoke from fires coats the bark walls and sago-leaf ceiling. Stone axes, bone charms, bows and arrows, and net bags are tucked into the leafy rafters.

The floor creaks as we settle cross-legged onto it. Most of the conversation is smiles and giggles punctuated by drags on a communal bamboo pipe. We did manage to communicate that we would really like a shooting platform constructed high on a particular banyan tree facing the house. It was a big ask, but once again, they obliged, and within a few days, we had a large tree platform with a roof to protect us from the vicious downpours and a ladder for access rather than a pole!

Fenelun excelled in overseeing the day-to-day practical aspects of the shoot. The crew bivac surpassed our expectations. It was a large hut, raised from the jungle floor and open on one side. It was solidly constructed with vertical and horizontal supports lashed with sago-palm fibres, woven walls, a sago leaf roof and a bark-covered floor. We had a sleeping area with leaf mats and mosquito nets provided by Jeed. Rupert had a corner where he could set up his laptop and work, and there was an open space where we could organise our kit, should it ever arrive. The tribes-folk are comparatively short and always sit on the floor, and Jeed must have explained that we weirdos were very tall and liked to eat seated on benches at a table. So they had lashed together a tabletop and secured it on a skilfully levelled tree stump at about chest height, with correspondingly high fixed benches. Much to the amusement of the ever-present kids, we ate like toddlers with our feet dangling.

We had a constant stream of visitors. Men would be passing with their bows and arrows on the way back from hunting trips, invariably empty-handed. We would have 'chats' exchanging English phrases and Korowai ones punctuated with peals of laughter. I had bought some postcards of London views, thinking they would be of interest. Somehow, a red bus in front of the Houses of Parliament didn't resonate and was so far from anything they could relate to that they were more interested in the card itself. When I pulled out the family snaps, it was a different matter. Dan was twelve, Tali was ten, and we had recently taken a camping holiday in western France. Spielberg's latest movie, *Jurassic Park*, was big in our lives, and the photos were of us messing around in the forest and posing outside a family-sized tent. I gave up trying to explain that this was not our home. Similarly, there was no interest in our state-of-the-art technology, which included Rupert's laptop and a satellite phone; that is until I showed my beloved Leatherman multitool with a saw blade that cut easily and cleanly through a small branch. Minds were blown.

Sleeping was comfortable enough. We couldn't hear the anticipated screech of cicadas because the deafening croaks of frogs drowned them out.

There was a river a kilometre away where the clan collected water, fished and bathed. We would wash there each day but soon learnt that being naked was not an option as our manhood was on display, i.e. not tucked away, which was shameful. It was wonderfully refreshing, but by the time we had trekked back to base, we were as sweaty and dirty as when we had left.

The sat-phone was at the cutting edge of tech. We all had experience in off-the-beaten-track filming, but none of us had encountered this luxury. It had a built-in base unit and an infrared dish that needed to be aligned with the satellite to precise coordinates. Fortunately, Tim is a great boffin, and I was happy to leave all this to the sound department. Making calls was very expensive, and we had strict instructions from

Richard to keep its use to a minimum. As things turned out, the production would have been a washout without it.

We are three days in the bush and still need good news about the arrival of our kit. This is now creating serious problems. Not least, the sago-grub harvesting and festival must be delayed, meaning the bugs are starting to mutate into beetles, causing much embarrassment for Yowo, the host. We will be very short on time, and I need a really good plan for shooting when it happens. Richard says to extend the trip as long as necessary, but that is not an option for us. No way are we not going to be home with our families for Christmas.

On another call to Jayapura, I spoke to the concierge at the hotel, and he said that John was on his way to Wamina, which meant that within a few days, we could start filming. We heard the chants from deep in the forest long before John, Jeed, and a stream of porters emerged, looking weary but happy to arrive. With the camera gear and film stock laid out in our bivac, John mustered the strength for a tour and to meet our new friends. Afterwards, he slept as Tim and I eagerly sorted through the equipment and readied it for work the next day. Everything vital was there. The only stuff that had 'walked' was a few rolls of gaffer tape and a few cans of Deet.

The nature of documentary filmmaking is rarely chronological for a myriad of practical reasons. But I had hoped this one could be shot spontaneously to avoid involving the subjects in the 'process'. Due to our now extremely tight schedule, all the elements had to be squeezed into about ten days of filming. I had to hatch a new plan of action.

27

Living with Cannibals

Oh, frabjous day! Callooh! Callay! Three weeks after leaving the UK, we are on day one of filming. Feyoko fells one of his hundreds of sago palm trees, which would have been planted about fifteen years earlier. The men lever off the outer bark to expose the fibrous pith, and then the women pound it with stone axes and load the pulp into holders made from the palm fronds, where it is soaked in water. When drained through a frond sluice, it leaves blocks of sago starch that can be cooked directly on the fire or wrapped in packages with meat or grubs. They carry the fruits of their labour home in sago-fibre string bags. People who say that British food is tasteless should try sago starch; it tastes how I imagine polystyrene does.

Dahale and his wife, Habil, visit their relatives to help prepare for the festival. They will turn out to be significant characters in the documentary, a young, attractive couple with whom I hope our audience will find some common ground. They prove to be very cooperative and enjoy helping us recreate a sequence of their day-long trek through the treacherous terrain. I obtained a good selection of angles from frog's eye view at ground-water level to bird's eye view from our tree-top platform. Dahale, whose name translates as 'Palm Heart', heralds their arrival with his signature chant. They climb the notched pole, Dahale carrying his axe and bow and arrows, Habil carrying a few belongings in the string bag strapped around her forehead. All the while, there is an exchange of dialogue about their journey. We are still on our platform as, predictably, the heavens open, providing the opportunity to get a good feel for the atmosphere of the clearing in a tropical downpour. Tim, the stellar sound recordist, always one step ahead of the game, had planted radio mics in the tree-house, and we film the verandah action and dialogue using my ever-handy 300mm telephoto lens. We will pick up in-situ footage to complete the sequence on another occasion.

L-R: Myself, John, and Tim on our tree-top shooting platform

Social interaction continues into the night, but their small fire doesn't give off sufficient light to register on the negative. In the larger film world, there are various specialist lighting options to recreate the effect of firelight; in the remote jungle, one has to improvise. John gently wiggles a carefully positioned, silvered collapsible reflector with an orange-gelled battery light focused on it—it works a treat.

In the morning, we followed Dahi and Fouari, Yawo's nephews, into the forest. As always, they carried bows and a selection of arrows, each metre-long shaft bound with vine to a head designed for a specific prey. Pig arrowheads are broad-bladed, those for birds are long and narrow; fish arrowheads are pronged, while the arrowheads for humans are carved from cassowary bone with several barbs on either side. Cassowaries are large, colourful, flightless birds and prime prey, but they are elusive, and I never got to see one.

Wild pigs are highly prized and believed to embody many human attributes. We hoped to bag one, but we encountered none, so Dahi grabbed his axe, and they proceeded to build a trap from felled saplings lashed together. They baited it with rotting sago bark with grubs in residence and constructed an elaborate trigger mechanism, all the while earnestly chatting away. On receiving the translation transcript a couple of days later, I was thrilled; they had been discussing their ailments and which corresponding part of the pig they would eat as a cure. After our return to base, Tim, John and I headed to the river to film some fishing. First, we came across a number of young boys collecting bait, mainly large insects pulled from the bushes. They grabbed grasshoppers, ripped off their legs to immobilise them and popped them alive into a string sack. A particularly juicy one was stuck behind an ear for a tasty snack later. Line fishing is the first hunting skill young boys master.

Waist deep in the cold river water, I filmed two men, submerged to their necks, patching up a sago leaf dam. They took large cone-shaped traps fashioned from strips of bark and pierced the dam wall, creating the only channels for the water to flow, thus trapping the larger fish. Such a catch provided a vital source of protein in a starch-heavy diet. Freshwater crayfish were the favourite. Our dinner that night was fried fish with green beans and noodles. Maria had been doing some bartering. As usual, we had an audience. Naturally, we offered morsels for tasting, but they didn't enjoy our spicy cuisine. When used to polystyrene, anything with salt and pepper is too much. Earlier on, I had watched (and filmed) one of our friends pounding a pandanus fruit into a luscious-looking deep red syrup. He licked the residue off his fingers with a look of sheer delight on his face. I eagerly accepted the offer of a taste—it had none.

John, Tim and I all fancied ourselves as musicians, and we had bought a cheap guitar in Jayapura. John had a great rapport with the kids, and his music created endless entertainment—something they could connect with. I had set up my Sony Walkman cassette player with a couple of small speakers hitched to the wall. Playing Pink Floyd's *Dark Side of the Moon*, one particular boy was open-mouthed, eyes flitting from side to side, transfixed by the stereo image of track two, 'On the Run'. The sounds of a panting man running left to right and back, plus an electronic version of planes taking off, mesmerised him. The only instrument I was aware the Korowai had was a bamboo version of a Jew's harp, and every man seemed to have his two-bar signature yodelling chant that he would repeat over and over.

When we checked the trap on the following day, fortuitously, there was a terrified boar within. To quote a thrilled Dahi (in translation), *"Usually, the first time we check a trap, it has only caught mosquitos!"* The now panic-stricken pig was screeching as the guys approached. It was quickly dispatched with a single arrow. I did a series of shots of them carrying the prey, swaying from side to side, hanging feet-bound from a pole. All of a sudden, Fouari dropped his end and, with a yelp, covered his crotch with his hands. His leaf had fallen off—how embarrassing! After regaining his modesty, they entered the clearing, announcing their arrival with a chant, and headed towards the festival bivac where the beast was laid down on a palm frond, and they proceeded to butcher. The men have an excellent knowledge of anatomy. They started at the back of the jaw and cut down each side of the torso using a razor-sharp split bamboo blade. Threading a length of vine under the breast bone, they lifted it and smashed the ribs with a stone axe all the way around so as not to damage the internal organs. The carcass and offal were cleanly divided for distribution. Tim told me that Dahi turned to him at one stage and said something. He said to Rupert that he would love to know what it was. That evening, after translation, he had the answer: "You butcher a human in exactly the same way." This was the first reference to the sensitive subject that I knew we had to broach. They were believed to occasionally practise cannibalism and it was an aspect of tribal life that I had to cover in due course.

 Meanwhile, Yowo and others of the family gather at Bulowal's tree house to cook and eat their share of the kill. Having developed our skills a little, we climb the pole, causing much amusement with our awkwardness. We hoist the camera and sound kit on ropes and start to shoot. The pork is put on a bed of sago flour, wrapped in banana leaves to retain moisture, and then sandwiched with hot stones. Meat is a luxury, and the smell of cooking fills the air with anticipation. Men, women and children smoke and chat excitedly. When considered ready, the parcel is unwrapped and shared. The women get the offal, and the men get the flesh. Much as I enjoy a rare fillet steak, barely singed pork is not to my liking, so I decline the offer of a piece. "Manop telobo." After eating, they lodge the bones in the roof supports as mementoes that embody special memories and spiritual meaning.

Evening and into dusk, Dahale chants his melodious yodel as he helps the young boys weave the 'Wendy House' roof—a lovely sequence. I feel we are getting the bonus of some insightful sync dialogue. On receiving Rupert's translation printout a few days later, it goes something like: "I hope that giant with the animal on a stick doesn't go too near the edge; if he falls, we will have to dig him out of the ground", referring to Tim—all six foot three inches of him—and his furry windmuff encased microphone on a boom.

On Bulowal's tree house verandah, the family waits for the pork to cook

28

The Price for Sorcery

For the Korowai, the forest is their world, providing all their material and spiritual needs. It is a domain that is revered and feared, where dangerous spirits may lurk behind every bush. As they wade across the jungle floor, bones underfoot embody memories of animals and people who have died, been hunted or eaten. They mistrust the spirit world, and any imbalance in their surroundings, such as extreme weather, poor sago harvest, illness, and death, is put down to sorcery. If someone feels sick, they will attribute it to being eaten from the inside by a sorcerer—even while asleep. They may well have suspicions as to who among their own or their neighbours is the culprit. An evil spirit inhabits this person, and they are no longer considered human. If there is agreement among the men as to who it is, their traditional fate is to be seized or ambushed, killed and eaten. They would often give the body to a neighbouring clan for consumption, who may offer a pig or a wife in return. As with the boar, eating equivalent body parts could ease ailments. They are aware that their Indonesian overlords consider it murder and punishable by law, even if the offender were a sorcerer.

It is crucial to the film that we address the subject of cannibalism, but I can't very well approach clansmen and ask them to please kill and eat someone so I can get some shots. I decided that the best approach was through story-telling, and as Discovery Channel disapproves of long dialogue sequences, I will find a way of illustrating them in the edit. We gathered at Bulowal's place and asked a small group of men if they would relate some stories, including tales of sorcery and its consequences. Fortunately, they were eager to oblige. We shot thousands of feet of film with absolutely no idea of the content. Still, they were very animated and acted out scenarios like grabbing a roof support and attacking it with a stabbing motion, so I was pretty confident we had something relevant.

As we all had such a busy schedule, I didn't receive Rupert's transcripts until I got home a couple of weeks later. I was thrilled with the results. There were a number of stories. Here is one of two that made the final cut:

> "As our people live and eat, we would wonder if one among us has become a sorcerer, and if so, will he try to eat us? When we are out in the forest, and we see what looks like cassowary or pig footprints, could they really be sorcerer's? Someone may be out walking, and the sorcerer would creep up behind him, shoot him dead, cut him to pieces and share the meat among his sorcerer friends. Old people would say, 'We must be careful.' The sorcerer would tempt men with the meat, and the men think, 'If we eat this, we too could become sorcerers.' We'd give it to our mothers and wives secretly at night,

and if they throw up, that's it, we would say, 'It's a good thing the women ate this and not us.'"

On reconnecting with Rupert twenty-seven years later, while preparing for this book, he clarified that this is not an act of chauvinism but a belief that the effects manifest themselves only mildly with women. Today (2024), Rupert is the world authority on the tribe and a senior professor at Cambridge University. He now speaks the language and points out that the stories' translations, at the time, were basic, and the tenses ambiguous.

The storytelling continues.

"As we sleep around the hearth at night, a sorcerer would sneak in and eat someone as they slept. He would wake feeling delirious. We would ask, 'Are you going to die?' 'Yes.' 'Who has eaten you?' 'That person, so-and-so, has eaten me.' His family would cry on and on. We'd bury him beneath his tree house wrapped in palm fronds. During the funeral, we would grab the unsuspecting sorcerer like this, this way, like this. 'He's running! He's free! He's getting away!' Eventually, we'd restrain him, shoot him dead and lie him down. We would carry the body along, letting the feet dangle. His head would shake back and forth, bouncing, making little noises as if he was talking. We would throw the body into a stream and cut his throat with a bamboo blade. We would twist his neck, and the head would break off. Someone would take a vine and put it in the mouth. The end would come out through the throat. We'd tie it up at the top. One of us would stand there holding the head and performing a war-like dance. We would split open the

body like we would usually butcher pigs, then pull out all the intestines. We'd give an arm to one group and the other arm to another group, and another would get a leg, another the other leg. Just like at a festival, we'd arrange the meat on palm leaves. Neighbouring groups would perform as they returned home, carrying meat on their shoulders. When we were done eating, we would gather the bones and put them where paths meet as a sign. From day until night and through to the morning, we would beat the walls, and then the sorcerer's relatives would ask us for compensation—dogs' teeth, pigs' teeth and cowrie-shell money. We would make peace, eat and drink together and say, 'Yes, he was a sorcerer, so we won't be demanding anything more.'"

Rupert and Fenelun translate sound rushes as curious onlookers watch and listen

Yowo is a quiet man and the eldest of the three Nandup clan brothers. It is he who has planned the party. Yowo lost his wife to another man many years ago. In most such cases, clans-people would have mounted a raiding party or negotiated compensation. He has received nothing, and if his festival is a success, it will help him regain some respect.

About ninety palms had been felled three moons ago to farm the grubs. For us to film the story, some more needed to be felled. Each tree has been personally planted and is individually owned, and there are many hundreds. Yowo fells the first one to the sound of whoops and cheers, and then friends from related and neighbouring clans join in to help. We film seven for a montage, much of it in slow motion, in order to see wood chips fly and the bounce of the crown and fronds as each tree hits the forest floor.

Young boys, chewing on the sweet palm tips, look on as the men prepare a tree for rotting. They split and wrap the trunk tightly in its own leaves. Rotting palms are the perfect environment to encourage the Capricorn beetle to lay its eggs, which, in turn, produce larvae, the sago-grubs, which are considered a great delicacy. These particular grubs will not be ready in time for the party.

We follow Yowo back to his bachelor tree house. As we film him, silhouetted against the daylight of the clearing, he engages in a shouted two-way conversation with Bulawao in his home about 40 metres away. This is a magical scenario, and when they finish, I ask if he would be happy to have a further such exchange in about thirty minutes (Fenelun was the timekeeper). Tim gaffer-tapes a radio mic to a roof support and plants another in Bulawao's platform. We climb to our treetop eyrie, from where I can pan back and forth between the two houses. It has the makings of a powerful and poignant sequence.

The festival hut has now become the centre of all activity. As the days pass, more helpers gather. They socialise in the hut and sleep on any available floor space. The time for the festival approaches. Women arrive laden with newly processed sago starch, jungle greens, fruit and vegetables, both gathered and cultivated. Yowo, as the party host, collects and distributes food from the centre of the hut, an honorary position he'll occupy throughout the festival.

As in the tree house, the women and men establish their own separate spaces. This is not strictly enforced, and during the festival, there is ample opportunity for flirtation. Although the main event is still a couple of days away, there is a buzz of excitement in the air. Yonale is already in a party mood. He is wearing his sexy cockatoo feather in his hair and entertaining his friends with innuendo jokes. There's a delightful moment where he has everyone's attention. I'm on a big closeup. His eyes are sparkling, his mouth neatly framed in a circular quill attached through his nose piercing. Grinning from ear to ear, he says, *"The girls came to my house only to look at my cockatoo feather."* A chorus of laughter. *"Heys"* and *"Whoops"* follow. He pauses and, with a self-satisfied smile and the timing of a pro comedian, he looks straight down the lens and exclaims, *"Good, eh?"*

Bones from birds' and bats' wings are popular as nose ornaments. Both women and men adorn themselves with anything attractive that their surroundings have to offer. Girls make new grass skirts out of young sago leaves so as to look their best. Although the light levels are very low inside, the shape of the light and the large amount of smoke from fires and tobacco make for a very moody look and with careful camera positioning and choice of exposure, it is possible to evoke the atmosphere that we are experiencing.

It's dead easy this directing business—you just leave it all up to the cameraman!

The moment of truth is nigh. The Nandups, their friends and helpers apprehensively head out to the felled palm trees that had been prepared three months ago, hoping that the grub harvest will be fruitful. Yowo and his team unwrap the first tree. It is stripped and pulled apart with disappointing results. Many cocoons are empty. The larvae have morphed into beetles and flown away, and he's worried they have left it too late. I feel awful. After all, the delay has been our fault. However, others are having more luck, and many of the hundred or so rotting trees are heaving, and the squirming grubs are quickly separated from their cocoons. The healthiest are about two inches long—plump with black heads. There are beetles, too, and many other creepy crawlies that the kids grab and put straight into their mouths. The overall yield is disappointing, but hopefully, there will be sufficient food for the guests to feast on. Thousands are collected and encased in large packages woven from leaves and taken to the festival hut for overnight storage. These will be cooked and served to the guests on the following day.

Yowo is anxious. For him, a great deal rests on the success of this festival. This is the climax of months of preparation and material outlay. Will there be enough guests? Will there be sufficient food? Will the rain hold off? Will people enjoy themselves? I am anxious. For me, a great deal rests on the success of the festival filming. This is the climax of the core story of the film. Will the rain hold off? Will the guests accept our intrusion? Will I get the variety of footage I need? Will the minimal amount of artificial light at my disposal see us through the night?

The Cameraman's Cut

Party day is upon us. Once again, my biggest technical and creative challenge is the lighting for when it gets dark. The viewer needs to see what's going on, but I have to create the illusion that it is unlit, all the while causing minimum disruption for the revellers. The small fires in the hut can only contribute a touch of flicker in the shadows on those closest. We clamp my three 100w Dedolights in the roof supports to give pools of side and backlight. They are each powered by a fully charged car battery and connected via a long lead concealed among the leaves. We rig the 800w Redhead lamp in a tree with a light blue colour correction gel to give some 'moonlight' on the area in front of the hut. In order to keep the noise level from the generator to a minimum, we run a long power cable into the bush. There's much guesswork as everything has to be rigged in advance. I'll be using my fastest lenses and fastest film and working at the lowest limits of the technology and chemistry.

We have sent scouts, from Maria's helpers, into the bush to warn us when the visiting tribes-folk are approaching. We climb up into the Wendy house, which I hope will give us a good bird's eye view of the arrival. It does not disappoint. We hear the chants long before we see anyone. In due course, the guests emerge from the forest, singing and performing. There must be close to one hundred. Adorned with their finest body accessories and dressed as if for combat, the visitors and hosts perform a mock war dance, moving around the hut's exterior in opposing directions. The men and boys punch the air with their bows and arrows. Some have large, colourfully decorated shields. Mothers, with babies in string slings or infants on their shoulders, bounce up and down in time with the music. With a selection of lens lengths, the top shots I am getting are magic.

I just hope I have left enough time for us to get down and shoot observational footage among the action before they tire out. My adrenaline is pumping, as is theirs. They have no intention of slowing down. To use well-established filmmakers' jargon, we 'shoot the shit out of it'. I have what I need outside and move into the hut where Yowo is already cooking the first course of grubs in sago flour pancakes. I grab an extra angle of the dancing and bow play framed from the inside, looking out and, as if on cue, they 'conga' in through the rear opening, through a convenient shaft of smoke-laden sunlight from a ventilation gap in the roof, and out the other end. They have quite a repertoire of different dance steps and chants. A curious mixture of harmony and cacophony, as well as whistling from the women. They are in a rapturous trance. It is also a heady experience for John, Tim and me. The revelry continues through the night. Their energy seems endless, only pausing to feast on the fare, banter, and flirt. To complete nature's cycle, the men return the now redundant food leaf wrappings to the forest with a special ceremonial dance.

Eventually, the exhausted and sated revellers succumb to slumber, huddled in small groups on the party hut floor. Yowo can sleep well in the knowledge that his sago grub festival has been a great success.

The shoot is virtually over, and I have one more requirement, which must be the most bizarre request that the tribesfolk have ever had. For geographical context and a pre-title sequence, I really needed to shoot some aerial footage of the forest and their location within it. The tangled forest floor makes it unsafe for a helicopter to land, so a helipad had to be constructed in one of their nearby clearings. MAF, the Mission Aviation Fellowship, who provided all our flights, supplied the dimensions and basic technical specifications via sat-phone. Overseen by Jeed and Fenelun, all hands, including our camp helpers, set to work using their well-honed construction skills and forest materials—extraordinary.

I managed to skive off by shooting some cutaways. Tim picked up some audio wild-tracks. John had the mammoth task of sorting and packing the rushes, along with the mountain of accompanying paperwork. We all had to pack kit and our personals, ready for flying. We had exposed seventy-one of our one hundred rolls of film. That is thirteen hours of content. Not a lot for a one hour film, but I am reasonably confident that I have what is needed.

It's time for farewells. I initiate a gathering of all, though the women and girls don't make an appearance. We are now well used to the chain-translation pace of communication. I make sure my sincere gratitude is understood. I am relieved to learn that my fears regarding disruption to their laid-back lifestyle and the delay we had caused to the festival may have led to some resentment were unfounded. The outpouring of affection profoundly touches me. They enjoyed the experience as well as the material benefits. There is much smiling, laughing, 'manop telobos' and exchanges of belongings. I have a fine bow and arrow set, a pig's teeth necklace, and a grass skirt on display in my living room to this day.

The gathered clan members and their friends may have seen the occasional Cessna fly high overhead, but the drama of an MD500 helicopter landing in their 'backyard' must be mind-blowing. The roar of the engines at a sound level they have never experienced. The rotor down and side-wash is akin to a tornado. Their new white friends being whipped off into the heavens—surely we must be sorcerers!

The reality is that there are a few shuttle flights to get the kit and crew back to Yaniruma. For the final one, the port-side door has been removed. I attach my patent 'Colimount' bungee camera rig, sit sideways with my feet on the landing skid, attach a safety harness, and we take off. John has loaded the three film magazines, and he sits alongside me for mag changes. With headphones and talkback on, I can communicate directions with the pilot. Shooting at the slightly faster frame rate of 32 fps to smooth out the bumps, all goes well until halfway through the 2nd mag. My beloved Aaton grinds to a halt with an air of finality. Probably a combination of moisture and creepy crawlies inside the camera. It is disappointing, but thank goodness it didn't happen a few days earlier.

The final stage of the process will be six to eight weeks of post-production, but before that, there'll be more familiar festivals to enjoy. I arrived home in the middle of the eight-day Jewish celebration of Chanukah, and in 1995, the final day coincided with Christmas. I had missed Yaffa and the kids so much and really looked forward to sitting around our hearth listening to and telling stories.

29

Korowai Post-Production

In the UK, Super16mm film was still king as an image capture format for broadcast documentaries and dramas. But the days of physically cutting and splicing film for TV were over. All our footage was synced to the time-coded audio and 'telecined'; i.e. the processed negative and sound would be converted directly to the new kid on the block, Digital Betacam tape. VHS cassette copies were made for home rushes viewing and a 'paper' edit. In this unconventional case, a Umatic cassette copy was also made so I could do an initial rough cut at home—another of Richard's economy measures.

He delivered a Umatic editing package to my home, and it was set up in the spare bedroom. The format was cumbersome and dated. It was considered 'industrial' quality but too low-spec for broadcast. It was tape-to-tape and linear. In other words, edits were destructive, and if you wanted to put a few frames back in, you would need to readjust everything that came after. Nonetheless, I enjoyed playing with the material for a while.

Allen Charlton is a good friend and a very experienced documentary editor, and he was to be the man for the job. Still, production had budgeted for only three weeks of his services and facilities, so he recommended we hire his colleague, Alex Zdan, to help out with the Umatic rough cut. Alex was a great asset. He would come to my home and work on the material in the evenings and through to the early hours, which suited his timetable. That first cut was a couple of hours long and included a fascinating story from the session that was somewhat Freudian, with disturbing undertones of repression and denial. A tape was FedEx'd to Discovery HQ in Washington DC (It was purely American back then). The rough cut was approved, but that story was rejected. I was requested to make the film with a twelve-year-old audience in mind.

By time I had received this feedback, I was in a grown-up edit suite in Soho, the heart of London's film production district, with Allen at the controls. Editing was now computerised and dominated by the Avid system, based on Apple Macintosh II computers with special hardware and software unique to Avid. The first job was to make low-resolution copies of the rushes that the computer could work fast with (even today, with massive computing power, the process is the same for high-end production). Aided by Alex's detailed, descriptive, and time-coded breakdown of the rushes and our rough cut, the offline edit was now underway. With Allen's prodigious talent and efficiency, the film rapidly started to take shape.

There was one very mysterious image. It was a static, high-angle wide shot, with a tree house to the right and jungle to the left. A ghostly, translucent, giant figure appeared to be half clambering through, half floating above the trees. It was definitely not a chemical or digital artefact. At home, Alex had made no sense of it, all the family and any visitors all had a look. None of us could work it out. In the edit suite, the same thing. Maybe the forest was indeed home to wandering spirits! A couple of weeks into the main edit, I was searching through the rushes for a useful cutaway when I came across it again.

Still perplexed, I looked at the previous shot on the roll. It was an extreme close-up of a silkworm climbing up its thread. I would have filmed it at the closest focus on the long end of the zoom lens. Photographers will now have guessed where this story is going. The mystery shot must have been taken on the wide end, focused on infinity without my realising that the silkworm was actually climbing through my shot close to the lens—totally defocussed.

When we came to cut the shouted conversation scenario between Yowo and Bulowal in the two tree houses, the visuals worked fine, but we struggled to make sense of the transcript. At the best of times, the Korowai dialogue was obscure to our sensibilities, compounded by the limitations of the basic translation system, but this was a level beyond. We worked through it as best we could. Eventually, we figured it out. The film soundtrack was mono, but to make the audio on this scene work, Tim had recorded each house on a separate stereo track, and only Bulowal's track had been transferred to Rupert's cassette for translation. Since it is unlikely that any Korowai speakers will critically view the film, I think we got away with it.

I was pleasantly surprised by the degree to which we were left to get on with the editing unhindered. I sent progress reports to Discovery in Washington, and everything ran smoothly.

The Korowai's storytelling is an integral part of the film's narrative. The clansmen were animated, and we scoured the rushes for suitable yet unused images to intercut with their synchronised dialogue. We chose material such as lightning flashes, blowing foliage, close-up arrow shooting, pig butchery, smoke, and fire. Allen slowed down some images, reduced others to monochrome with selective colourisation, and used all sorts of visual tricks that are considered two a penny today but were innovative at the time. They gave the sequence a dream-like, surreal feel.

It had been agreed that translated dialogue would be subtitled, but the storytelling translation would be voiced. I arranged to hire the actor Jonathan Tafler for the role. We hired a voiceover studio and engineer. I asked Jonathan to create a neutral accent that was subtly and unrecognisably 'foreign', and he did a fine job.

John Hurt was one of the few English accent narrators on Discovery's approved list, so I was delighted to comply with that choice but somewhat intimidated to write a script to hand to such a renowned thespian. My approach was to use voiceover to fill gaps in the story that the pictures didn't tell. Discovery felt that their audience preferred a narration that reinforced the visuals. I found a middle ground and faxed the script to Washington. They seemed happy with it, though there was one line that someone wanted to alter. It was over the sago starch processing scene. Men, women, grannies and children all had different roles. My version went, "Everyone *is* involved." They wanted it changed to "Everyone *gets* involved." In my opinion, their version had a slightly different connotation and was poor formal English. Numerous faxes flew backwards and forwards across the Atlantic over this disparity. In due course, I gave in—sort of.

The Cameraman's Cut

It was more cost-effective to fly me to Dublin, where John Hurt resided, than to bring him to London. I spent an enjoyable day in his company. We discussed the script over a pint of Guinness and settled into a local audio studio to record the narration. I recorded both versions of the disputed phrase and dropped mine onto the soundtrack, and no one noticed.

The cut was approved. Now comes the final part of the procedure—the 'online' edit, a confusing term today, but it has nothing to do with the internet. Due to computer processing limitations, the 'offline' edit had been done to a below-broadcast standard resolution, so we are now in a very hi-tech facility. We go back to the Digibeta master tapes. We have the cutting copy and an extremely detailed edit decision list (EDL), which includes all the dissolves, fades, subtitles, digital effects, credits, etc. Under Allen's supervision, the online editor has to conform all of this to a frame-perfect master copy. Also, we have to apply shot-by-shot colour correction, do a final mix to the soundtrack and ensure that the programme meets the stringent technical delivery specifications. The process is very time-consuming, and the facility is expensive, but production had budgeted for only one day.

Upon arrival that morning, I was surprised to find Richard sitting in the green room sipping a coffee. He revealed that Discovery had decided they didn't want Jonathan's voiceover for the storytelling, opting for a more local accent. He introduced me to Monovi Amani, an affable young man who was studying at Huddersfield University International. Far from local, he was from Bougainville in the Solomon Isles, 1,300 miles from the Korowai. He had no relevant experience, basic English, and an accent so thick that I had trouble understanding him. It was a fait accompli, and a frustrating morning was spent burning dollars in a sophisticated edit suite without a sound booth, striving to get a suitable performance from this bewildered young man who struggled to read the script, let alone fit it to picture. I was incensed and seriously considered having my name removed from the credits. The online process was rushed through, albeit with a few pricey hours of overtime, and the project that had dominated my life for the previous six months came to an abrupt end.

Discovery was happy, and the film was broadcast internationally. A while later, I heard that it had received a US cable award, but I had not been informed.

I would have liked to have made a more profound film with more time and more research. In reality, to do the subject justice, I would have needed to live alongside the clansfolk for many months, observing and filming life as it unfolded—not a realistic prospect. Making this documentary was a once-in-a-lifetime experience. Despite the hardships and frustrations, I consider myself fortunate to have had the opportunity to glimpse the last remnants of a fast-disappearing world and to document a small slice of ethnographic history.

30

America Flies

Aerial filming is a vital tool in the box for many documentary cinematographers. Each platform has its characteristics. Hot air balloons are slow, graceful and at the mercy of wind direction; airships can fly low and slow over an area where other aircraft aren't allowed, and microlights present the nightmare of keeping the struts, structure and pilot's head out of shot, but can reach parts that others cannot. Fixed-wing planes are fast but generally need to fly in a straight line while the camera is running. By far, the most versatile aircraft for this purpose has always been the helicopter. It is highly manoeuvrable and flies at any speed from a hover to 250mph (depending on the model). Of foremost importance with all these options is the skill of the pilot.

Over the last ten years, drones have changed everything, making a massive impact on all areas of filmmaking. What had been a costly, time-consuming process only accessible to well-funded productions is now readily available to everyone.

Although they cannot achieve some shots that helicopters can, they can achieve a hell of a lot that helicopters cannot. With unprecedented manoeuvrability, they can fly low and through small gaps. They can be programmed to track or circle subjects and use GPS waypoint navigation for precise pre-planned flight paths. And, if the weather conditions or the light are unsuitable, the kit can stay in its cases while you carry on with other filming tasks. They are now used extensively in documentaries, current affairs, and dramas, usually to great effect. For the big screen, larger and more sophisticated models with specialist crews carry higher-spec cameras.

Back in 1996, *Flights of Courage*, or *America Flies* for the US version, was the story of the birth of the United States Air Mail. Bill Cran was the executive producer, and he put me forward for the job. The co-directors were Greg Barker and Liz Dobson. Liz, I knew from the Japanese railway shoot. Greg was at the early stages of what was to become a stellar career.

At the end of World War I, manned flight was still under twenty years old, and the US Post Office announced its hopes for this new service. It was the brainchild of a desk-bound Washington bureaucrat, Otto Praeger, who knew nothing about aviation and cared little about the dangers to which he would subject his pilots. Still, many young war-experienced aviators were eager to sign up. Initially, they flew Curtis 'Jenny' aircraft, wartime trainers nick-named after the stubborn female member of the mule family. They were constructed from ash and spruce, held together with wire, and the fuselages covered with Irish linen. Pilots could expect to fly about 800 hours before being involved in a crash—light bulbs had a longer life expectancy. There were no charts, compasses, radios or emergency landing fields. They flew in all weathers by instinct and landmarks, referring to railway tracks, when visible, as 'iron compasses'. These were tough young men who revelled in the adventure. They were pioneers in this futuristic endeavour, epitomising the spirit with deeds of derring-do. Armed with revolvers to protect the US mail, they were the new 'cowboys', living by their own rules.

Telling such a story and entertaining the audience in a one-hour TV programme took a great deal of directorial skill. There were archive newsreels, photographs, and interviews with historians and surviving pilots, but that could only go so far. What was needed was dramatic re-enactment footage on the ground and in the air.

On day one, we filmed atmospheric, moodily lit tracking shots in the sorting area of the Old Post Office in Washington, DC. Framed through a window was the Capitol building in the near distance—Praeger, in his ignorance, had insisted that if he could see the roof of the Capitol from his office, it was safe to fly. Fortuitously, the weather was wet and dismal, and with the aid of an ND grad (neutral density graduated filter) in front of the lens, I could make conditions look suitably threatening.

We flew on to New York and drove a hundred miles North to the Old Rhinebeck Aerodrome, an excellent museum of historical aircraft, many still operational. The weather was awful, and we couldn't shoot a thing, putting us a day behind schedule—a problem that would dog us over the coming weeks as we tried to play catch-up. Fortunately, the following day offered beautiful conditions. We rose early and covered a lot of ground.

We had a good selection of early biplanes at our disposal. We filmed several sequences featuring the 'Jenny' and the

'Standard'. I donned the supplied World War One leather flying helmet and goggles, and resembling Biggles, I was strapped into the forward open cockpit, from which I could film POV (point of view) and detail shots looking forward and to the sides.

We also needed to mock up a crash. I had every faith in the pilot's competence, and the restored aircraft's mechanical and safety features were vastly improved from the original. We climbed as high as possible, stalled and spiralled earthwards at a terrifying speed, pulling back up at the last moment. It was exhilarating in the extreme, and the roaring wind, the spinning, the G-force and the inertia effects were palpable. Still, it never ceases to amaze me how removed one is from reality when concentrating on maximising the image in the viewfinder. In the moment, I was oblivious to any potential danger—one of several reasons I never considered accepting a war zone assignment.

We filmed from the ground, having mounted two GSAP cameras to the underside of the fuselage to get dramatic angles of take-offs and landings. Another, we clamped to a cross-bar between two wing struts facing the well-briefed pilot. This was to illustrate a story of one aviator who would calculate the distance he had flown by the number of cigars he smoked his way through. They must have burnt pretty quickly with 60mph of wind in his face!

I was then taken up in a slightly more modern, more manoeuvrable 'Stampe' biplane to shoot alongside the Jenny in flight. It had been a high-value day, but we were behind schedule, and we still had to make the five-hour drive to the next location, Bellefonte, Pennsylvania.

The first Air Mail route was from New York to Chicago, a 700-mile flight. The planes had to refuel every 200 miles, and

Bellefonte, population 5,000, made a pitch for the prestigious and profitable role of the first staging post and fuelling stop. The town fathers had received a telegram saying that a plane would land in a field on a given day, and they were tasked to supply fuel, water and anything else the pilot requested. Depending on the operation's success, they could win the honour, so they went all out to impress the Post Office. Max Miller, the service's star pilot, gave the thumbs up. An airfield was built, and in due course, hotels and bars flourished with the regular custom of the now socially elite, glamorous and hard-partying aviators.

It was the most exciting thing to have happened to this small town. Apparently, the second most exciting thing was the arrival of our small film crew, which included my assistant, Catherine Brandish, Conrad Slater, a sound recordist from LA, our fixer and two extra production assistants who were students from the New York Film Academy. TV and the local press were there, recording our every move. Mind you, we did make quite a significant impact.

The Centre Square was emptied of modern vehicles and cordoned off by the local police department; 1920s cars were brought in, and extras from the community were dressed in period costumes. Greg, shot from behind, made a couple of appearances as a pilot. The State Fire Service provided us with a 100ft platform crane truck for high-angle perspectives and jibbing moves.

The appearance of the historic centre had changed little since the time, so we could get plenty of shots, carefully composed to frame out indications of modernity, such as street furniture, signposts and TV aerials. There were several scenarios to film, such as one particular pilot who would fly low over Main Street and throw out a mailbag containing his laundry so that the laundress could get a head start. We didn't have a suitable aircraft at our disposal, so I followed a bag, in slo-mo, dropped from the crane to the ground—not as easy as it sounds. What we did have was a Robinson two-seater chopper for a fly-over POV.

At the time of the initial test flight, the nuns at the local Catholic school, realising this was a historic event, took the pupils out to experience it. We shot a scene of suitably attired kids and nuns rushing out to the field to greet the arriving plane. We did a series of close-ups, wides and running shots as they excitedly waved to the empty sky, and then I climbed aboard the chopper and repeated the action, shooting it from Max Miller's POV.

We went on to film the Allegheny Mountains from the air. It had been a hazardous part of the route, known as 'Hell's Stretch'. The area's geological structure features a series of ridges that create extreme up-draughts and down-draughts, causing turbulence that these early aircraft, with their primitive equipment, had great difficulty handling. Many an aviator's life was lost.

We took an early commercial flight to Chicago, where we shot an interview and some 'GVs' (General Views), or 'B-roll' in American industry jargon. We checked into a hotel; I was upgraded to a magnificent suite with wardrobes that could each fit in a couple more bedrooms. Exhausted from the extreme work schedule, I felt like sinking straight into the luxurious bed. However, I had to experience something of this glorious city, with its bold modern architecture and views over Lake Michigan. We also had a few hours free in the morning, so I went shopping; not a pastime generally on my list of leisure pursuits, but thanks to the exchange rate, everything was so cheap.

I bought a Canon exposure meter, which was then unavailable in the UK, a new Leatherman multitool, and, for Yaffa, an American-made winter coat ironically branded 'London Fog'. For Dan and Tali, now fast-growing ten- and twelve-year-olds, I scoured the city for the ultra-cool Chicago Bulls bomber jackets. When I eventually found some in their sizes, they were $500 each. They got sweatshirts and baseball caps.

Forty miles away is the town of Naperville. I knew what we planned to film there, but was surprised when we pulled into the driveway of a detached house in what appeared to be a sleepy suburban housing estate. Our host greeted us with coffee and cookies and led us into his 'garage'—well, it was not a garage but a hangar, and inside was an immaculate, recently completed replica 'Jenny'. I looked around and noticed that all the houses had hangars and backed onto an airstrip—it was a community of flying enthusiasts.

Our first setup was to be the opening shot of the film. I carefully aligned the camera with a symmetrical composition behind the aircraft and set the exposure for the exterior daylight. With all the interior lights switched off and doors closed, the image was black. Our helpers, recruited from neighbouring enthusiasts wearing cloth caps and other period-relevant garb, opened the hangar doors from the centre to reveal the 'Jenny' as the light flooded in. Again dressed as a pilot and in silhouette, Greg walks into the shot and guides the plane from the tail as the ground crew wheels it out onto the taxiway.

This labour of love had been twelve years in construction, and this was its first outing. It had yet to fly, but that was not what we had in mind. Liz and Greg needed plenty of images to tell the many stories of hazardous flying conditions. We had hired a lighting crew and a special effects team from Chicago. They provided and operated cracked-oil smoke machines, creating a nasty and carcinogenic pea-souper through which the plane could taxi. I sat on the ground, getting a low-angle perspective, suggesting it was in flight. I also photographed close-ups of the spinning propeller, pounding engine rocker arms, and shots of the struggling pilot. I was in among it and could barely breathe; the camera, tripod and I were covered with moist black soot, but the shots were dynamic. That type of smoke machine is no longer legal. Today, there is a safer mineral-based oil version; benign water-based ones are good for indoors, but the mist is too thin for outdoor conditions and disburses too quickly.

One of the many tales of derring-do was Jack Night's contribution to the inaugural eastbound mail route delivery from San Francisco to New York. He flew from the North Platte airstrip to Omaha, Nebraska, landing in foul weather at 1:00am. The forecast worsened, and the pilot scheduled for the following leg refused to fly in such hazardous conditions. If cancelled, the grand experiment in night flying would be jeopardised. Though he had never flown the route and was extremely weary, Night took on the challenge. He took off in pouring rain and driving wind, and the field manager put out word that he was pressing on. Across the prairie, farmers lit bonfires to guide his way. He landed at the next fuelling station in Iowa. Having rested for the two hours until daybreak, though exhausted, he flew on. As he approached Chicago, his engine packed up; he glided to the airfield and landed. A relief pilot took the mail on to New York. The speed was bewildering—the airmail had beaten the train by three full days.

We needed a sequence to illustrate the story. I had an

obliquely positioned 2kW Xenon follow-spot mounted on a scaffold tower, a water tanker, and a rain machine. For close-ups, we used the spray directly on and in front of the subject matter. For wides, I shot through a three-quarter lit 'wall' of rain in front of but not too close to the lens. We filmed the ground crew and pilot preparing and positioning the aircraft and taxiing into the distance, three-quarters backlit by the follow spot. The bonfire sequence was filmed a couple of days later. We wrapped at 2:00am and drove back to Chicago.

In the morning, we flew to Denver, from where we boarded a small aircraft for North Platte—the hometown of the legendary cowboy, 'Buffalo Bill' Cody. We met up with Ted Long, a renowned artist specialising in imagery from the Old West. On his ranch, he had a beautiful home, resplendent with varnished wood features and filled with his stunning oil paintings and bronze sculptures. He was a larger-than-life character with a beaming smile under his ten-gallon hat. He had no part in the film, but he drove us miles across fields and hills in his four-wheel-drive Chevrolet to prime spots for filming the most beautiful scenery in the area.

Later, I went up in a Bell 47 two-seater chopper to shoot the landscape from the air. As per usual, we removed the door, and I attached my simple bungee rig. Greg had bought a used Super8 home movie camera, which we wrapped in foam and gaffer tape, and I threw out of the chopper from 500ft for a shot to cut into a crash sequence. We landed and retrieved it, and miraculously, it was still working, so we took it up again for a Take 2. We also flew low, buzzing some cattle, causing them to scatter; this was for a later scenario where Slim Lewis, one of the star pilots, had to make a forced landing, hitting a prize bull, causing the Post Office great embarrassment and expense.

Liz had arranged for the local fire service to build and light bonfires for the earlier-mentioned night flying sequence. We lit and shot the process, and Greg wanted aerial POV shots. This was to be a complex operation involving many personnel and radios for communications. I expressed my doubts, explaining that all we would see would be small flickering points of light in a sea of black. Still, he insisted, and indeed, a brief shot did work well in the finished film.

All aboard our crew vehicle, towing a U-Haul trailer packed with camera, sound, lighting, and grip kit. We crossed yet another state line, heading for the Wyoming Hereford Cattle Ranch, where Slim had had his altercation with the bull. It was an impressive place and the oldest livestock operation in the United States. We filmed images for the story. I ran through a herd of cattle, filming blind from the hip, and, of course, did shots of their top prize bull and his harem.

Break of dawn at the local aerodrome, Greg and I met up with Roy, a 73-year-old World War Two pilot. He had recently completed building a replica of a De Havilland DH-4, the other aircraft featured in the Air Mail story. Chopper pilot Lyle Gurley joined us with a Bell Jet Ranger helicopter. I rigged my 'Colimount', which by now had evolved and been simplified from a complex 'spider's web' of bungee cords to a single doubled-up, tightly knotted one fed through two solid rings on the top Aaton handle and attached to two hooks on the fuselage above the door space. Pulling the camera down onto my shoulder—fighting a fair bit of resistance—the tensioned woven elastic cord absorbed much of the vibration and battering from the slipstream, still offering me flexibility of movement.

We filmed the flight over the stark, barren countryside to

The old and the new. Roy checks over his replica De Havilland DH-4 as I strap into the Bell Jet Ranger

Laramie Airport, where we met up with the rest of the unit, ate breakfast, refuelled, and Catherine reloaded the three film magazines for the next leg.

Aerial filming tends to be pretty stressful. It can be fraught with problems such as unsuitable weather and flying conditions, simple camera adjustments that can't be dealt with in the air and difficult communications. Getting the pilot to understand the shot you are trying for can be tricky; after all, he faces forward, and you face sideways. Positioned half outside the fuselage, you are continually battling 60 to 100mph of wind. It is extremely noisy, making it difficult to interact with the pilot and director over the intercom headset. Paying by the minutes you are airborne is costly. With an ambitious shot list in mind, you are invariably fighting against the clock—there's a great deal of pressure to get it right.

Nevertheless, the shoot that ensued was the antithesis of this. First, Lyle was a next-level pilot with extensive filming experience; he fully understood everything we were trying to achieve, and he was flying a powerful and manoeuvrable aircraft. The weather was good, with minimal turbulence, and the mise-en-scène was stunning.

We filmed Roy in his DH-4, flying en route to Saratoga, Wyoming, initially over desert and then through the snow and glacier-covered Rocky Mountains—awe-inspiring vistas. He flew mainly in a straight line, and we swooped around, above and below him. As we crabbed sideways or tracked alongside, Lyle tilted the flight angle of the chopper so that I could avoid getting the rotors in the top of the shot—a common pitfall with air-to-air filming, as the fast-spinning blades are easy to miss in the flickering viewfinder of a film camera. Adrenalin ran high, and the whole experience was wonderfully exhilarating.

Medicine Bow is a small, unassuming town with a population of only a few hundred, many of whom live in trailers. Despite its modest appearance, it holds a unique historical distinction as the site of the only surviving original Air Mail landing strip. The runway, however, was very bumpy, and Roy wasn't willing to risk landing there. Instead, we filmed multiple approaches, with him pulling up at the last moment. For close-ups of actual landings and takeoffs, we used a nearby farm airstrip—all while being viciously devoured by oversized mosquitoes.

We stayed at the Virginian Hotel, a designated National Historic Landmark. Poor 'New World' America—so little history; my house in London is fifteen years older. The hotel was completed in 1911 and named after the classic novel written a few years earlier, the first 'Cowboys and Indians' fiction, later made into three movies and a TV series. The layout and decor lived up to the promise and exuded Old American West ambience and hospitality. The ceilings were painted with imagery from the era, horse tackle, and period pictures of cattle adorned the walls and pillars. We filmed another scene of 'aviators' knocking back whisky at the bar and then returned to the airfield to catch an electric storm that serendipitously offered itself up.

There was a crowd of around thirty men staying at the hotel. I had a drink and a chat with the head honcho. An otherwise delightful guy, he had travelled the world shooting animals—not my idea of a worthwhile pastime. He was a businessman and the publisher of a hunting magazine. He explained that they had driven over a thousand miles from Dallas, Texas, for their annual visit to shoot prairie dogs, considered vermin by the local farmers (they are not dogs at all but of the squirrel family). They planned to thunder across the prairie in their SUVs, playing loud classical music, taking potshots as their prey stood on their hind legs to check out what the commotion was; they reckoned to kill 10,000 over the weekend.

Everyone we met in these small western towns was genuinely friendly and welcoming. They were happy that we were interested in telling their story and went out of their way to be helpful. We were treated like celebrities, and local press and media documented our progress.

After a ten-hour drive through stunning scenery, we reached our final base, Salt Lake City, Utah. What a contrast. This western city is the world centre of the Mormon faith. Yes, everyone was still friendly, and we were greeted with broad smiles. Despite the blistering June heat, the men seemed cool with shiny scrubbed faces, neat haircuts, slacks with razor-sharp creases and immaculate white shirts. The traditionally feminine women were modestly dressed and appeared to float rather than walk as they wandered around town with large numbers of children in tow. That's how I remember it anyway.

We had a few free hours to explore, so we visited the Salt Lake Temple, a wonder of 19th-century religious architecture hewn out of granite and laced with artistic symbolism in the form of carved statues, hand-painted murals and ornamental stones. We also checked out The Great Tabernacle with its substantial wooden dome roof and spectacular 11,623-pipe organ.

But the city was not our purpose. We rode the Interstate 80 highway into the desert and across the Bonneville Salt Flats, an extraordinary environment. We were in the searing heat, looking across miles of what looked like a frozen lake. In the far distance was a range of mountains with its mirrored reflection in open water near the horizon. Of course, there was no water; it was a mirage caused by the heat haze, the hot air bending the light and creating the illusion. This area had been on the Air Mail route, and I clambered onto the SUV roof with the tripod to get a little height for landscape shots.

Our destination for the day was yet another historic airstrip used by the mail, where we filmed our final interview. Our drive took us to Wendover, a small desert-surrounded city that straddles the Utah/Nevada border. Utah is a conservative, puritanical state with laws that embrace the Mormon ethics of temperance and abstention. Nevada, on the other hand, embraces and profits from indulgence and hedonism—gambling, prostitution, and the selling of alcohol are legal. You are greeted by Wendover Willy, a 63ft tall neon-embellished cowboy, enticing you to spend, spend and spend some more in the plethora of casino resorts. Not for us. We returned to base and indulged in a fine celebratory WRAP meal—Greg and Liz funded the feast, and I, the champagne.

31

Soviet Sport, Space Race and Oligarchy

The USSR dissolved in 1991 after the collapse of communist regimes in Eastern Europe and the fall of the Berlin Wall in 1989. Two decades of flawed democracy followed before Vladimir Putin seized total power—an era with repercussions that will undoubtedly have evolved by the time you read this. During this period of 'opening up,' I had a few diverse filming experiences in Russia.

Vladimir Lenin, revered throughout the socialist world, was a brilliant intellectual and idealist, driven by a vision of a global communist utopia. As the first leader of the Soviet Union, he wielded immense power. For decades, secret files about his life were locked deep underground, secured in vaults behind blast-proof steel doors designed to withstand a nuclear attack. Producer/director Bill Cran gained access to these hidden dossiers, uncovering a different Lenin—a man tormented by personal struggles and ill health, whose political reign was marked by terror tactics to hasten revolutionary change. It was an intriguing project to work on, resulting in a compelling film for BBC's *Timewatch*.

Bill went on to series produce *Red Files* for PBS (the American Public Broadcasting Service). I was delighted by the offer to shoot two of the episodes to be directed by Greg, a filmmaker for whom I had acquired a great deal of respect.

Soviet Sports Wars explores how the Soviet Union used sport as a propaganda weapon during the Cold War. Ironically, Soviet athletes were once forbidden to compete in the Olympics. Kremlin ideologues denounced the games as capitalist, saying the very notion of victory was bourgeois and anti-communist. However, in the early 1950s, Stalin changed his mind. He wanted to defeat the West at its own game, and the Soviet sports machine set out to mass-produce Olympic champions. It became a giant industry. Stalin demanded victory, whatever the cost. It was all about government prestige—if sport was strong, the state was strong.

Secret Soviet Moon Mission recounts the Cold War space race from the Soviet perspective, centering on their enigmatic chief designer, Sergei Pavlovich Korolev. His identity was kept secret to protect him from assassination. Korolev, a brilliant rocket engineer, had endured six years of torture and imprisonment in a Gulag during Joseph Stalin's Great Purge of anyone with a good brain. He was reinstated at the end of the Second World War and tasked with replicating the German V-2 rocket, the world's first long-range guided ballistic missile.

Under Nikita Khrushchev's leadership, Korolev was ordered to build a rocket capable of delivering a five-ton nuclear warhead across 5,000 miles to the United States. The R7 rocket was the most powerful the world had seen and, in

1957, it launched Sputnik 1, the first human-made satellite, into orbit. Initially dismissed as frivolous by the military, the Kremlin saw the international excitement at the achievement and Khrushchev became aware of the propaganda coup. He ordered another to be launched within a month. Korolev upped the ante by carrying a dog named Laika aboard—the first living Earth creature in space. Sadly, with no way to return, Laika perished after five hours.

In 1961, the cosmonaut Yuri Gagarin became the first person to travel to space. He orbited the earth once and landed safely in the plains of southern Russia. This made the Americans sit up and take notice. President John F. Kennedy expanded the U.S. space program, vowing to land an American on the Moon by the decade's end. The race was on.

Korolev's innovative lunar lander, the LK-1, might have secured Soviet victory, but he died from cancer in 1966, and there was no one on his team to match his brilliance. It was never completed. In 1969, NASA's Apollo program saw Neil Armstrong and Buzz Aldrin step onto the Moon's surface.

We filmed cosmonaut Alexei Leonov creating art in his home studio and then interviewed him. In 1965, he was the first person to conduct a spacewalk and was selected to be the first Soviet to land on the moon, but the project was cancelled. Other major interviews were with Korolev's daughter and Khrushchev's son. Thanks to Tim White's audio expertise, Greg, the translator, and the contributor, had simultaneous translation via earpieces, and I understood nothing—a recurrent frustration with foreign language exchanges.

We did a series of shots with a vintage limousine, using locally hired car mounts, to connect Star City, still the main centre for cosmonaut training and family accommodation,

Filming Korolev's LK-1 lunar lander, which never left Earth

with various government establishments and aerospace facilities. We filmed the 'Monument to the Conquerors of Space', an impressive titanium obelisk that depicts a rocket soaring 110m into the sky. We filmed the LK-1 and other space travel artefacts and much more. But the highlight was a visit to the Baikonur Cosmodrome in the desert steppe of southern Kazakhstan, the world's first and largest operational space launch facility, where all Soviet and modern-day Russian launches have taken, and still do, take place.

We are here to film the preparations for and launch of a crewed mission to the Mir space station, the first continuously inhabited long-term research station in orbit. The Mir element is not relevant to our story, but the present Soyuz spacecraft that will transport the crew is a development of the original R-7 rocket and similar in appearance.

I am amazed by the 'access (almost) all areas' Greg has acquired. The extent of the enclosure is vast. The bleak steppe terrain has scatterings of abandoned vehicles and other ferrous junk, and in the centre is mission control, a cluster of giant hangars, workshops and peripheral facilities. From an exterior gantry above the main hangar doors, I point the camera down to the wide-gauge embedded rail tracks that will be used to transport the massive, fully fuelled spaceship, and I tilt up to the launch site about one kilometre away. The herculean task of moving it to the launch pad and lifting it to the vertical commences. The doors open, and a powerful diesel-electric engine pulls the laden transporter at a snail's pace—the slow progress is handy for us to reposition ourselves to obtain a variety of angles. Lots of useful close-up details. Serendipity is our friend as a large daylight moon presents itself in the clear desert sky, positioned perfectly for a reveal as the rocket clears the shot.

Travelling the short distance takes a couple of hours; a giant arm lifts it to the vertical. Then, two counterweighted service gantries rise, resembling giant crocodile jaws, and attach to the ship. Technicians are set to work preparing and checking everything for tomorrow's launch. We get in our vehicle and drive to a suitable spot to get the site silhouetted against the glorious desert sunset. We hang around a little

The manned R-7 rocket stands ready for liftoff at Baikonur Cosmodrome, Kazakhstan

longer for a twilight shot of the distant floodlit rocket as it patiently awaits its destiny.

Today is the big day—for me anyway, and doubtless for the three cosmonauts and the senior technicians. It appears like just another day at the office for the multitude of people on site.

Greg wanted some impressionistic imagery to drive the

narrative. I suggested using an effect I had developed for *Sports Wars*. Normally, shooting at 6 frames per second (fps) creates a fast, jerky 'Keystone Cops' effect when played back at the standard 25fps. However, by transferring the footage to videotape at the same 6fps, the playback remains in real-time. The longer exposure of each frame results in blurred motion during movement and brief flashes of sharpness during still moments. Combined with unusual angles, erratic camera movement, crash zooms, and later intercut with conventional and archive footage, the effect is captivating.

Through an observation window of a low-contamination room, we film the cosmonauts suiting up. I then join them on the bus to the launch pad. At a particular point, it pulls up, and they all get out and proceed to pee on the rear right-hand tyre. "Curious," I think. It turns out that back in '61, Yuri Gagarin had been caught short en route and did the same. Now, it has become a tradition and a good luck gesture before each mission. Apparently, women cosmonauts take a prepped vial of their urine to splash onto the wheel.

The main gantries have been lowered; now, there are just four small supports around the base and an elevator tower. We are first out of the bus. Standing close to the rocket, I get a feel for the immensity of what is to follow. In the heat of the desert, the metal of the rocket's body is thick with layers of ice condensed out of the atmosphere against the bitterly cold fuel tanks. We film the three cosmonauts walking silently to the base of the lift—I wonder what thoughts are going through their minds as they enter the wire cage that is delivering them to the spaceship that, after ejecting the rocket stages, will propel them to their rendezvous with Mir in a couple of days. As they ascend, they are soon enveloped in the white mist of water vapour.

It's time for us to board a UAZ Jeep for a bumpy ride to our assigned vantage point for liftoff. Not as distant as I imagined. At NASA launches, the closest unprotected viewing platforms are around four kilometres away; this must be about one. Great for shots, but not if the rocket explodes on liftoff! Nothing to do about it now. Having dropped off the four of us and the kit, our ride has sped off, trailing a cloud of dust.

There's only one go at this, and never having shot a rocket launch before, I am unsure of its trajectory or how fast things will happen. Nadia, my assistant, attaches a fresh magazine and a fully charged battery and prepares the 15x zoom and the 600 mm for speedy lens changes.

The thick cloud of vapour from the ice and the venting of excess liquid oxygen that has built up in the fuel systems partially obscures the R-7 Soyuz rocket as it stands in readiness. We have no audio connection to mission control, just information regarding the planned time for liftoff. It would be awful to miss the moment of ignition, but neither do I want to waste film in anticipation, risking a run-out at a vital moment (another scenario where video, with 40-minute tapes, has an advantage over film). Greg has an eye on his watch and cues me to turn over. There are about thirty very long seconds before the dramatic instant when a brilliant flash of flames and smoke bursts from the clusters of rocket nozzles at the base. A plume of exhaust smoke rises to one side as it billows from the flame deflector trench. A deep rumble pre-empts a roar as the ground shakes. I can feel the vibration under my feet and up through the tripod.

We are struck by a blast of heat. The immensity of the thrust forcing 340 tonnes of rocket off the ground is phenomenal. Without the aerodynamic lift that aids other forms of flight, it is wondrous to see this miracle of engineering climb into the sky as it accelerates to the 25,020 miles per hour needed to break free from Earth's gravity.

With my right eye glued to the eyepiece, I view the small ground-glass screen, one step removed from reality. With my left eye, I take in the surroundings. I tilt the camera with the action, tracking the flight, letting Soyuz exit the top of my picture. Then, I hurriedly reframe, and it re-enters and leaves different-sized shots, finishing on the long lens only when the brightly glowing spec gets swallowed by the vast blue nothingness. Wow!

It is twelve years later. Shooting from a 100ft height truck-mounted cherry picker, I crane up a giant statue of Lenin. The shot develops to look over his shoulder, revealing a sprawl of industrial hell. As far as the eye can see, tall chimneys billow dark smoke, and the whole town has a visible blanket of polluted smog hovering above it.

We are in Norilsk, Siberia, Russia's second-largest city within the Arctic Circle (after Murmansk). Having discovered rich deposits of nickel, copper, and cobalt in the 1930s, half

a million Gulag prisoners were put to work for twenty years to build a massive metallurgical complex. Thousands died in the process. Every year, more than two million tonnes of toxic gases are expelled into the atmosphere. In one of the world's top ten most polluted cities, foulness is ever-present, and we are aware of it with every intake of breath. The average life expectancy of locals is ten years less than elsewhere in Russia; the risk of cancer is twice as high, and respiratory diseases are widespread. The area is extremely remote, and there is still no direct access by road or rail—only by air. Freight is transported to and from Norilsk via an Arctic port in Dudinka, 90km away.

The series is *Commanding Heights: The Battle for the World Economy* for PBS. Once again, it was produced by Bill with Greg at the helm. Following the collapse of the Soviet Union, this area became the main centre of Norilsk Nickel, the world's leading producer of nickel and palladium. We are filming the industry and the oligarchy that runs the show.

Dressed in protective suits and wearing heavy-duty gas masks with charcoal filters, we film in a copper smelting facility. You cannot help but get dramatic images as roaring furnaces feed giant melting pots and glowing molten metal splashes about with little attention to health and safety.

We are loaned a chopper for aerial filming. As we approach, I become wary; it's a bit of a rust bucket. I should say something, but the pressure is on, and I don't. It's July, so there is no snow. We are on the outskirts of town and would expect to see a healthy growth of tundra vegetation on top of the permafrost, but everything is withered due to the pollution. All is going well as I feel the familiar buffeting on my legs from the chilly wind. But I also experience an unfamiliar stinging sensation. Concentrating on the job at hand, I don't give it much thought. After we land, I realise that my Rowan padded trousers are saturated with liquid—it's aviation fuel that has been spurting from a leak in the engine. The following day, the chopper falls from the sky. Fortunately, no one is seriously hurt.

The next airborne experience is much classier. We are with the CEO in his personal helicopter; he is giving us a tour of the area. Undoubtedly a PR exercise, we land near an indigenous reindeer herder's encampment, where our protagonist, proffering bottles of vodka, is greeted warmly by the Dolgan tribe elders as the herd looks on inquisitively. He is invited into the conical, skin-covered tent for a brew. He sits on the floor that is carpeted with fur and skin rugs. There's a fire burning in the centre, with smoke being drawn through the gap at the apex. Despite a lack of fluency in common languages, there's an enthusiastic exchange accompanied by broad, toothy smiles from the characterful, weathered faces of the hosts. I would relish the chance to absorb more from the experience, but we are soon on our way back to the chopper, and the camera hasn't stopped running since we disembarked

He announces that we are going for a picnic. This will not be part of our story. The pilot lands us at a predestined spot by a beautiful lake miles from any civilisation. As he shuts down the engine, we hear the now familiar rhythmic throb of other rotor blades as three more helicopters approach at speed, landing with a flourish and disgorging the other guests—our oligarch's buddies. Two long trestle tables have been set up. One is laden with fine finger food and large jars of black and red caviar. I had succumbed to caviar's charms in Armenia, where sprinklings had delicately garnished the blintzes; here, we join the crowd shovelling it into our mouths by the dessertspoonful. The other table had lines of vodka bottles and shot glasses. I'm a real lightweight when it comes to alcohol consumption. The toasts come thick and fast, and for every shot, I neck, five are discreetly discarded beneath the table—similarly, for Greg and soundman Andy Cottom. The liquor stock runs low, and one of the choppers takes off on a vodka resupply mission.

Meanwhile, the guests strip naked. They are all men, and many are very overweight. The fat could well be a blubber-like advantage as they plunge into the icy Arctic lake, validating their masculinity and justifying the subsequent vodka shots. We Englishmen display our traditional reserve and look on impassively.

32

Presenter-Led

Presenter-led documentary series come in many forms, as do presenters. Dr David Bellamy was a botanist, environmentalist, broadcaster and writer with instantly recognisable facial features surrounded by wiry white hair, a matching beard and an endearing speech defect; many a standup comic affectionately mimicked him. A true eccentric, beloved by the British viewing public, he would invariably appear in shot in the most unlikely way to deliver his 'piece to camera' (PTC) in his signature enthusiastic and energetic style. For *Blooming Bellamy*, one chilly spring morning in the Kew Royal Botanic Gardens, David, fully dressed, clambered into a pond, drew a deep breath, submerged himself long enough for the ripples to disburse and, on a cue from me, popped his weed-covered head from below the water to deliver his ebullient PTC.

Taking a comic approach to a serious subject can be an effective means to get a point across. *Sex, Drugs and Dinner* is about starving labourers in developing countries slaving to produce profitable cash crops for the West. Alexei Sayle, the prominent satirical comedian and actor, fronted the film with a style that was a Pythonesque, sarcastic comedy performance befitting his on-screen persona.

I shot a short travelogue film, *Jackie Chan's Hong Kong*. Jackie, an icon of Hollywood action cinema and a legendary figure in the world of martial arts, is a megastar on his home territory and was mobbed by adoring fans wherever we went. He had an enchanting manner and a cheeky smile. He didn't only talk to the camera, but he would faux-attack it with strikes, punches and kicks to within a centimetre of the lens—seriously freaky when looking through the viewfinder and trying not to flinch. He took us to his favourite restaurant for an authentic Chinese meal. I'm a sucker for dim sum or crispy Peking duck, but duck's tongues, chicken's feet, and pigs ears are only one step up my culinary experience ladder from the Korowai's Sago Grubs!

Classical Destinations: Series 2 was a thirteen-part series about great classical composers and the regions from which they came. We visited landmarks, museums, and other historically significant sites. It was presented by Simon Callow, the highly respected British actor, director, and writer known for his eloquent and articulate way of speaking. He had an extensive knowledge of, and a profound passion for, music. He provided insights into the area's musical heritage, discussing the composers and the impact of the location on the music. He has an engaging and affable on-screen demeanour and was the perfect choice.

Spread over two years, it was a delightful project to be involved in. Peter, an Australia-based producer, had a background in music production, not film, so the visuals were left entirely to me, which was great; the primarily European

Jackie Chan delivers a Punch To Camera in Hong Kong

Simon Callow about to deliver a Piece To Camera in a Budapest concert hall

Bettany Hughes in position for a PTC on location in Spain

Presenter-Led

locations were very photogenic, and the music performances were exquisite. Also, he employed our daughter Tali, who had recently graduated in film production, as an assistant editor in his Sydney cutting rooms.

Unfortunately, the experience was soured by Peter never settling my £10,000 invoice for the final filming trips. It was not just payment for my time but for extra equipment rental, subbing his failed credit card payment for the whole crew's hotel bill in Moscow, and my flight to Sydney to shoot music recording sessions for the series. I should have deduced that, although the pay rate was satisfactory, invoice settlements were invariably prolonged and generally resolved just before the start of the next shoot. Sydney is a long way to travel with a baseball bat!

Tim Copestake was pursuing a niche in producing presenter-led documentaries about ancient civilisations. There were many wonderful photogenic locations, but there was often the risk of the subject matter being rather static. Tim and I were keen to inject some dynamic 'cinematic' production values. The trouble is we didn't have cinematic budgets or schedules to play with. Today's lightweight electronic stabilising gimbals were not around then, and there was rarely the chance to hire grip crews with dollies, cranes and mounts, or Steadycam equipment and operators. I had invested in a lightweight dolly and plastic tracks. Out of doors, a conventional dolly would have steel tracks on top of plywood boards laid by grips with the aid of blocks, wedges and a spirit level. Though I did carry a bag of wooden wedges, the plastic tracks were usually laid directly on the rough ground in all sorts of uneven environments, including caves, mines and forest floors. They were not designed for this, but if the shots were carefully chosen, the tracks would yield to absorb any bumps.

I also had a first-generation ABC TopShot crane assembled from interlocking aluminium tubes and mounted on a tripod. It was a Heath Robinson affair with adjustable cords and pulleys to control the camera angle as I lowered or lifted the jib arm. A degree in higher mathematics would have helped with calculating the geometry so the camera would tilt down to the right degree as the jib arm rose—we made do with trial and error. The rise had an excellent lens/height range from ground level to nearly five metres. We improvised counterweights from sand, rocks or water as the barbell weights I used in the UK were not excess baggage friendly. To monitor the shots, we connected a new-fangled monochrome video 'tap' that relaid a low-resolution image from the film camera viewfinder to an LCD monitor.

Documentaries about ancient Egypt are always popular, and our first was *Pharaohs and Kings: A Biblical Quest*, a three-part series for Channel 4. David Rohl presented it based on his book.

David's thoroughly researched theory suggests that the conventional Egyptian chronology is out of sync with other historical records. Key events, such as the identification of specific pharaohs and their reigns, need to be adjusted to match a more biblically based timeline. More than anywhere in the world, Egypt has a wealth of potential evidence in the form of archaeological information and hieroglyphic data, creating ample opportunity for alternative views. Still, the establishment does not like to be challenged—good TV.

We have all seen photographs and films of the impressive ancient Egyptian monuments, but experiencing them first-hand, I was awe-struck by their magnificence and abundance. The colossal pyramids of Giza and Edfu, intricate hieroglyphs, and the ancient temples of Aswan and the Luxor region— the 'World's Greatest Open-Air Museum'. They are all lasting memorials to the pharaohs and their legacy; each structure tells a story of power, ambition, and religious devotion.

The intricate carvings, paintings, and sculptures adorning the temples and tombs display breathtaking artistic skill and aesthetic sensibility. How do I do justice to what I am seeing? Challenges like this are what motivates me. It is all about choosing or creating the best light, camera movement, pace and composition, often against the clock, striving for excellence though rarely achieving it.

One photographic highlight of the trip was filming from a hot air balloon. We arrived at the chosen takeoff point before dawn. The operators already had the envelope spread on the desert floor, with the attached burner and wicker basket lying on their sides. I filmed the inflation process, first by a fan and then by the propane burner, as helpers held the balloon's skirt open. I was surprised to be invited by the pilot to get shots from inside the partially inflated envelope. The burner was idle as I crawled through the throat and headed to the apex. There was a mighty roar as it was fired up again. The intense heat it produced had sufficiently dissipated to a comforting warmth by the time it reached me. I got rare and magical footage as it inflated, revealing the translucent, imposing emblem of a pharaoh's crowned head backlit by the rising sun. I was directed to exit before another blast lifted the envelope off the ground.

The pilot, David, Tim, and I climbed into the now-upright basket. With another brief blast from the burner, we gently rose from the desert floor. The sensation was surprisingly

Inside the hot air balloon

smooth and gradual; I felt a sense of weightlessness as the ground slowly slipped away. The silence was interrupted only by the occasional roar of the burner; the balloon moved with the wind, offering a gentle and effortless journey. All the pilot can control is the altitude. We floated low over the surrounding hills to reveal the fabled Valley of the Kings—a necropolis of splendour and ambition, a sprawling gallery of tombs where generations of pharaohs sought a final resting place and an eternal gateway to the realms beyond. With the tripod lashed to the edge of the basket, I pointed straight down, filming slow, drifting top shots of the epic monuments casting long shadows on the valley floor.

David was an accomplished writer and an established Egyptologist and academic but an inexperienced presenter. After one long day of filming, eager for dinner, we had one final PTC to get in the can. It was beautiful 'golden hour' light. After three takes, we still hadn't got it. As the sun dipped below the horizon, we all climbed higher up the hill to keep him bathed in the soft, warm light. This scenario repeated itself many times until we were exhausted. We reached the very top, caught the last rays, and to everyone's relief, he nailed it.

The other occasion Tim and I did a shoot in a hot air balloon was on *Britain BC*, filming with Dr Francis Pryor, flying over Glastonbury Tor in Somerset as he explained its connections with Celtic mythology, particularly in myths linked to King Arthur. Francis is an archaeologist and author known by British audiences for his TV appearances (most famously *Time Team*) and his work in the study of prehistoric Britain. He is also a farmer specialising in rare breeds of sheep. He comes across on-screen, as in life, as the sort of guy you could have a cosy chat with over a pint in a country pub. He draws you in, explaining complex archaeological concepts in an accessible manner. On this and a second series, *Britain AD*, we drove more miles than I care to calculate and covered the UK from the northernmost tip to the southernmost—the Orkney Islands to Penzance.

Professor Bettany Hughes is a highly respected classicist, historian, author and broadcaster—another consummate professional. As we set up a shot, she would wander around, apparently talking to herself, formulating her lines. Bettany can bring history to life through storytelling, weaving historical facts, anecdotes, and narratives together. She would address the camera and enchant the audience with a hint of a smile, often in a closeup.

Tim directed two series with her. Shot mainly in Granada, Cordoba and the Moroccan city of Fes, *When the Moors*

Ruled in Europe was about the changes Islam made to Europe during the Moors' 700-year reign in Spain and Portugal, ending in the 15th century. The second was *Athens: The Dawn of Democracy*, which was about the 'Golden Age' of Ancient Athens and how it became the first democracy 2,500 years ago. A privilege of this style of documentary-making is the special access to some extraordinary sites at times when they are closed to the public. To feel the history and express the atmosphere of the Alhambra in Granada or the Parthenon in Athens without the distraction of tourists wandering around adds authenticity to the stories we tell.

It was interesting to observe the difference in dynamics between the two productions. On *The Moors*, Tim and producer Rowan Deacon had scripted the series, and Bettany was happy for them to write the PTCs, which she would then 'Bettany-ize'. However, on *Democracy*, she was in her academic home territory and insisted on crafting her own, which did cause a little discord—gladly, not my department.

33

Quest for the Lost Civilisation

Graham Hancock is a master of talking to the camera. His easy-going, engaging manner, balancing speculation with hard evidence, captivates the audience. If he believes it himself, he could convince you that a square wheel is more effective than a round one—usually in a single take.

He had, and still has, a massive international following. At the time, it was through selling books and appearing on television; today, it is also online with regular appearances on the *Joe Rogan Experience* podcast. He is a best-selling author with his thoroughly researched alternative theories on prehistory. Graham does not see himself as a professional historian but as an investigator and journalist, and he ruffles many feathers along the way.

I am all for challenging the establishment in all areas of life. Regarding his theories, it is not my place to give an opinion. However, it was my place to squeeze out the best-looking images from many wondrous locations. I worked with Tim on two series based on two of Graham's books.

In *Quest for the Lost Civilisation*, Graham presents his hypothesis that the orthodox theory of human prehistory is flawed. By examining myths and legends from various cultures and reinterpreting clues from ancient sites that are continents apart, he uncovers hidden evidence of a shared human heritage. He builds a compelling case for the existence of a lost, culturally advanced maritime civilisation that thrived on a global scale, only to be nearly wiped out by a cataclysmic sea level rise caused by a comet colliding with Earth. Such an impact would have melted the ice sheets and caused tidal waves, unleashing flooding on a devastating scale and bringing an end to the last Ice Age over 10,000 years ago—was this the work of the gods? The survivors travelled the world passing on their knowledge—a legacy of wisdom and a warning to the future.

His theory includes the idea that these ancients understood the concept and significance of precession (the Earth's wobble on its axis). He proposes that their architects aligned significant monuments with specific celestial constellations during defined times in its twenty-six thousand years cycle. This knowledge was passed down the ages and is reflected in the construction of monuments such as the Egyptian, Mayan and Aztec pyramids.

The first of four trips started near the village of Callanish on The Isle of Lewis in Scotland's Outer Hebrides archipelago. We were there to film an impressive five-thousand-year-old stone circle overlooking the Atlantic Ocean. Within an hour of our chartered plane landing on the Stornaway airstrip, we were filming Graham by the stones telling us about astronomical alignments, and we worked through sunset and then shot a mid-summer moon alignment. This happened after 11:30pm as it was mid-June and far North. We were up again at 3:30am to position a shot where two megaliths with kinks carved into them aligned to target sunrise on the summer solstice.

They were long days and short nights, but it didn't stop there. The nature of the story demanded solstices and equinoxes in scattered locations, and we had to be seven hundred miles south at Stonehenge for the next sunrise (it was cloudy anyhow, so we could have shot at any time). The following day was the solstice sunrise in Carnac, the world's biggest megalith site, in Brittany, France. Along with aerials at each location and filming modern-day Druids, we, the crew, could have retired on the overtime payments and penalties had it been a few years earlier when the ACTT union was all-powerful! Andy Cottom, who actually fainted from exhaustion at Stonehenge, bowed out of the subsequent shoots.

Though there was a degree of public awareness of humanity's abuse of the planet, the term 'carbon footprint' wasn't coined in 1997. I would not like to calculate the number of miles we would fly over the coming three trips. On trip two alone, we flew eighteen commercial flights and three aerial filming flights in thirty-two days.

Travelling with forty cases of equipment, filmstock, and personals is a chore. There are usually airport porters with large carts who are glad for the business. Then you have to haul everything to customs, where the wad of preprepared paperwork, in the form of a British customs 'Carnet de Passage', is scrutinised. Randomly selected items and their serial numbers are checked against the detailed list. Invariably, a lens with a £12,000 value tag from page one and, from page five, a disposable battery for an exposure meter buried at the bottom of the bottom case in the pile. Once the local customs officer is satisfied (or, in certain countries, bribed), they will gleefully ink their stamp and thump it on each page. This procedure happens again in the country of arrival. The next step is to check in to the flight. At this juncture, it is smiles and well-rehearsed charm (or, in certain countries, bribes) to acquire the best possible deal for excess baggage. We have to maximise hand baggage; most vitally, it is the film stock, often including the extremely valuable unprocessed exposed film.

First, you must convince security that their beloved X-ray machines are not film-safe. If they insist on checking inside a can, the assistant would get out a film-changing bag. Then, having removed the tape that seals the can, put it inside, direct the officer to slip his hands into the light traps, open the can, feel inside the inner bag and then close it up again. It is stressful, and it's a palaver.

Seven of us travelled on this series: Tim, Stef Wickham, the co-producer; Catherine Brandish, my assistant; Danny Hambrook on sound; Graham and his wife and photographer, Santha Faiia, and myself.

After thirty-three hours of travelling from a grey, overcast London, we finally arrived at Cambodia's colourful, overcast Siem Reap. It was rainy season and lived up to the description, with extended downpours and electric storms. Bicycle rickshaws weaved through the motor traffic, and massively laden trailers towed by 75cc motorbikes transported their wares. The inviting smells of street food mingled with exhaust fumes, market stalls filled every spare space, and a sea of umbrellas was on the move.

As we drove through town, I commented to our fixer/driver how beautiful and well-postured the young women were. He immediately offered me his sixteen-year-old niece, who was "looking for a European husband." I explained that I was taken but would see what I could do.

We were here for the main reason that most outsiders go to Siem Reap—to visit the magnificent masterpiece of ancient Khmer architecture, Angkor Wat. It was built in the eleventh century as a Hindu temple dedicated to the god Vishnu. Later, the country converted to Buddhism, and now monks wander in contemplation, their orange robes a delightful contrast to the grey sandstone walls.

We filmed Graham and Santha walking through the grounds, passageways, and intricate galleries, pointing out the bas reliefs, carvings, and inscriptions as Graham expressed his interpretation of their meanings. The weather-worn walls had very little contrast, so we side-lit the details with battery lamps or collapsable silvered reflectors to make them stand out.

We featured the rainy conditions—after all, we will have plenty of sunshine and blue skies in our later locations. But, a crucial part of the narrative is the sunrise on the spring equinox, and that required some clear sky. Also, we needed dry weather for aerial filming, which offered a vital plan view of the area's seventy-two major temples, laid out mirroring constellations as they were orientated 10,500 years ago. In line with Graham's premise, seventy-two is a precessional number as the world's axis shifts one degree every seventy-two years. Also, various precessional numbers feature in the dimensions and alignments of the temples. I will not attempt to go deeper into the mathematical aspects as my head may explode. Suffice it to say, Graham suggests that these builders were masters of maths and astronomy and had built an interface between ground and sky. Angkor was built just 800 years ago, but recent satellite photos reveal very much older structures beneath.

Executing a camera move with the TopShot crane; Tim drapes a jacket over his head to view the monitor

We had three and a half days in Siem Reap, and the gods of the ancients smiled upon us on day four. We were positioned dead centre, lined up in front of the main temple before dawn. The sun rose, silhouetting the stunning towers. The sky slowly transitioned from darkness to a beautiful array of colours, with orange, pink and purple hues mirrored in the reflecting pools in the foreground. It was a couple of days after the actual equinox, and I could see the sun appearing a little off-centre, so I quickly shifted the tripod a few feet to the left—there'd be no take-twos! The orange sun perched momentarily on the top of the central tower. The sight was magnificent, but there was no time to relish the moment; every second was precious as we built a sequence featuring Graham and Santha's reactions.

All too soon, the sunrise was over, but the morning light was gorgeous, and we had to milk it for all it was worth. We took various craning and tracking shots around the site and squeezed in the aerials before flying on to Phnom Penh.

That evening, Stef took Danny and me to a bar he had found on the recce a few months earlier. It was named 'The Heart of Darkness' after the Joseph Conrad book on which Frances Ford Capola's Vietnam War film *Apocalypse Now* was based. We got there by the local taxi transport called 'xi om'— pillion on a small 75cc motorbikes. It was a buzzing place, with a mixture of ex-pats and locals. We sat down and ordered a drink, and the waiter placed a complimentary snack dish on the table. Was it peanuts? Maybe olives? No, it was a generous portion of marijuana leaves (fortuitously, Stef had some skins with him!). From what little I remember of that evening, we had a wonderful time with delicious food, beer like nectar and a colour-infused environment that swirled. Danny only stayed a short while, the party-loving Stef remained till the early hours, and I left at a much too sensible time in anticipation of our early start the next morning. As I floated out of the door, I was mobbed by 100 eager 'xi om' drivers (it was probably ten), all fighting for my custom. Dazed and confused, I jumped onto the nearest bike and yelled my hotel name, and we blasted off with a jerk, accelerating to 80mph (it was probably thirty). I held on for dear life as we snaked through the chaotic traffic. Of all the supposedly hazardous activities I had undertaken in the pursuit of documentary filming, this was the closest to potential death I had ever felt.

We lost a day to bad weather and frustrating flight cancellations, but a few days (and a few flights) later, we found ourselves on the beautiful island of Yonaguni, Japan's westernmost—though it is 1,200 miles from the mainland and only 67 miles from Taiwan. Graham and Santha were guests of Japanese industrialist Yasuo Watanabe, who owned a substantial chunk of the island and an exotic mansion on a cliff top. He was also hosting John Anthony West and Robert Schoch, expert contributors and friends of Graham, who would appear on screen every so often during the programmes, and a few of Watanabe's business colleagues. We stayed in a hotel but still enjoyed his luxurious hospitality in the form of the most delicious BBQ feast—possibly the finest meal I have experienced before or since. His Cordon Bleu chef and team served a non-stop stream of every imaginable seafood, meat, vegetable and confection, all exquisitely seasoned and presented—my mouth is watering as I write.

Ten years previously, while looking for a good place to observe hammerhead sharks, a director of the local tourism association noticed some seabed formations resembling architectural structures. Shortly after, a group of scientists directed by a prominent marine geologist, Professor Emeritus Masaaki Kimura of Okinawa University, visited the site. He concluded that the formations are human-made stepped monoliths and that the last time they could have stood on dry land was over 9,000 years ago. The geological establishment did not take the claim seriously. Watanabe had sponsored Graham's expedition to investigate further. He supplied the boats and extra diving personnel. I was in my element as we sped through the water, filming boat to boat and on board the dive boat.

Unfortunately, underwater cinematography is not included in my skillset, so the diving footage was shot on video by Stef, who did a wonderful job. Anyhow, it would have been unrealistic to come, soaked and breathless from the sea and start filming the vital onboard sequences. As Graham climbed the ladder dripping from the dive, he enthused to camera about what they had seen. We filmed Schoch, West, Graham, Santha, and the dive team viewing the video footage on a monitor and excitedly pointing out all the elements that suggested it was indeed a massive human-made structure. The edges were perfectly geometrical; there were straight line channels with celestial alignments and large round holes that may have anchored wooden roof supports.

Hungry work, all this excitement, and I hadn't noticed any lunch supplies. Foolish me for doubting. A surreal and welcome sight, a fast launch was heading our way and sitting on the sunken foredeck was a chef in his whites and toque hat—how didn't it blow off? The launch came alongside, and the chef stepped aboard with a mountain of freshly caught and prepared tuna sashimi. I love Japanese food and have always treated sashimi as a delicacy savoured in small mouthfuls. As with the oligarchs' caviar in Siberia, the ravenous unit smothered the raw tuna with fiery wasabi, and we all shovelled it down as if it were fish and chips.

"WHERE THE HELL IS POHNPEI? 158°15'E, 06°55'N." That's what's emblazoned on the T-shirt, which I still have thirty years on—a bit shabby and washed out, rather like me. I had never heard of the place or of Micronesia, where it is situated. Micronesia is an archipelago of about 2,000 small islands in the northwestern Pacific; it felt like our 'island hopper' flight from Guam touched down at most of them. But once we arrived there, it was a tropical idyll (despite being in the heart of the rainforest belt). Yes, it was humid, but what's a bit of sweat among friends? Palm trees swayed gently in the minimal breeze as we sipped cocktails in 'The Village' resort overlooking the sea. Like the rest of the facilities, the bar area had a floor woven from jungle materials, a reed roof, and waist-high walls beneath large openings to encourage airflow. Ceiling fans spun lazily, and there was an ambience of calm.

In an instant, it changed. I was no stranger to tropical rainstorms, but this was next level. I won't use the word 'downpour' as 'down' did not come into it—maybe 'crosspour' is a better description. A mighty, warm wind blew the tumbler-sized raindrops horizontally through the dining area. We donned our Gore-Tex weatherproofs and sat at the bar, backs to the wind, ankle-deep in water, sipping our aperitifs. The protective garments absorbed some of the impacts, but we were drenched head-to-toe. The staff, unperturbed, carried on about their business as usual.

My chalet, of a similar design, somehow remained dry and, much to my surprise, beneath the hanging mosquito net was a large waterbed. These had been all the rage in the '70s, but now we were heading towards the new millennium; the rest of the world had moved on. All the same, it was rather pleasant. The buoyancy created a sensation of weightlessness, and I felt like I was floating. The next day, I was. Danny and I hired sea kayaks and explored the crystal clear waters. It was rare leisure time—what a delightful way to spend it.

The following morning, we set off in two open boats, a crew boat and a featured one carrying the 'talent' (on-screen contributors). The route was about a 45 min 25 knot ride around the coast from The Village. We sped through the water; the helmsman sat atop one 55 hp outboard with the tiller between his legs and a broad smile while operating the other engine by hand. We circled Graham and Santha's boat a couple of times, picking up travelling shots as they pursued their quest.

Nan Madol is an ancient city constructed on a coral reef centred on the tiny Temwen Island. It is believed to have been built around 1,200 years ago on a network of man-made islets, but no one really knows by whom. I was wowed by the magnificent sight of the towering dark maroon walls fashioned from columns and blocks of basalt. Tall palm trees pierced the sky, and mangrove-like growth matted the ground.

As we approached, it became apparent that the silted-up channels were too shallow to take our boats, and we had to wade barefoot through the slime. Keeping an eye out for venomous sea snakes, we carried the camera kit and sound kit and disassembled TopShot crane to dry land. It was a great spot for getting dramatic jibbing shots of the grand edifices.

As Graham delivered his PTC, we all stood shin-deep in the warm, muddy water with sea cucumbers nibbling at our feet. He theorised that the builders possessed a knowledge and skill set far beyond what we currently attribute to their era. Might they have tapped into a reservoir of wisdom, now lost to us, that enabled them to accomplish such feats of engineering and architectural brilliance? Moreover, he suggested the placement of Nan Madol amidst a latticework of tidal channels and surrounded by an intricately designed wall system, prompting questions about the site's purpose. Was it a ceremonial centre, a place of governance, or perhaps something more esoteric, a link to a spiritual realm or cosmic connection?

Graham believes that the geographical locations of Nan Madol, Easter Island, Angkor, and Giza are not randomly located but linked as part of a deliberate plan. No one could have done this without surveying the entire world—something modern man has only achieved in the last few hundred years.

So ended trip Number Two.

Graham delivers a PTC as he surfaces from investigating underwater evidence near Nan Madol, Micronesia

34

The Quest Continues

Rapa Nui, to the locals and Easter Island to outsiders, is a magical place located 3,500 kilometres off the coast of Chile. It is the world's remotest inhabited island, with a population, at the time, of around 2,000. However, the airport had a disproportionately sized runway as it had been designated a USA Space Shuttle abort site in 1987, the only place a distressed Shuttle could make an emergency landing in the Southeast Pacific. Consequently, this small island could host wide-bodied Airbuses, resulting in day trippers stopping en route to Tahiti from Santiago de Chile. I understand that tourism is flourishing and fundamental to the economy today, but in 1997, it was minimal.

The major attraction and our reason for coming was the 'moai', close to 1,000 colossal monolithic statues that stand as a testament to a vanished civilisation. Their stoic expressions have weathered the test of time, gazing across the ages. Their creation and transportation remain a puzzle. It struck me that some resembled Hasidic Jews in their 'shtreimel' hats.

Like everyone, I had seen pictures but had yet to learn of the scale, complexity, variety and quantity. Crafted from the island's volcanic rock with remarkable skill, these figures, some towering over thirty feet, are an enigma. There are many theories about the details of their history, and, naturally, Graham has his version, including the notion that their positioning and aspects are rooted in astronomy. Petroglyphs, ancient images carved into rock, are located all over the island, etched into almost every suitable surface. The motifs that stick in my mind are bird-men, fish-birds and canoes, and the only ancient writing script found in Polynesia. No one has been able to decode it.

I found the numerous incomplete statues 'growing' out of the ground in the Rano Raraku volcano crater fascinating. This is where they were carved in situ before being transported or, as folk tales suggest, they 'walked' to their final positions. Whatever ended this devotional work seemed very sudden—maybe cataclysmic. Perched on the crater's edge, Graham said to camera, *"Archaeologists see it all as a great folly which came to an end as follies do. The ancients weren't stupid; they didn't do all this for nothing."*

The island is naturally barren, and the few palms and trees are modern additions, though there is scientific evidence that it once had lush forests and, in more recent history, productive grazing.

We had a welcome day off. Catherine and I took a pleasant walk around the area; then, I indulged my interest in people-watching. I sat on a low wall near the Catholic church that dominated the town centre and watched the world go by. There was an eclectic mix of ethnicities—Polynesian, Hispanic and Caucasian. The atmosphere was very laid back; people stopped to chat in the middle of the road. At the only

Moai and me

tarmacked section of said road, a smartly uniformed police officer was directing traffic. A purposeful-looking little old lady on a dusty dirt bike chugged along, followed by a hippie with a flowing ponytail and bandanna who galloped past her on a noble steed. A young woman with long, wild, red hair approached on a sparkling new high-powered motorbike. I was fascinated and thought there was a great subject for a human interest documentary to be made here. I filed it away in that corner of my brain with all the other documentary ideas that were never to see the light of day.

There followed two weeks of hectic travelling and filming around South & Central America.

Inevitably, we experience hiccoughs with scheduling; half of our baggage went missing at Lima airport, a less than competent fixer here, weather delays there, and Graham had a suspected heart attack elsewhere (it turned out to be stress-induced indigestion)—the list goes on. To quote Tim from a trade publication article about the shoot, "Never get upset, even when things go wrong. They always will. Use problems as a chance to find new solutions."

For the sake of logistics, the shooting chronology rarely coincides with the script, and in this type of multi-location production, the final film jumps back and forth throughout.

Though Graham is responsible for the primary content, I take my hat off to Tim and Stef for keeping on top of all the material, editing and moulding the PTCs, and maintaining continuity between pieces that may be shot weeks and continents apart.

Nestled in the Andes on the border between Bolivia and Peru, at a height of 3,812m (12,507ft), Lake Titicaca is the highest navigable lake in the world and is a marvel to behold. The lake stretches out in serene grandeur, the surface reflecting the azure sky. Along the shoreline, totora reeds sway in the breeze, and it is with these that the last generation of artisans weave their traditional boats. The high prows and curved sterns are almost identical in design to the ancient Egyptian papyrus reed boats, suggesting to Graham the sharing of knowledge between civilisations 12,000 kilometres apart, as an exhausted crow would fly, and much further by sea. The air is crisp and thin at this altitude, making breathing difficult. We chew coca leaves (yuck!) and munch kola nuts to fend off altitude sickness as we traipse our kit along the tracks. With the added elevation for aerial filming, I feel really queasy.

Spelt 'Xacxaguaman', pronounced 'Saxy-woman', is the remains of a citadel on the outskirts of Cusco, Peru, the historic capital of the Inca Empire. The stone blocks that make up the walls are so closely spaced that a piece of paper will not fit between them. This precision, combined with the rounded corners, the variety of their interlocking shapes, and the way the walls lean inward, meant the ruins have survived earthquakes that have devastated the city in more recent times; yet another example of sophisticated ancient engineering that testifies as to how advanced the builders were. Graham argues that the Incas may not have built these megalithic structures and others nearby, as mainstream archaeology maintains, but were constructed by an earlier, more developed society with a sophisticated understanding of solstices, equinoxes, and other celestial events, consistent with other ancient sites worldwide.

The camera with a wide-angle lens is lined up at ground level, skimming across rust-coloured iron oxide-coated pebbles. There's a shimmering heat haze in the distance. Two pairs of booted feet step large into the frame, and we crane up high to reveal Graham and Santha walking into the centre of the giant stylised spider etched into the floor of the Nazca desert over 2,000 years ago. The design is intricate, with legs stretching out in dignified precision from the symmetrical abdomen and thorax; it is a testament to a bygone civilisation's artistry and craftsmanship.

The 'Nazca Lines' consist of hundreds of such zoomorphic figures and geometric shapes engraved into the ground of the desert south of Lima, Peru. The most famous are the spider, a hummingbird, a monkey, a condor, and a parrot. Their purpose is shrouded in mystery, as is their execution, considering they can only be seen in their entirety and correct proportions from the air (at around 500m [1,600ft]). It wasn't until the advent of modern aviation in the 1930s that the figures were identified.

There are numerous theories; the most outlandish was that of Erich von Däniken, expressed in his best-selling book, *Chariots of the Gods*. He speaks of the Nazca lines, not as etchings but as runways for alien visitors—landing strips for celestial chariots. All I can say is that they must have been very small spaceships with tiny occupants. Not that extraterrestrials should necessarily share scale with humankind, but diminutive beings would have barely cut it as 'God-like' with the natives. Needless to say, Graham does not go along with such ideas; he points out that many of the figures match astral constellations and that the spider is an exact model of the constellation of Orion, a recurring theme within his rationale.

They have survived for so long because they have remained undisturbed; the arid desert's climate is so dry, and the light winds sweep sand out of the grooves. For this reason, the local conservation organisation vigilantly restricts ground-level admittance. We are privileged to have access and are monitored closely as we go about our work. I must admit, the crane tripod does leave small marks, which we try to cover. In years to come, maybe archaeologists and historians will be theorising and squabbling over the significance of the three little holes at the base of the spider!

Working against the clock, we need last-minute aerials before a chartered flight to Lima. Time is tight, and the charter pilot is getting very twitchy as the local airstrip is not equipped for after-dark takeoffs. Catherine, Danny, Stef and our fixer had overseen the kit loading and are strapped in. The turboprop engines are already running as Tim, Graham, Santha, and I climb aboard. By the time the door is closed, the plane is already taxiing along the runway.

About fifty kilometres northeast of Mexico City, the Mayan city of Teotihuacan, which translates as "The place where men became gods," has to be the most impressive of all the ancient sites, if only for its scale, fine condition, layout, and extent. Unlike many archaeological sites, where we had seen impressive constructions amid desert rubble, here we entered the main thoroughfare to a vista of the substantial remains of a complete city centre. I could envisage the population that once thrived here, generations who gathered to celebrate, mourn, pray and live out their everyday lives. The Pyramid of the Sun rose majestically before us. As we climbed its monumental steps, bearing our heavy equipment, I couldn't help but wonder about the hard labour of the workers who had meticulously placed each stone.

The oldest part of Teotihuacan is below the pyramid. We went through a long tunnel, Graham lighting the way with a Dedolight powered by a heavy battery belt; this provided a sufficiently even, powerful circular spot that no regular battery light could match. The natural phenomenon formed from lava was held sacred before the pyramid was built. The tunnel and the pyramid above aligned precisely with a significant astronomical event over 2,000 years ago, but only when the sun first reached its zenith directly overhead.

We filmed a conversation with Hugh Harleston, an engineer who had made nine thousand site measurements over many years. He concluded that a network of repeating numbers is woven into the design. The dimensions of the citadel represent the circumference of the Earth on a scale of precisely 100,000:1, and the side of the main structure represents the radius of the Earth. He also determined that there are measurements of time in the dimensions of the building, which are connected with the revolutions of the Earth, meaning they could measure distance with time, one being directly proportionate to the other. This suggests a highly sophisticated knowledge of precision astronomy. He went on to measure other ancient sites worldwide and found evidence of this knowledge in Stonehenge, Egypt, Tiahuanaco—indeed everywhere, once again, suggesting a common source.

We arose early, before the site opened to the hordes of tourists, to catch the best light for the crucial aerial shots. We had a Hughes 500, my favourite chopper for the purpose, and a good pilot who understood what we were after. We flew along the Avenue of the Dead, past the Feathered Serpent Pyramid, also known as the Temple of Quetzalcoatl (I have to mention it because I love the sound of the name), up to the Pyramid of the Moon and turned to approach the Pyramid of the Sun. As we circled it, the shot was developing beautifully, but the magic was lost as a man appeared at the summit frantically waving his arms. I don't think he was being friendly—he was a security person who felt we were flying unacceptably low.

I had not heard of Graham or his ideas before working on this production. He was my age (47). I found him to be a gentle, empathetic man and assertive in expressing his tenets. I was taken aback when, sitting in the site's café, he was mobbed by a crowd of Japanese tourists, mainly young women, excitedly calling out his name in their distinctive, melodic accent. They crowded around to be photographed with him (no selfie facilities yet). He did appear to enjoy the attention. Apparently, he already had film star status in Japan.

We moved on to Chichén Itzá in the Yucatán Peninsula to film more stunning pyramids adorned with intricate carvings and reliefs depicting aspects of Mayan life, mythology, and history and El Caracol, an observatory-like structure believed to have been used for astronomical observations.

Finally, we visited La Venta, where the oldest discovered signs of an advanced society are displayed. The 3,500-year-old Olmec heads predate the Mayan and Aztec civilisations; some are three metres high. Their relevance, for Graham, is that they clearly depict bearded caucasian and African-featured faces, reinforcing his theory that civilisers must have travelled from other continents, spreading their knowledge and wisdom.

Three trips down and one to go.

For this sort of filming, the DoP can only prepare a certain amount in advance of the shoot. Tim and I would meet over a pint to talk about the scenarios he has in mind. We would discuss the overall look and style, choice of camera and lighting equipment, any special lenses and filters, and the proportion of daylight to artificial-light film stock.

Beyond that, the practical elements of documentary camerawork involve arriving on site and assessing the situation and how to make the very best out of it photographically—quickly and efficiently. It is all about the light, whether daylight or nighttime exterior, available-light interior or lit interior. It's not about having enough light—that's illumination—it's about creating and maintaining the ambience. In a controlled situation, the first consideration is how to light it to best effect without blinding your contributors or casting unwanted shadows and how to get a variety of camera angles with the minimum amount of resetting. Even in purely observational scenarios where you are going with the action, you are effectively 'lighting' by choosing your camera position in relation to the light source.

Directors and producers have enough to think about, controlling the content and managing logistics. If they have faith in the camera and sound crew and have developed a trusting relationship, it makes for a smooth, efficient process.

Unlike some directors, Tim has a good understanding of lenses and the visual perspectives they offer, as well as lighting and composition. We have similar aesthetic tastes. He would often suggest shots but, more generally, leave them to me. Filmmakers are perfectionists by nature, so even if there is a healthy budget, they will invariably push the envelope and squeeze the schedule to inject some extra production value.

My approach is that it is insufficient to shoot a handful of great shots and intersperse them with fillers—every shot

There's Invariably a way to find a more interesting angle

counts, and each one should have a little something special. Often, it's a very subtle touch. I don't expect the viewer to sit in front of their TV and take heed of a quirky detail highlighted in the defocused background of a brief shot. Still, accumulatively, it does make a difference to the audience experience. A beautiful or dramatic-looking location is always a great help, but if the story demands a sequence in an urban car park, it still has to look interesting.

Maybe this is the point at which to digress and share a personal secret I have harboured for the past fifty years—I live with congenital red-green colour blindness; not something that looks good on a Director of Photography's CV. For me, sighting that distant red Hangul stag on a green foliage-covered hillside, or indeed, a bright red flower on a green bush, is well nigh impossible. The problem has not been easy to conceal, but I have developed strategies. The most difficult situations have been specific conversations around colour palettes; I would steer the dialogue to hear the director or designer's opinion. I have a good knowledge of colour temperatures in degrees Kelvin, of different types of light sources, and which lighting gels have what effect in front of which kind of lamp. In a colour grading session, I would make requests using vague terms such as 'warmer' or 'cooler' and 'crushing' blacks or 'compressing' highlights. I could tell when a shot didn't look quite right, but I would not have the confidence to verbalise it. I'd pull a face and grunt, at which point the grader would hopefully say, "Oh yeah, that shot does have a slight magenta cast," and he'd fix it.

If I had worked mainly on light entertainment, commercials or dramas, it would have been more problematic, but I usually dealt with naturalistic colour, and surprisingly, my deficiency sometimes had an advantage. Because I visualise more tonally, I have a subtle approach that apparently translates into nuanced colour choices. I smile inwardly when complimented on my eye for colour.

Glad I got that off my chest—is this how a therapy session feels?

OK. I'm now back on script. When filming in Western Europe or North America, the booked hotel accommodation is generally fairly basic, but as soon as you are in less developed or more unpredictable countries, production ups the level drastically. Nowhere was this more apparent than in Egypt. As with David Rohl, we stayed in The Oberoi-Mena House, Cairo, the epitome of five-star luxury, offering breathtaking views of the Giza pyramids from every room. I bagged the best room by suggesting a sundown time-lapse shot of them from my balcony, leaving the camera running at six frames per second while we dined in style downstairs.

Of our thirty-four cases of equipment, three vital ones went missing c/o Egypt Airways, so our hard-negotiated rest day was moved to the beginning of our stay, which somewhat defeated the object. What can you do?

Dealing with the bureaucracy and, indeed, getting anything done in Egypt needs a miracle-working local fixer. Romany Helmy is just such a man. He was with us on *Pharaohs and Kings* and other shoots in the region. He arranged access to never-before-filmed parts of the Great Pyramid.

But the man you need on your side for any filming of Egyptian antiquities is Zahi Hawass. He was then 'Chief Inspector of Antiquities' in Giza and a force to be reckoned with. He considers himself the ultimate authority and is a staunch defender of orthodox interpretations of the history, much of which he claims credit for discovering. His powerful presence can be seen on screen in almost every documentary on the subject. I have worked on five different productions in which he appears.

Thanks to maintenance work in progress on the iconic Great Sphinx, we could climb the rickety wooden scaffolding onto its back, where we filmed Hawass and Graham in conversation about its origin. This segment was to be intercut with interviews with Robert Schoch and John Anthony West. They have convincing scientific evidence that the severe weathering erosion on the monument and the trench surrounding it could only have been caused by thousands of years of heavy rainfall. When the Great Pyramid was built in the Fourth Dynasty, 2,600 BC, the weather was much like today—arid with light winds. The days when the Nile Valley was green and wet were 5,000-7,000 BC, thousands of years before the first Pharaoh sat on the throne. Schoch staked his considerable reputation on this being the proof of the Sphinx's age. This fitted neatly with Graham's ideas, along with the fact that the lion-bodied Sphinx's gaze faced the constellation of Leo at dawn on the spring equinox as it was in 10,000 years BC. Hawass, however, rejected any radical redating outright. Waving his arms in the air, he said that there are new theories thrown out every day: *"...if you gave everyone with a new theory permission to investigate, it would be a riot!"*

According to Pharaonic era belief, the Duat—the Kingdom of Osiris—was the region of the skies through which the sun god Ra travelled from west to east each night. It was also the place where people's souls went for judgment after death. Graham believes that Khufu or Cheops, the second pharaoh of that era, built it not as a tomb but as a gigantic model of the

Duat sky region. He came there during life to learn about and prepare for the journey he expected to make after death. There is no evidence of anyone having been interred there, and it does not have the plethora of hieroglyphs found in other tombs. What have been discovered in both the 'Queen's Chamber' and the 'King's Chamber' are ducts that connect to the outside surface. Robert Bauval, a friend and colleague of Graham's, on researching his hypothesis, calculated that they align with specific stars of great significance. Graham suggests, *"The Great Pyramid was nothing less than a flight simulator for the Pharaoh's journey to heaven."* All this was illustrated with a later-shot sequence of star maps on a laptop and post-production graphics.

There's a network of corridors and low-ceilinged passageways to access the chambers, tricky conditions to navigate with kit, but we had sufficient helpers. Within the chambers themselves, there was little light, mainly from low-wattage bare bulbs hanging by their own wires; acceptable for us to find our way but not conducive to creating an atmosphere of exploration and discovery. It was always a challenge to create the right mood. With strategically positioned, carefully hidden lamps creating pools of light and deep shadows, Graham moved around the awkward environment, talking to camera and pointing out features that told the story. The available power supply was minimal, and we were, once again, operating at the very edge of what the film stock could handle.

We also had rare access to a 'relieving chamber' at a higher level. No, it was not a place for the builders to take a pee but assumed to be a structural device to distribute the immense weight of the pyramid's massive stones. A comparatively recent discovery, Victorian explorers had

Filthy and exhausted, we take a brief lunch break in the relieving chamber. L-R: Tim, Stef, me, Graham

blasted their way through with dynamite. Our entry was via a vertical squeeze hole with an iron ladder precariously bolted into the stonework. I filmed from below as Graham climbed, dislodging gritty stone dust onto me and the camera. Then the camera, sound and lighting kit was hauled up with ropes, and I followed. It was an unlikely sight. No hieroglyphs or paintings; the surfaces were smothered in 19th-century graffiti. The only sign of original wall art was a blast-damaged cartouche (identifying inscription), believed to be that of the builder, Pharaoh Khufu.

Knowing we had a five-thirty call in the morning to climb the Great Pyramid for a sunrise sequence at the top, I headed to my room and slumped, exhausted, onto the bed. Maybe I had inhaled too much of that dust. I felt nauseous and had a pounding headache. I was still feeling rough when my alarm rang. I dragged myself from bed, dressed, splashed my face with cold water and headed out with a hotel trolley, laden with kit, to help load the crew bus. We set off from the base of the pyramid, clambering up the jagged face that had, in its heyday, had a smooth finish of fine white limestone. As is invariably the case, the crew had a tougher job than that of the intrepid protagonists. We had to get ahead with the equipment, set up, and shoot a sequence with a variety of angles of Graham and Santha from above, alongside and below.

I was feeling worse, but this was the production's only chance to get this rare access, so I pushed hard to get through it. When, at last, we reached the apex, I was burning up with a fever, and I made it known how awful I was feeling. The unit first-aid kit was in the bus, so apart from sympathy, expressions of concern and an improvised compress for my fevered brow, there was nothing to be done. I managed to shoot Graham's arrival at this extraordinary viewpoint. He delivered his PTC as the sun rose and, a few metres below us, the peak of the adjacent Khafre pyramid emerged from a blanket of mist.

There was no realistic rescue option. I had to make my own way down; because of the nature of the environment, helping hands would only hinder. I relieved myself of any responsibility for carrying equipment and started my descent. I was on the edge of collapse. Fuelled by adrenaline, I mustered every last ounce of my being to scramble down to the bottom, keener on speed than safety. I made it to the bus and collapsed. I was rushed to the hotel, where a doctor was already waiting. He did a quick examination and plunged a needle into my arm.

I have suffered a couple of bouts of illness on location over the years, but this was the only time before or since that

I was completely incapacitated. Tim and Stef postponed the flight we were meant to take to Luxor that afternoon and juggled the schedule for the rest of the shoot. Meanwhile, I lay in bed feeling very sorry for myself. I made a phone call to Yaffa, and when I told her that the doctor had not used a disposable syringe, she freaked out. This was the era when the AIDS virus was rife and deadly, and contaminated needles were second only to sex as a form of transmission.

I can't recall the details of the diagnosis, but a couple of days later, bolstered with drugs, I was back on my feet and filming once again in Luxor. As I shot Graham boarding a felucca (traditional local sailboat), I see the boat's name blazoned across the transom—'Aton', named after the Solar Disc sun god worshipped as the sole deity during the reign of Pharaoh Akhenaton (around 1353-1336 BCE). It has the same route as the company name of the beloved 16mm film cameras that I have relied on for the previous 20 years: 'Aaton'.

We filmed at other wonderful sites and locations, such as Dendera and Saqqara, and the series went through other titles, such as *Heaven's Mirror* (kept for the American version) and *Temples of Stars*, before the powers that be settled on *Quest for the Lost Civilisation*.

All the Channel 4 series mentioned in this and the previous two chapters are, at the time of writing, viewable on their streaming sevice, the earliest being *Pharaohs and Kings*, first broadcast thirty years ago in 1994. Most originated on Super16mm film and some on Digebeta video, but all the master finished edits were on PAL Digital Betacam tape, 625 lines standard definition. Back in the day, I was a bit lavish when it came to home viewing (all tax deductible). I had the latest 28-inch Sony Trinitron widescreen TV (almost as deep as it was wide). Today, I can watch these same programs, upscaled with the aid of some fancy software, on my 60-inch 4K UHD screen (three inches deep) at four times the resolution of the original. I am blown away by the amazing image quality new technology can achieve.

35

Tech Moves On
(Skip it if you want!)

As a cameraman/owner, you develop a relationship with your camera and lenses. Your fingers instinctively know where to go for all the settings. You can feel the focus and adjust it with the subject as it or you move. With film, everything was mechanical. You could hear if there was a problem with the film transport mechanism. On my first Aaton camera (7a), there were no electronics at all; the second (XTR) had through-the-lens metering and a timecode option, an early scheme for encoding a signal in the frame margins that offered post-production synchronisation with audio and with other cameras when required. The image was directed to the viewfinder via a prism from the mirrored revolving shutter onto a ground-glass screen with markings that showed the picture edges. You could usefully see outside of the picture area to accurately anticipate when a character was about to step into the shot, to gauge if the boom mic is in danger of entering the shot, or if a lamp or other unwanted artefact or person is at risk of appearing in the shot.

Portable single camera, broadcast quality, analogue video arrived on the scene in the early 1980s. Although it was great for news gathering and fast-turnaround programming, the image quality was a step backwards. The cameras were cumbersome and unergonomic; the viewfinders displayed a low-resolution monochrome image, and the sound recordist, who had been freed from a physical hookup to the camera since the '70s, once again required a cable connection. Film was still the capture format of choice for quality documentary and drama productions, but you can't halt the march of progress or the influence of production budgets. The cost of video and film cameras were similar, but a 40-minute videotape cassette cost £14 and needed no processing, and an 11-minute roll of 16mm film stock plus processing cost £160.

I reluctantly worked on video when required, and it was invariably on the day-to-day jobs that paid the bills between the more substantial shoots. I learned to adapt my lighting and choice of shots to minimise its limitations. Often a director would say, "I want to go for a film look," to which I would reply, "Then let's shoot it on fucking film!" Well, maybe not out loud—I'd stick on a Promist diffusion filter to reduce the electronic 'edge' and flash a smile.

However, in the mid-'90s, the game-changer came: a digital video camera, the Sony Digibeta DVW-700WS. It was superior to analogue video in every way—the colour rendition, sharpness, resolution, and dynamic range (the ratio between pure black and the brightest white). It still did not match film on any of the above criteria, but it was a big step forward, and more productions requested it.

For the first few years, I would rent a camera kit to my specifications, as and when required. In the year 2000, the improved second-generation model came out (DVW-790WSP), and I celebrated the new millennium by investing £65,000 in a camera, lenses, and accessories and an eight-inch colour field monitor. It was a small fortune, but it paid for itself in the first couple of years and was a trusty workhorse for ten, by which time High-Definition TV was the new kid on the block.

Film was still top for picture quality, and in my opinion, it would remain so until 4K UltraHD came to our TV screens twenty years later. It had an organic quality with a random grain structure that differed in each frame as opposed to video's consistent lines of pixels. It could capture more detail in shadow areas and offer more subtle colour variations. Even today, many arthouse and Hollywood blockbuster movies are originated on film as an aesthetic choice (mainly 35mm or 65mm).

From an operational point of view, I could list a hundred pros and cons for both formats, but fear not—I'll keep it brief. Film cameras and lenses were more robust. You could happily take one camera kit to almost any environment and feel confident that it would not let you down. Film cameras had no sensitive electronics that could fail due to dampness or condensation. They only consumed power when they were actually running, whereas video sucked it up for all its operations, even when in standby mode, meaning you needed a lot of bulky rechargeable batteries to hand and nearby facilities to charge them. The 16mm Aaton was smaller and lighter, with a sleek profile and a low centre of gravity—much better suited for smooth handheld shooting. It was ergonomically designed and engineered with a great deal of input from camera operators. In contrast, Digibeta, though superior to earlier video cameras, was seemingly designed by a committee made up of Sony's electronic engineers. On film, the sound recordists were independent. Working with a mono or stereo Nagra quarter-inch reel-to-reel recorder and, later, a Digital Audio Tape (DAT) recorder, they were free to position themselves optimally. With video, they had a mixer connected by cables to two camera audio inputs and a return output—a hindrance to them, the cameraperson and anyone or anything in between. Later, this could be worked around by Velcroeing radio audio receivers and senders with protruding aerials to the camera body. As if that was not encumbrance enough, someone invented a video-send transmitter so the director could wirelessly watch a monitor. All these had cables to various sockets, and the camera appeared like a laden Christmas tree.

The clapperboard was now redundant as video generated timecode, and audio was recorded directly onto the tape. It did have a renascence some years later when it was realised that separate sound was more flexible and visual idents, rather than electronic codes, were often more useful for the editor.

A lightbulb moment for the production money-men, whose hands-on filmmaking experience was limited to VHS home movies of their kids, was the realisation that no one had to load magazines or put on clapperboards; therefore, camera assistants were surplus to requirements on documentaries. This change was a blow to everyone. The equipment was more bulky, and the setup more fiddly. There were monitors, cables and batteries to deal with, cassettes to be labelled, and we still had to erect and set lights and dollies, etc. Local fixers would arrange for helpers, but they didn't know how to handle or pack kit and weren't around to help with paperwork, airport transfers and customs.

Most importantly, there was no on-location training for

the next generation of DoPs. I'll stop whingeing for a moment and introduce some positivity. The 790 was a marvel of late 20th-century precision electronic engineering. It had dozens of menu pages you could access in the electronic viewfinder or on a monitor, only a few of which I dared to touch—the rest I left to engineers. You could also create alternative 'looks' and save them to programmable data cards.

Curiosity kindled by this writing, I have just retrieved my obsolescent twenty-four-year-old camera from its retirement home of fifteen years—my under-stairs cupboard. I lift it from the case. The handle is sticky and deposits black gunge on my fingers from the now-perishing rubber cushioning. The camera body displays a decade's worth of battle scars and three large patches of superglued male Velcro that once supported the aforementioned receivers and senders.

Cosmetically, it is a mess, but I have little doubt that it could run and record as sweetly as ever. I counted the controls; in handheld ready-to-shoot mode, weighing in at 10.7 kilos, it has 14 inputs and outputs and 69 switches, knobs and buttons, each of which has a genuinely useful purpose. It is a very different animal from a film camera, and it has inevitably changed the dynamics of the filming process. To start, you could connect to a CRT monitor. This was like a high-spec tube TV. The director, along with continuity, production and a passing astronaut or traffic warden, could add their two penn'orths to the choice of composition and lighting—even before I had put my eye to the viewfinder. As well as watching the shot in real-time, it could be played back afterwards to check that everyone was happy, an aspect that continues to the present.

It does relieve the DoP of some responsibility—if the director is satisfied with the shot, there is no comeback.

Frankly, I prefer the responsibility and control to be with me—that is my role. Fortunately, many directors I worked with came from a similar professional background and were happy not to have a monitor. Nevertheless, it does come in useful for controlled situations involving complex lighting. The pre-LCD viewfinder was in black and white, as a colour one would have been very bulky and had too low resolution for accurate eye-focusing. Lighting was different for standard definition video; it was less forgiving in terms of contrast, so a monitor could be handy, especially when trying to match with a second camera. Whichever way you look at it, it does slow down the process.

The physical dimensions of a lens are determined by the size of the image sensor (or 'gate' for film). The image sensor on the 790 was smaller than the Super16mm film gate, so the same size lens was a lot more powerful. My standard optical zoom had a massive ratio of 21x. Beyond that, it had a built-in doubler. I could be set up for a wide-angle shot of a presenter doing his thing, see a backlit donkey pulling a hay cart in the far distance and whack in on the zoom to capture the magic.

The camera had two behind-the-lens filter wheels with neutral density and colour-correction filters. This meant less heavy glass went in front of the lens, leaving space for diffusion, polarising, or graduated filters.

You could not see outside the picture area in the monochrome viewfinder, but you could use the other eye to see what was going on beyond the frame. I had done that previously, but now, with the monochrome image to the right eye, the real world in colour to the left and the brain doing its clever stuff, I had more awareness of what was happening around me—especially beneficial for vérité filming. Other handy optional features were 'peaking', a focusing aid that offered a white highlight on edges within the image, and 'zebras', an exposure aid, offering striped markings in bright areas.

The most significant difference was the low cost of recording the image. It was a double-edged sword. On Digibeta, you could run continuously for 40 minutes, swap cassettes and carry on within seconds. This was very handy for long runs on sensitive interviews and other unpredictable situations. But, the low cost inevitably led to overshooting. Directors, especially the younger generation who had only worked with video, asked for extra angles to give them more options in the cutting room, and there was a tendency to shoot superfluous sequences "just in case." It removed much of the discipline from the process, making the shooting days longer and creating extra work for the poor editor. The knock-on effect was that, in many cases, the preproduction phase became shorter, the postproduction longer, and the shoot more intense. Oh dear, I'm whingeing again.

However, the amazing thing was that, at the end of the day, you would hand over tapes with high-quality, colour-balanced, edit-ready images with a synchronised, professionally mixed soundtrack.

36

Death, Deceit and the Nile

Since childhood, I have seldom been happier than when on the water; whether aboard a sailboat, a canoe, a yacht, or a narrowboat, there is always a smile on my face. Therefore, I was delighted by the opportunity to cross from Zanzibar to the Tanzanian mainland on a traditional seagoing dhow. The hemp ropes, wooden block and tackle, indeed the whole structure, creaked as we plied the waves in this remarkable craft. The wind filled the triangular lateen sail, and the helmsman steered with his foot on the tiller while the crew slept on sacks of cargo. All parts, including the hull planks, were lashed together with fibres. No nails or staples—the only metal on board was the loaded cooking pot that simmered on an open fire resting on the wooden foredeck.

In the Victorian era, Africa south of the Sahara was a vast dark wilderness barely reached by white men. It was a place of myth and danger that fed a passion for exploration. To the man who could solve the ancient puzzle of the source of the

Ploughing the waves in the sea-going dhow; Stephen is in the foreground

White Nile, the world's longest river, would fall the greatest geographical prize since the discovery of America.

For Channel 4's *Ends of the Earth* strand, the film was titled *Death, Deceit and the Nile*. It was directed by Stephen White, for whom I had recently photographed two dramatised historical documentaries, and it was the first off-the-beaten-track shoot with my new Digibeta camera.

Explorer and writer Michael Asher followed in the footsteps of Sir Richard Burton and John Hanning Speke on their 1885 quest. Both were former British army officers and eccentric upper-class gentlemen, but their similarities ended there. Burton was a multilingual polymath. He translated the *Kamasutra* and *The 1001 Arabian Nights* into English and, controversially, wrote scholarly articles on the sexual practices of various ethnic groups.

While on this expedition, he had gone around Zanzibar measuring men's penises and concluded that Africans were better endowed than white men (mentioned in the narration, though not illustrated visually). In contrast, Speke was every bit the Victorian Englishman—prudish and disinterested in anything more than the most functional interaction with the native people. Though of high intellect, he had great difficulty with maps and figures (most probably dyslexic) and was intimidated by Burton's brilliance and confidence. It did not take long for their relationship to sour.

As the dhow beached at Bagamoyo, we, the crew, waded ashore to film the disembarkation of Michael and Umi, a contributor who was granddaughter to a chief we were to meet later. As Michael lowered himself into the thigh-deep water, the generously proportioned Umi was carried to the dry sands on the shoulders of a slight young man, in the same way a dignitary or an esteemed visitor would have been in the past. When Burton and Speke arrived, any previous intrepid European had only survived for a few days, having been hogtied and dismembered to the ritual beat of a drum. Later, only a handful of missionaries had set foot on these shores, and very few had survived. We visited a nearby Catholic church, built in 1870, with a graveyard filled with missionaries who had died in their twenties, mainly from malaria and other unfamiliar diseases. The original expedition took 132 men and 30 asses and struck out for the interior. They trekked for four and a half months, 600 miles, to the small Arab trading post of Tabora—we took the 17-hour steam train ride from Dar Es Salaam. It was an achievement to get all our equipment on and to find our allotted compartment among the bustling throng of travellers, several of whom jumped aboard the overcrowded train as it pulled away. Seeing and filming the endless savanna and semi-desert as we sped along the track gave us a good idea of the environment the expedition must have endured. We filmed Michael reading from Burton's journal, explaining the difficulties they experienced and the severe bout of fever and delirium that Speke suffered.

After several stops at stations, where village children would wander past the train windows selling plastic bottles filled with dubious, brightly coloured liquids to quench one's thirst, we arrived at our destination.

In 1885, Tabora was a centre for the slave and ivory trades. The dominant tribe was the fearsome Wanyamwezi. For safe passage to the centre of the continent, Burton had to gain the support of the all-powerful chief Bhundu Khira, whose favoured choice of punishment was to crack open the heads of the 'guilty' with a wooden vice. He had seventy-two children from thirty wives, and one of his great-grandsons was today's chief, bearing the same name. He was Umi's cousin, hence the introduction for an audience. With a little trepidation, Michael approached him with us in tow. We were introduced to the chief and his fellow elders. They were dressed in suits and ties and sat in a line in the shelter of his porch. Colourfully attired women of the family looked on from a respectful distance, undoubtedly bewildered by our presence and the strange antics of a documentary film crew. There's no blending into the background in such circumstances. This was an excellent opportunity for Michael to gather research and for Stephen to further the story.

Michael's wife, Mariantonietta, herself a seasoned explorer and talented photographer, and their young son, named Burton after the great man, joined us for the next leg.

Michael was keen to live through something of the original expedition's experience. He hired three porter/guides and all of the six donkeys that Tabora had to offer. I don't know their purpose in the village, but these animals did not consider themselves beasts of burden; they had no reigns or harnesses. If there was ever a film sequence to demonstrate the stubbornness of donkeys, we shot it that day. Most of the village turned up for the entertainment as Michael and his team tried to strap the expedition paraphernalia and supplies onto their backs. They grunted, squealed, kicked and bucked, and jettisoned their loads; a couple broke loose from their tethers and bolted. I'm unsure who made more noise, the braying donkeys or the laughing onlookers. After a great deal of resistance, the asses eventually gave in, and the caravan headed west towards the next objective—260 miles to the banks of Lake Tanganyika.

We, the crew, had the luxury of a Land Cruiser and driver, enabling us to get ahead for filming and to avoid holding up the expedition's progress. Also, using the roof rack allowed me to get some elevation in a rather flat environment. A second Land Cruiser, towing a trailer, drove ahead to set up camp and kitchen for the night. This team was efficient and well organised, as their usual role was support for safaris. The food was superb and very welcome after a hard day's filming in challenging conditions. Naturally, Michael and his team were included in the hospitality package, but that aspect was omitted from the film.

The villagers told Michael that donkeys really hated water. He was sceptical and dismissed it, that is until we reached the banks of the Malagarasi River. It was tens of metres wide and waist deep; the donkeys were having none of it, and the only option was for the whole team plus some of our crew to drag them across one at a time, pulling them by their rope reigns and their ears and pushing and coaxing them from behind. The fear of a crocodile attack was also at the front of all our minds. Burton had written about their encounters with ferocious crocs, and there were plenty of contemporary tales of recent human deaths. Memories of my encounters in Madagascar came to the fore as we crossed a couple of times to get shots from the two banks and midstream. Word had spread, and once again, we had an audience of bemused locals cheering us on from both sides; some were sitting on hillocks to get a good view while others stood leaning on their spears. Burton wrote that it had taken them seven months to get this far.

We continued filming their arduous journey from the comparative comfort of our transport, though it was no picnic. The daytime heat was searing; at times, there were thick clouds of tiny flies drawn in swarms to every facial orifice—mouth, nostrils, ears and, worst of all, eyes. At one point, the guide led the walkers through the middle of a huge patch of thorns, where we needed to join them on foot. The waist-high thorns tore at our legs, and the cracked, creviced ground was hard to navigate; the donkeys were not cooperating and had to be manhandled; nobody was enjoying themselves. Michael was cursing and moaning about the guides' incompetence and the donkeys' bad behaviour—one kept butting his bottom. At one point, I had a distant panning shot, through foreground growth, of the Asher family progressing through this hellish environment. They were oblivious to the fact that we were eavesdropping on their dialogue via the radio mics. Young Burton was whingeing, wanting to stop, and Michael and Mariantonietta were irritably egging him on. It sounded just like a weekend family walk in the park.

By this point in the original expedition, both leaders had suffered long bouts of sickness, and many porters had died along the way. Burton had been so sick that he was semi-paralysed and suffering from depression. The two

Englishmen's relationship had deteriorated further, and they increasingly resented one another. Speke was discontented with Burton's decisions and complained of not being consulted, confessing that he found it unbearable to be part of an expedition of which he was not the leader.

The rigours of their own journey caused Michael to reevaluate the characters on the original expedition. We filmed a conversation around the campfire at night. He said to his wife, "*I must admit I started off with the view that Burton was the goody and Speke the baddy, but I've changed that considerably on this journey because I felt travelling with a large group of people—the camera crew and the rest of it, I felt that I was no longer the leader of the expedition and I felt sidelined and I think that's what Speke must have felt—sidelined. He had these abilities; he had led expeditions before and lived very rough, and the only way he could make this journey was by being subordinate to Burton, who was this sort of overwhelming figure. He couldn't compete with Burton in certain spheres, but I think he was every bit as physically tough—perhaps more so. He had great determination and great courage and endurance, and those are qualities to be admired, yeah."*

Burton had been severely ill for eleven months, unable to walk and suffering psychotic episodes. The only thing that kept him going was the knowledge that somewhere in front of them lay this vast lake, and they would be the first people from their own culture to be there. When they finally arrived, Burton was ecstatic to see it in its full glory, but Speke missed the experience due to a severe eye disease, only giving him a vague impression of mist and glare. We arrived after dark, and Michael was very disappointed not to be able to share Burton's initial wonderment. Next morning, we filmed Michael and Marieantoinetta crawling from their tent as the sun rose behind them, and they had their first glance at the magnificent site of the world's longest and second-largest lake, spread in front of them. The far bank was well beyond the horizon, so it was like looking out to sea.

Burton's sickness had been at a crisis point. Thinking he was at death's door, he sent Speke, whose sight symptoms had improved, on the only sailing boat on the lake to search for a clue. Lacking Burton's language skills and tact, Speke had antagonised the Arab boat owner and, four weeks later, came back empty-handed. However, there was some good news. He'd heard that a river flowed from the lake to the north. Excited by this rumour, Burton got off his sickbed and arranged to hire two giant canoes. He could not endure being left behind. Eight men carried him in his hammock and put him in the front of the lead canoe, where he sat under a fluttering Union Jack, as they set off once more into the unknown.

They travelled northwards, hugging the coast towards the lands of the fearful cannibals of the Wabembe tribe. Burton was frustrated at their slow progress. As time ran out, he knew that the odds of finding the source of the Nile and of their survival grew worse every day. The conditions were horrific. The boats were overcrowded; it was the rainy season, and everyone was constantly drenched, but he never lost the desire to go on.

After paddling north for several weeks, they were close to where Speke had been told the Ruzizi River flowed from the lake near the village of Uvira. Although Burton had met some Arab traders who insisted that the river flowed into, not out of it, he was determined to see for himself. Just one day before reaching their goal, the boatman refused to go on for fear of the Rovira cannibals. Low on food and unable to persuade the men to continue, the expedition had no alternative but to return to Tabora defeated.

To illustrate the story, we filmed Michael negotiating to hire dugout canoes and boatmen. The whole village was in attendance at the event, and half of the men were involved in the haggling process. We set off onto the lake and filmed every conceivable shot and angle both on board and boat-to-boat. Throughout this shoot, we capitalised on the glorious sunrises, sunsets, twilight and dusk that this part of the world has in abundance.

Meanwhile, back in the 19th century, Speke had decided to travel north with just a few men to verify reports of an even larger lake. But to ensure their survival, Burton stayed in Tabora to beg for supplies and porters to get themselves home. As a result, he never shared the extraordinary sight that awaited Speke at Mwanza, where he gazed out over this incredible expanse of water that a local told him "…stretched to the end of the earth." Inspired by what he saw, along with faulty altitude calculations, Speke determined that he must, at last, be looking at the source of the Nile and renamed the lake 'Victoria' in honour of the Queen. He declared that he had solved the mystery. However, there were many assumptions and little evidence, so he failed to convince the more methodical and scientific Burton.

Speke sailed for England ahead of Burton, having promised to tell no one about the two great lakes. Still, when Burton arrived at the Royal Geographical Society two weeks later, he learnt that Speke had double-crossed him and addressed their sponsors in his absence, claiming sole credit for finding the source of the Nile. His reward was the command of a well-financed second expedition. Burton was devastated. He was never again able to raise funds for expeditions. Despondent and still suffering from his tropical illness, he took to heavy drinking.

Two years later, Speke discovered a river and waterfalls flowing out of Lake Victoria's northern end, but he failed to prove beyond a doubt that this was the Nile. Far from settling the controversy, the expedition had further muddied the waters. It failed to quash Burton's idea that Lake Tanganyika might still be the source. To evaluate Speke's claims, a public debate was arranged where Burton and others could test their theories against his. The day before the debate, Speke went shooting on a relative's estate. He clambered over a wall, carelessly carrying a loaded and cocked shotgun which went off. A few minutes later, he was dead. Was it an accident? Many people at the time believed that he'd shot himself, fearing he would face humiliation in the face of a challenge from the pedantic and eloquent Burton.

As it turns out, Lake Victoria is now known to be the source of the White Nile.

For all the documentary shoots that have taken me to far-flung locations, the final day's shoot of this one was a two-minute drive around the corner from home (I'd have walked, but for the kit). In Mortlake, the St Mary Magdalen church cemetery has a mausoleum in the form of a Victorian expeditionary-style tent decorated with symbols of Islam and Christianity. At the back is a fixed ladder up to a small glass panel through which you can observe the coffins of Sir Richard Burton and his wife Isabel, surrounded by dust-covered artefacts from his travels in Arabia, India and Africa. Isabel had tried and failed to get him buried in Westminster Abbey, a much more worthy place for a hero and a man of such high regard.

37

Nefertiti Revealed

"*A child bride, a queen, a pharaoh, a living goddess and a heretic—a revolutionary who tried to transform Egypt and failed.*" So says a line of commentary read by Kate Winslet summarising the known life of Nefertiti.

For five centuries, most pharaohs and their families were entombed in the Valley of the Kings. Tomb KV35, rediscovered in 1898, was built for Pharaoh Amenhotep II. Later, it was used as a cache for numerous royal mummies from different periods. Although thieves had breached the tomb in antiquity, Amenhotep's mummy was restored by priests; it and several others now rest in the Egyptian Museum.

Dr Joann Fletcher, an Egyptologist whose doctorate thesis had been on hair and wigs in ancient Egypt, had a hypothesis that one of three unidentified mummies known to have been left in situ, sealed in a walled-up side chamber, could be that of Queen Nefertiti.

Unaware of her theory, the ever-present Dr. Zahi Hawass sanctioned her access to inspect them. I filmed her as she hovered in the hieroglyph-adorned adjoining chamber, barely able to contain her excitement and anticipation as workers chipped away at the wall. But Discovery Channel was paying the bills, and filming had priority, so I, not she, had the first look through the aperture in order to suss the shooting and lighting plan. A shiver ran down my spine as I peered through the hole in the barrier that had not been breached for decades.

As a whiff of musty dust hit my nostrils, my torch beam picked out the three figures facing me in a neat line. Their gaunt facial features and skeletal bodies were in repose as they had been for over three millennia. The mummification and embalming processes must have been extraordinarily sophisticated to preserve them so well. The bodies were shrouded in tattered linen wrappings, and the heads were exposed. Two of the faces were locked in peaceful rest, but the third had a vicious gash across the lower half and a piece of cloth stuffed into the mouth.

I was momentarily frozen in awe by the occasion's significance, but this was not my party. I examined the space. There was not much of it and no signs of adornment. It was more like a cave than a room. The floor was sand and dust, a significant lighting challenge. I needed to film Joann first looking through the hole and, after the workers removed the rest of the wall, entering the chamber and inspecting the mummies. The reality was total darkness, but that is not photogenic. I chose to set up two small Dedolights, throwing subtle splashes of three-quarter backlight to outline the ghostly figures and another for Joann's face. Sitting on a binliner on the dusty floor, I filmed Joann silhouetted against the comparatively bright outer chamber as she climbed into this little cavern and reacted to what she saw. She positioned herself on the opposing side of the three figures and examined them with her small torch, excitedly commenting on her observations. There was no room for other crew; Andy, on sound, had radio-miked Joann and given a feed to the producer, Kate Botting. Hawass had fortunately wandered off, as what she was suggesting was not for his ears.

Based on many years of research, she hypothesised that one of these mummies could be that of Nefertiti and here was the opportunity to gather more evidence. She believed the left-hand mummy was that of her mother, Queen Tiye; the middle one, her brother-in-law, Tutmosis; and the third, with the gashed face, Nefertiti. After her reign, she was hated by the priests and much of the population for her heresy and, along with her husband Akhenaten, for presuming god-like status for themselves. It is believed that her original tomb had been ransacked, not just for valuables but to disfigure her face, as without her mouth, she could not speak her name to the gods, thus losing access to their realm.

Who knows what we were inhaling in this musty, dusty, airless space, but it cannot have been healthy. We only had three hours before the chamber was to be resealed, so we kept at it. Joann took some hair and wig samples essential to her research, and a plan was made to mount a major scientific project to be headed by her colleague, forensic anthropologist Don Brothwell. They were to use the latest hi-tech digital X-ray imaging to study the mummy in detail, including facial mapping to digitally recreate her appearance and compare it with Nefertiti's famous bust. We filmed this on a future trip when the chamber was reopened and, this time, filled with heavy-duty equipment and flooded with light.

Joann was a delight. With her big, curly, bright red hair, nose stud, black Goth clothing, and black umbrella to protect her fair skin from the desert sun, she emanated joy and enthusiasm as she expounded her theory on camera. But Hawass was unimpressed, and when he eventually discovered that he had been kept in the dark about her theory, he was not happy. He banned her from working in Egypt, saying, "Dr. Fletcher has broken the rules, requiring all prominent discoveries be subject to approval by the Supreme Council of Antiquities prior to publication in popular media."

There have been several claims before and since to have discovered Nefertiti's whereabouts, the most recent by Hawass himself. None have been conclusive. Her ban was lifted five years later.

It was a two-hour film, and much of it consisted of dramatised re-enactments of Nefertiti's life.

Measured by area, Atlas Studios, situated five kilometres west of Ouarzazate in Morocco, is the largest in the world. Most films or TV dramas you have seen featuring desert landscapes will have been shot there, and since there is so much space, many of the big movie sets are not dismantled but left as a facility for smaller productions such as ours. We shot much of our footage on sets from *Asterix & Obelix: Mission Cleopatra*, skilfully adapted for period accuracy.

Directed by Mathew Wortman, the production was epic by docudrama standards, and I was delighted to flex my drama lighting and shooting muscles. I was also happy to be back on Super16 film. Apart from my first assistant, Nigel Meakin, the camera department was in-house. I had a week of on-site pre-planning. The local gaffer and key grip spoke good English and were very helpful and efficient, and I had the luxury of choosing from a large variety of lamps and dollies. We had a lot of material to cover, and the pressure was on.

Nefertiti had lived a privileged life as a child, surrounded by the splendour and ritual of Pharaoh Amenhotep III's reign and was probably hand-picked and groomed, from a

Mathew checks a tracking shot with stand-ins for Nefertiti and Akhenaten

young age, for marriage to the future pharaoh, Amenhotep IV. Their first meeting as ten-year-olds was reenacted in a luscious palatial setting using carefully cast Egyptian actors. This docudrama style rarely used up-front dialogue, letting the images tell the tale, aided by ambient sound, music and narration.

We moved through the story; five years into his reign, Amenhotep changed his name to Akhenaten, 'Effective for Aten, the sun god' (yes, him again). He sought to break away from the traditional polytheistic worship and founded a new monotheistic religion solely venerating the Aten. He searched for a site to establish a new capital city, Akhetaten, which he later renamed Armana. It was a monumental undertaking that reflected his desire to establish a new religious and political order. At its heart was the Great Temple, the primary religious structure, which included an open-air altar for the worship of the sun god. We filmed building sequences with actors and extras as construction workers and slaves, using wooden cranes and painted polystyrene blocks from the studios' enormous cache of props from previous productions.

The exceptionally beautiful Queen Nefertiti was not mere eye candy on the pharaoh's arm; she is believed to have been the brains of the couple. In hieroglyphs and other works of art, they are depicted as the dream family—mother and father joyfully playing with their young children, the solar disk of Aten shining its rays down upon them all. We filmed scenes of family life and of the majestic couple being revered and adored by the masses.

To make his new religion succeed, Akhenaten needed Nefertiti. She was elevated to co-equal status in the worship of Aten. She enjoyed prestige and power more than any other woman in Egyptian history. One way of cementing her image in the public psyche was to display her prowess as a charioteer. We shot a thrilling action sequence of them competing in a friendly race; she, wearing a dazzling tunic and the iconic headdress synonymous with her image, and Akhenaten, in equally splendid attire. It started on the studio lot with the palace in the background and rows of pillars adorned with vibrant banners fluttering in the desert breeze. With stunt double charioteers at the reins and roars of encouragement from the crowd of extras, the chariots burst forward in a flurry of dust, wheels spinning and hooves pounding against the compacted sand. With Peter operating a second camera, we shot a selection of angles of the start and swung around with them as they raced off into the open desert.

I was then strapped onto a quad bike, sat on a dense foam cushion, facing backwards and executed a few extremely bumpy handheld tracking shots in front and alongside, plus close-ups of hooves, wheels, and various details. Utilising almost every muscle in my body to stay upright and in control, we sped and swerved around the course. It was excruciatingly uncomfortable, exhausting and exhilarating in equal measure.

After a brief break to dust down the camera and wash the dust from my eyes, a chariot was hitched to the quad bike. Our 'Nefertiti' actor took the reins, cracked her whip, and, with a jolt, we were off. It was a great angle and brought the scene to life. We did the same with 'Arkhanatan'. The bumps weren't a problem for the shots as my body acted as a shock absorber. The images were dynamic and the jerkiness actually heightened the tension. The fact that I was barely able to move my limbs or sit down for the rest of the week was put down to 'suffering for my art'.

In due course, the pharaonic duo elevated themselves to gods, and the only way for the mortals to convene with the Aten was through them. This radiant, outwardly divine couple gradually became despotic, suppressing their subjects and smiting their enemies. We filmed Nefertiti personally beheading prisoners, tastefully edited with a final shot of her walking off with blood dripping from her 'khopesh' sword.

Nefertiti is known to have had six daughters, but the long-awaited son was probably born to a secondary wife, Kiya. The boy is believed to have been Tutankhamun, who would take over after his father's death nine years later. Kiya's relative obscurity in historical records is a mystery. Could a jealous Nefertiti have had a hand in that?

We shot several scenes of public and palace life in the years that followed, up to and including Nefertiti's lying in state, embalming, and funeral procession. That said, there is some speculation that she took the throne after her husband's death, ruling under the name Ankhkheperure Smenkhkare, and guiding her country into the reign of Tutankhamun.

Finally, a reconstruction of the sacking of her tomb, which would appear early in the finished film as a precursor to Joann's investigation. By the light of flaming torches, four men in turbans and masks broke in. Though they stole the valuables, they had a more sinister motive. They viciously slashed her face with an axe to obliterate her identity and made fast their escape. The Egyptian Book of the Dead speaks of a curse; if the face is mutilated, they will be forever trapped between the world of the living and the world of the dead.

The new religion had unsettled an entire culture, with an extensive network of priests, temples, and worshippers. After Akhanatan and Nefertiti's reign, Egypt returned to its old faith. Their successors tried to erase their names and legacy.

Artworks featuring their likenesses and names were defaced. The Egyptian capital returned to Thebes, now Luxor. Armana was abandoned and has languished in ruined obscurity for more than 3,000 years.

Filming finished in 2003, and this was the last production I shot on film—Aten had ceased to be, and my Aatons were laid to rest (actually, they retired to a film school).

38

Docudrama

The concept of intercutting dramatised re-enactments with documentary footage was not new, but from the mid-1990s, it experienced a significant surge in popularity, largely for historical themes. From a director's point of view, getting the balance right and achieving the audiences' high expectations of performance and production values was a tricky tightrope to walk. Many DoPs saw the genre as a gateway to shooting TV dramas and movies. I had no such aspirations; I loved the spontaneity, unpredictability, variety, travel and excitement of working as part of a tight documentary team. Nevertheless, creating images from scratch, collaborating with other creatives in a controlled environment, and having appropriate lighting budgets was appealing.

The segments varied considerably as a proportion of the programme. Sometimes, they were brief stylised interludes (as with *Red Files*), and others (such as *Zulu Wars*) where virtually the whole production consisted of re-enactment, interspersed with the occasional interview and archive image or map. Sometimes, there was scripted dialogue, but more often than not, the soundtrack consisted of background chatter and ambience, with voiceover, narration, or music.

Zulu Wars was a three-part series produced, directed and co-written by Richard Wawman shortly after I completed *Korowai* for him. It was the first I shot and the most ambitious in terms of scale. I photographed half of it. It documented the rise of the Zulu nation under the great warrior king Shaka and its fall under Cetshwayo.

We filmed in KwaZulu-Natal, South Africa, close to the original locations. In the Battle of Isandlwana, the Zulus won a significant victory by overwhelming the Brits despite being armed with only spears. We had hundreds of actors, stunt people, horsemen and extras, all attired in authentic costumes and carrying replica weapons. I was kitted out as a British officer to film handheld amidst the melee, so as not to be spotted in the wide shots that my first assistant, Catherine, was filming with a second camera. Engulfed in smoke, It was quite a bewildering experience; I was almost trampled by the onslaught, with 'bloodied' bodies falling all around me.

As Zulu regiments advanced towards their eventual defeat at Rorke's drift, they faced a new formidable weapon that was a game-changer for war worldwide. The Gatlin gun was the first rapid-firing machine gun with multiple barrels rotated by a hand crank. It was capable of firing 600 rounds per minute. We had a rather pitiful mockup and had to be inventive with our shots—thank goodness for smoke machines.

It was a memorable shoot, as much for the days off as for the filming ones. We were led on a horse ride through the beautiful and diverse terrain: rolling hills, lush grasslands, and picturesque valleys. The scenery was breathtaking, with the Drakensberg Mountains in the distance.

Never one to take the conventional route, in place of a wrap party, Richard decided to marry his girlfriend with a 'traditional' Zulu wedding. I don't recall any family negotiations regarding the bride's price or cow slaughtering for fertility and prosperity. Still, the bride was radiant in a vibrantly coloured, beaded wedding dress and hat. And the sight of Richard with his ample body draped in animal skins was more than compensated for by the beaming smile on his face as we partied through the night.

Throughout the 1980s, Diana, Princess of Wales, won the hearts of millions in the UK and worldwide. In contrast to the customary remoteness of the royal family, she was renowned for her empathy and willingness to engage with individuals from all walks of life and her hands-on involvement with the charities and the humanitarian causes she championed. She was beautiful, glamorous and a fashion icon—rarely out of the tabloid newspapers. She became referred to as 'The Peoples Princess'. By 1987, cracks in the royal marriage had become visible, and speculation about her love life, and that of Prince Charles, was rife. In 1996, they were divorced, and a year later, she died tragically in a car crash in Paris while being pursued by paparazzi on motorbikes. The outpouring of public grief and emotion displayed was unprecedented and profound. The royal ceremonial funeral was hurriedly organised, and the massive BBC live television coverage (which had an estimated two-and-a-half-billion viewers) speedily recruited every available person who could operate a TV camera. My role for the day was to cover the funeral cortège, with the horse-drawn gun carriage bearing her coffin, along a stretch of Hyde Park.

Not long after this, I was filming a different horse-drawn hearse in a reenactment of her great-great-great-great aunt's funeral. It was the opening sequence of the Channel 4 docudrama *The People's Duchess*, which tells the similarly controversial and tragic story of Diana's ancestor, Georgiana, Duchess of Devonshire.

In the late 18th century, the seventeen-year-old English aristocrat Georgiana Spencer was contracted in marriage to William Cavendish, Duke of Devonshire, with the expectation that she would bear him a male heir. She became a leading light in fashionable society. She was renowned for her charisma, beauty, political influence, generosity to the poor, unusual marital arrangements, love affairs, and a ruinous gambling addiction.

She had a colourful and tragic life, played out and largely filmed in the opulent setting of Chatsworth House, a stately home in the Derbyshire Dales and home to the present-day Duke of Devonshire, her great-great-great-great grandson. What an excellent location and subject matter for creating luscious visuals.

Newspapers for the masses were then in their infancy. Among the common population, each copy of *The Morning Post* was passed on many times, and those who were literate would read aloud to an audience hungry for gossip and scandal. Georgiana was perfect fodder for the 'paparazzi' of the day, which we alluded to by firing camera flashes from out of shot in scenes where she was open to the public gaze. She was adored by everyone but her husband. So many parallels. Her closest friend and possibly lover, Lady Bess Foster, moved in. She became a mistress to William. There were now

three in the marriage—a 'ménage à trois'. Bess bore him two children, one of whom was a boy. Georgiana had two girls, but that did not suffice.

It was my first dramatised production using Digibeta. Lighting conditions were under my control, and despite my misgivings about video, I was happy with the picture quality we achieved. The 'look' we were after was warm and soft, much of it as if by candlelight. Everything was shot using Black Pro-Mist diffusion filters front of lens. One advantage of video is that you can control the colour temperature in-camera, reducing the need to attach luminance-reducing colour gels to the front of the lamps (today, with LED sources, you can wind in your colour temperature of choice).

Supported by high-voltage effects technicians with their Tesla coils and plasma display panels, we shot a sex scene with Georgiana and William in a 'Celestial Bed' designed to enhance fertility and sexual pleasure. It was a large ornate bed draped with colourful silks, purportedly connected to electrical and magnetic currents. Erotic dancers swayed to sensual music, and incense burned as the couple had intercourse in the hope that this would produce a male heir. It didn't. But, at a later time, a son was born to Georgiana. The pressure was off, and at last, she was released to pursue her political and charitable objectives and partying lifestyle. Beset by declining health for many years, she died at the age of 48. I had my moment in the spotlight playing the clergyman, giving her last rites, albeit in a very wide shot.

Biddy Hodson played Georgiana. The production was based on a biography by Amanda Foreman, produced by Paladin Pictures and directed by Justin Hardy. Ten years later, a movie was released, which was also based on Amanda's book and starred Keira Knightley.

Who Killed Julius Caesar? was a fascinating story of a CSI-style investigation into ancient history's most famous assassination. It was led by Brigadier General Luciano Garofano, head of forensics for Italy's military-affiliated Carabinieri police force, with the help of criminal profilers from Harvard. History is clear as to those directly responsible, but the investigation suggested that symptoms of his epilepsy could have played a significant part in his downfall.

It was filmed for Atlantic Productions between shoots for *Nefertiti* and with Mathew directing. We did the documentary filming in Rome and the dramatised sections in Malta on the adapted sets of the recently completed movie *Troy*. They had Brad Pitt, Orlando Bloom and Brian Cox; we had principal actors whose names I have long forgotten, but they did a great job. Once again, we had access to big film studios' facilities. To enhance the scenes and expand the scale, we rigged greenscreen flats to multiply cheering crowds within the central square and to create depth beyond the sets in post-production.

There was a vital scene in which Caesar climbed the imposing steps to the majestic Senate building, applauded by dignitaries and onlookers. A soothsayer pushes his way to the front to warn of his premonition about the emperor's impending death on the 'Ides of March'. Mathew wanted a point-of-view shot. It was early morning, and the sun was aligned with the front elevation of the set. There are several aesthetic reasons to avoid filming with the low sun directly behind you, not least that you are at risk of casting your own shadow. Rather than pointing out the scheduling error, I suggested I don a laurel wreath and a toga, hold the camera at waist height beneath, and shoot the emperor's POV ascending the steps, featuring my 'noble' shadow in the bottom third of the shot. On-screen again!

There followed a violent and bloody scene of the assassination where Caesar suffered twenty-three stab wounds (shot in a London studio), rounded off with the grand state funeral.

Few BBC festive-season schedules pass without a rerun of *Dickens and the Invention of Christmas*. Shot in 2007 and directed by Paul Tilzey, it was written, fronted and executive produced by Griff Rhys Jones, a comedian, writer, and actor whose success, along with that of the cream of '80s British TV comedy, had rocketed out of BBC's *Not the Nine o'Clock News*.

Since medieval times, Christmas has been celebrated with a mixture of religious observance and merrymaking. There were nativity plays, carol singing and such, but come the Protestant Reformation and Puritanism in 16th century Europe and the holy day's perceived pagan origins, it became much lower-key. The Victorians were now coming around to a new approach.

The film opens with a night exterior sequence of the young Charles Dickens hurrying through the frosty cobbled streets of Victorian London, clutching a bunch of parcels. It was Christmas Eve 1843, and he was heading for his 'rather comfortable' home near Regents Park in London. The filming location was actually the 'rather comfortable home' of Griff Rhys Jones in Fitzrovia (near Regents Park). We employed the time-tested style of moody lighting and smoke to invoke the period's winter ambience. In a piece to camera, Griff showed the viewers a copy of the Monday, 25th December 1843 edition of *The Times* newspaper, pointing out that there was not a single reference to Christmas, "*...just as if it was any other day.*"

At the age of thirty-one, Dickens was already a literary giant, and his latest best-selling book, *A Christmas Carol*, spread a message of redemption, hope, and the transformative effects of embracing kindness, empathy, and the true spirit of Christmas. It was a powerful piece of social commentary, drawing attention to the plight of the poor and highlighting the importance of compassion and generosity. In counterpoint to his anti-hero, the miser Ebenezer Scrooge, he painted a picture of a wholesome family celebration with presents, decorations, turkey, plum pudding and goodwill to all. The book sold 6,000 copies in its first five days, and how Christmas was celebrated in Europe was transformed. He was the first celebrity author and an 'influencer' long before the term was coined.

PTCs from Griff, documentary segments, and interviews were interspersed with the dramatised sequences. These segments we gave a contemporary look, using a different colour palette and lighting style. Sir Patrick Stewart, a renowned actor long before international stardom as *Star Trek's* Captain Jean-Luc Picard, *X-Men* and *Dune*, was a substantial contributor to the programme. He is an authority on Dickens and something of an *A Christmas Carol* aficionado, having narrated the Audiobook and played Scrooge on screen.

We recreated Dickens' household enjoying the holiday; he had four small kids. They say 'avoid working with children and animals'—our mini actors were a delight. Dressed in Victorian attire, they relished the joyous ambience, dressing the tree, opening parcels, dancing to the piano playing of Dicken's friend, John Forster, and being absorbed in their 'dad's' storytelling and magic show. Oblivious to the lights, dollies and all the paraphernalia, they had a wonderful time. I did, too. I enjoyed creating a dreamlike atmosphere with warm, glowing light. I used a square cut from a 10-denier, black silk stocking tightly stretched over the front element of the lens to spread highlights and add a glow to the image, especially around the candle flames and in-shot gas lamps. Much as I would like to take credit for the technique, it actually dates back to the silent film era. I always carry a pair of silk stockings among the dozens of bits and pieces in my accessories kit, often causing a snigger and knowing glances when a customs officer rifles through my equipment cases.

39

A Life in Higher Definition

I have a vivid childhood memory of my first cinema experience—*The Wizard of Oz*. Watching through a gap in my fingers, I was terrified by the Wicked Witch of the West. She had green skin, a hooked nose and the most malevolent manner—the personification of evil. So, it is an anathema to me why, fifty years after those nightmares, someone would produce a stage musical glamorising her and giving her an empathetic backstory. But *Wicked* has broken box-office records worldwide, so what do I know?

My first shoot in High-Definition was an Electronic Press Kit (EPK) for *Wicked's* UK launch. Directed by Greg Barker, it took the form of a cinema trailer with sweeping camera moves, using the stage lighting supplemented by our own.

There had been unwieldy high-definition studio and OB cameras around for a few years, but the ground-breaking CinAlta Sony HDW F900 in the year 2000 was to dominate as the first broadcast field camcorder. Ergonomically, it was similar to the Digibeta camera with the same dimension sensors but now capable of recording a 1080p, 2.2-million-pixel image. None of the British terrestrial TV channels could yet broadcast in High-Def, and few households had the TV sets. It was expensive, but any productions deemed worthy of futureproofing had to follow that route. As for the *Wicked* EPK, I saw it played as a commercial at the BFI IMAX, the UK's largest screen, and though it was not projected onto the entire screen, the picture quality was outstanding.

There was a buzz among the TV camera fraternity that it would make life more complicated. With the higher image resolution, you would need to employ makeup people on all shoots and be more aware of all the fine details. In reality, I added a clothes brush to my kit to clear away contributor's dandruff, and I already carried flesh-coloured face powders to dull the occasional highlight hotspot. In fact, it was a delight to work with the extra picture detail and exposure latitude it offered.

The Sony camera was a wonder, and other manufacturers joined the fray, but these were still tape-based camcorders, so inevitably, a variety of solid-state formats followed.

For some years, they stuck with the same 3 x 2/3-inch sensors, and then, the nasty (in my humble opinion) 'revolutionary' PMW-EX1 appeared on the scene. Despite being small, it had 3 x 1/2-inch sensors, which was good. It was, supposedly, a professional camera, and yes, it ticked the HD boxes, and yes, it was compact and great for one-man-band, fly-on-the-wall documentaries and news stories. But in terms of having any control over the image, it had its own mind, and any of the manual override options were well buried; ergonomically, it was awful. Production companies loved it. They seemed to think that because they only had to pay the rental on a £4,000 camera channel rather than a

£65,000 one, they could also offer the cameraman less. As if that were not enough, there was a tendency to expect him to do the sound, too (I didn't go along with that except, reluctantly, on the occasional interview).

The only whole documentary I shot on it was about the infamous pair, Burke and Hare, who murdered at least sixteen people in 19th century Edinburgh and sold the corpses to an anatomy school. It was an early directing job for Rowan Deacon, who knew me from when she had been an assistant producer for Tim Copestake. I mumbled and cursed under my breath, exasperated by this confounded machine. Extremely unprofessional of me and disconcerting for her. She never called me for another shoot. I wonder why?

In the realm of miniaturising cameras, the amazing new toy was the HD GoPro Hero 3, launched in 2012. It was developed in California to capture high-quality onboard surfing video and action stills. The basic package came with a waterproof housing and a selection of mounting options. It only cost a little over £300, and I bought one.

Initially, I didn't even charge rental; it was just there in my kit. I would pull it out every so often and say, "How about…?" When you have it to hand, a world of opportunities presents itself. The sorts of images that would have been significant production numbers if planned were now a cinch—shots such as car-mounted interiors and exteriors and body-mounted POVs. In plentiful light conditions, the picture quality was superb, and the technical limitations were more than compensated for by the dramatic impact of the shots.

In due course, the camera became more commonplace, and productions would rent in kits of three or more for particular purposes. One such shoot was *Nova – Iceman*

Murder Mystery for PBS. In 2010, nineteen years after his chance discovery beneath a Tyrolian glacier, the immaculately preserved 5,300-year-old freeze-dried mummy, known as 'Ötzi', provided an unprecedented glimpse into the life of a person from the Copper Age.

In the Italian Alpine city of Bolzano is a Museum of Archaeology built around the star exhibit, which can be observed through glass in his deep-frozen crypt. On display in adjoining galleries are articles of his clothing, weapons, and personal artefacts that had also been beautifully preserved in his icy grave. I understand from local hearsay that, at the time of discovery, Italy and bordering Austria were in dispute over Ötzi's ownership. However, when the science suggested signs of homosexual activity, the Austrians were happy to grant him to the Italians (not verified)!

The documentary's central event was a rare nine-hour thawing to +4ºC for scientific probing. An international team of over twenty pathologists and other specialists had flown in to investigate, perform new scans, and collect samples of his DNA, tissue, and stomach contents.

Suitably attired in surgical scrubs and a face mask, I was the only TV crew member allowed in the crowded theatre. I poked my lens through any gap in the throng of bodies surrounding the mummy. We had rigged a few GoPros in advance. Three of the principal team members wore them as bodycams; one was mounted on the surgical lighting boom directly above the action, and another pointed at the endoscope monitor.

Meat and plant remains found in Ötzi's intestines provided a valuable insight into his diet and lifestyle, and pollen from different altitudes suggested he had travelled across the mountains a great deal in his final few days. The collected samples would be studied and analysed for years to come.

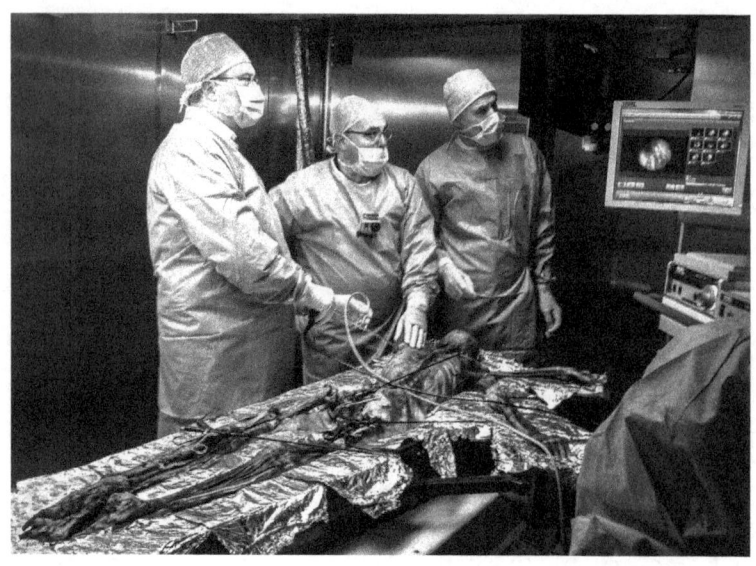

There were many theories about the cause and circumstances of his death, but there was no evidence to support them. It was the oldest and coldest of all cold cases—that is, until that day they discovered an arrowhead lodged in his left shoulder and signs of trauma on his body, suggesting he had died from injuries sustained in a violent encounter. The plot thickened.

Nova is a science series that has been running since the early '70s. It is broadcast by PBS in the United States and syndicated worldwide. The series was inspired by and often co-produced with BBC's *Horizon*.

Another *Nova* episode in which GoPros were handy was *Building Pharaoh's Chariot*. It was a film documenting the research, construction and trials of replicas of the extremely fast and sophisticated 'war machines' that spearheaded ancient Egyptian military advances for centuries. For the chariot trials, the rugged little cameras were mounted in all sorts of places: on the undercarriage, positioned to show the innovatory suspension and wheel construction, facing forward to film the galloping horses' hooves and facing backwards to get the chariot behind, as body and headcams on the driver and bowman, and on the desert floor to be driven over. We also used them on the dramatised reconstruction of the biggest chariot battle in history when Ramesses II took on the Hittites in Syria, 1,258 BC, involving thousands of chariots and, for us, plentiful CGI to multiply our dozen replicas.

A few years later, the Canon 5D Mk 2, a professional DSLR stills camera, introduced an HD video facility—almost as an afterthought—for photojournalists to shoot short clips to support their news stories. The full-frame sensor was substantially larger than that of any professional video camera, and with the long history of developing fine prime lenses, the image quality was sensational. The low-light shooting capability was superb, and the pleasing shallow focus aesthetic (depth-of-field) was on par with 35mm movie film. It was a godsend for students and low-budget filmmakers and captured the imagination of many in the professional market. Initially, it was perceived as an expendable 'crash camera' to capture specific shots or angles in potentially hazardous situations. Subsequent innovations overcame some of the shortcomings of a camera whose design was optimised for still photography.

However, the best outcome of these developments was the rise of relatively inexpensive, large-sensor professional video cameras capable of delivering stunning images up to 8K resolution. Today, a significant proportion of TV is shot on these cameras. Ironically, this new tech tends to be bulkier than the HD equipment it has supplanted. Despite the compact sensor block, the larger sensor requires larger lenses, and the modular design demands an array of add-ons, typically mounted on an aluminium 'cage'—viewfinders, shoulder rigs, follow focus, matte boxes, high-capacity batteries, monitors, as well as video, audio, and timecode senders and receivers—and that's just a starting point.

In the grip world, there are now gizmos that can make any camera move you can dream up. Then there is 'Motion Control', where robotic systems precisely control the tracking and positioning of a camera to achieve complex moves, visual effects, and compositing shots with a level of precision and repeatability that can be achieved no other way. Camera and image stabilisation have advanced enormously, using combinations of gyroscopic and digital tech in the field and software-driven wizardry in post-production.

As technology develops at such an extraordinary pace, ever-increasing image quality can access ever-decreasing spaces, and small details on the planet's surface can be filmed from orbiting satellites. With the right equipment, software, technical talent and budget, any image the creative mind can envisage can be realised.

On the other hand, driven by ever-developing trends, social media, internet connectivity and fashion, the pace of visual content has become more intense. Traditional concepts of picture composition, fluid camera moves and smooth picture edits have changed. Long developing shots or slow pans with a hold at either end have essentially given way to jump cuts, fast cutting, unconventional eye-lines, erratic camera movement and in-shot hunting for focus. Film grammar has moved on, and these elements have become a style choice. My generation of DoPs has had to move with the times, learning to appreciate the new aesthetic in the same way as our predecessors did in the mid-20th century.

Along with the emergence of online platforms such as YouTube and Vimeo, the advent of high-quality phone cameras, inexpensive handycams, and advanced software, which remove much of the need for knowledge or experience of the craft, has led to the 'democratisation' of filmmaking. It is fantastic that people have the opportunity to express their creativity or articulate their message for minimal outlay. They are also great platforms for aspiring filmmakers to experiment and get noticed. But it is a double-edged sword. The market is flooded with largely unregulated content, some of it profound, some of it perilous, and much of it harmless.

Conventional television viewing is now dominated by streaming platforms, leaving traditional terrestrial and cable stations behind. As a viewer, I contribute to these statistics. As their audience shrinks, advertising revenue for commercial television has decreased, along with funding for the BBC. This has resulted in tighter budgets and a reduced willingness to take creative risks. It saddens me that programme commissioners have become increasingly cautious, opting for safe, predictable formats. Apart from news and current affairs, much of factual television is shifting towards visually flashy gimmicks and overly enthusiastic presenters, perhaps in the belief that the audience may be lost to the allure of the remote or the click of the mouse. The listings tend to favour formulaic reality shows and celebrity-led travel and lifestyle programmes, leaving little room for thought-provoking or experimental content.

40

Looking Back

As I write, AI is in its embryonic stage; I'll not speculate as to where it will take us, but whether there will be a camera, let alone a cameraperson, involved in visual storytelling, I cannot say. I like to think that documentaries will always have an audience and that people will be required to film people.

Television still has its part to play in Western society. Whatever the future holds, there will always be a role for the moving image, and those involved in creating the content will be storytellers. Whether it is fact, fiction, fantasy, or something in between, the story is at the centre, and no amount of method, style or sophisticated technology can overshadow that.

From a documentary cinematography perspective, there is no shortage of talent in the upcoming generation. However, there is no longer a clear progression through the ranks—no apprenticeship-type roles in which to hone the necessary skills, but the cream will still rise to the top.

It was forty-eight years ago, in 1966, that I made my first tentative steps into the world of professional photography. I had no strategy for the future, nor did I possess a burning ambition to dazzle the world with my talent. I didn't know or worry about whether I could make a viable living; I scraped by in my chosen field. I had no ties and was unconcerned about the insecure lifestyle of a freelancer. Looking back at my younger self, I see that I had low self-esteem and little drive. I was naïve, content to go with the flow, and perhaps a bit too easy-going (or maybe lazy). However, as time went on, my passion grew as I realised that I actually had a flair for visuals, and dreams of combining this with travel and adventure could possibly become a reality.

Though I had mixed feelings about it at the time, film school gave me the grounding I needed and the notion that there could be a place for me in this daunting industry, peopled by confident, purposeful creatives. Without the fortuitously timed break when offered the BBC assistant cameraman contract, I really think my career could have floundered in 1976. Through the early '80s the competition was tough, and the finances stretched, but with support and encouragement from Yaffa and the need to provide for my new family, I had the drive to progress, and the offers started to flow.

Being a poor networker, I always feared work would dry up, and there were periods of drought. The job was demanding and sometimes stressful. However, through the '90s and into the new millennium, I enjoyed a fascinating variety of assignments.

Now, in my mid-seventies, in good health but lacking the stamina for those arduous shoots, I keep my hand in with occasional filming offers from people I have a special connection with. Beyond that, I have largely returned to my first love—still photography.

What began as a fanciful idea evolved into a passion and a vocation. Over the past five decades, capturing irreplaceable moments and often creating unique ones has been both a privilege and a joy. I am grateful that my career has coincided with a golden age in television history. It has been a wonderful and fulfilling way to earn a living. I urge anyone with a passion for photography, in any form, to persevere.

Acknowledgements

Family has been fundamental. Betty Clarke (1922-1990), my mother, had the insight to envisage a future for me in photography and Denis Clarke (1916-2003), my father, had the faith to lend me a substantial sum towards the vital investment in film equipment. More than I can express, Yaffa's love, support, and sacrifice over thirty-five years of often unpredictable and worrying comings and goings have been the foundation on which I have been able to build my career and pursue my dream. Dan and Tali had no choice in the matter, and I hope the long periods of absence were compensated for by some long periods at home. Today, as mature adults, I am grateful for their encouragement and words of wisdom during my long struggle to complete this book, and I am overjoyed that both have become parents this year to Jack and Azra, to whom it is dedicated.

I am thankful to Colin Young (1927-2021) for recognising my potential and offering me a place at the National Film School, which provided a crucial jumpstart to my aspirations.

Acknowledgements

I am also indebted to the numerous photographers and DoPs I assisted in my earlier years, from whom I learnt so much.

All filmmaking is a collaborative effort. The end credits of any production show how much work and how many people are involved. This account is from a cameraman's perspective and mainly focuses on the most intensive part of the process—the shoot. In addition to the core camera and production crew, various local technicians, fixers, translators, and helpers have played vital roles, although only a few have been mentioned in the book.

I have been lucky to work alongside many outstanding professionals, some of whom have reminded me of situations and anecdotes I had forgotten. In other cases, their versions of my recollections were entirely different! Thank you for your input.

Thanks go to Stef Wickham, Ian Lewis, Barry Clarke, Charles Harris, and Harriett Vered for their valuable contributions, guidance, and meticulous manuscript reviews and to Prof. Rupert Stasch for bringing added clarity to the Korawai story.

Filmography

(Many can be found on YouTube. Search: 'colin clarke dop')

Television

ARENA – MENTIONED IN DISPATCHES (1hr 16mm)
Dir: Chris Sykes. BBC 2 1980
Portrait of Tim Page – Vietnam War photographer.

POLICE – OPERATION CARTER [2nd unit] (5x1hr 16mm)
Dir: Roger Graef. BBC 2 1983
'Fly on the wall' series on the Thames Valley Police. BAFTA award 'Best documentary series'.

THE GREAT BIRD RACE (1hr 16mm)
Dir: Major Steadman. Channel 4 1985
Sponsored ornithological 'race' for charity, with Bill Oddie.

MADNESS – THE VIDEO [part] (90min 16mm)
Dir: David Robinson. MTV(US) 1986
Zany 'Rockumentary' on pop group, Madness.

ASSIGNMENT ADVENTURE – ON ANGELS' WINGS (1hr 16mm)
Dir: Peter Mc Pherson. Discovery Channel (US) / Channel 4 1986
Hang gliding adventure from the world's highest waterfall – the Angel Falls, in the Venezuelan rainforest.

TRUE STORIES – PEACE FOR OUR TIME? (90min 16mm)
Dir: Jan Němec. Channel 4 1988
Munich 1938 and the fate of Czechoslovakia.

ANKARANA (The Wilds of Madagascar) (1hr 16mm)
Dir: Philip Chapman. National Geographic TV (US) 1988
Caving/canoeing expedition to explore undocumented and virtually inaccessible sunken forests in Madagascar.

MOVING STORIES – A STEP ON THE LADDER + THE FIVE MILLION POUND HOUSE (2x1hr 16mm) BBC 1 1989
Dir: Steve Poole. *First-time buyers + the other end of the scale.*

Filmography

ENTERPRISE CULTURE – BEYOND THE DIVIDE (1hr 16mm)
Dir: Peter Symes. BBC 1 1989
'Tebbit's Express' victims from the north seek work down south.

BY-LINE – THE BLASPHEMER'S BANQUET [part] (1hr 16mm)
Dir: Peter Symes. BBC 2 1989
Salman Rushdie's situation through the eyes and prose of the poet Tony Harrison.

ICEWALK (1hr 16mm)
Dir: Simon Normanton. Channel 4 1989
Robert Swan's multinational expedition walks to the North Pole + student expedition to study the Arctic's environmental problems.

ENTERPRISE CULTURE – BEYOND THE DIVIDE (1hr 16mm)
Dir: Peter Symes. Prod. co: BBC Bristol. BBC 1 1989
'Tebbit's Express' victims from the north seek work down south.

DARK RIVER (100min 16mm)
Dir: Malcolm Taylor. 1990
Feature / TV film set in colonial Africa, starring Tom Bell, Ian McNeice, Rosemary Leach, Kate Buffery.
Screened at Cannes + *'Montreal Jury Selection'* 1990

EVERYMAN – FROM GRACE TO MERCY (30min 16mm)
Dir: Jane Treays. BBC 1 1991
The story of a charitable children's clinic in the Arab Quarter of Jerusalem's 'Old City' and its' fight for survival.

WORDS ON FILM – XANADU (1hr 16mm)
Dir: Kim Flitcroft. BBC 2 1992
A Rochester housing estate through the eyes and prose of the poet – Simon Armitage.

EVERYMAN – THIS LAND IS OURS (1hr 16mm)
Dir: Jane Treays. NBC (US)/BBC 1 1992
This is a study of Jewish fundamentalism in Israel, specifically the Gush Emunim, the Natura Carta, and the Chasidim.

THE NEW EUROPEANS (3x1hr Betacam)
Prod. co: MPT (Washington)/Rias TV(Berlin) PBS (US) 1992
European life from the Champagne harvest, chez Bolinger, to the struggle of adapting to capitalism in the East.

999 (4x12min Betacam) DEATH BOAT, FIRE ESCAPE, WASP STING, STRANGFORD LOUGH. BBC 1 1992
Dir: Phillipa Cousins / Nick Shearman.
Dramatised reconstructions of rescue operations.

SEX, DRUGS AND DINNER (1hr 16mm)
Dir: Charles Harris. BBC 2 1992
Black satirical documentary with Alexie Sayle. Starving Third World produces cash crops for Western consumption.
'Premiere Award' – One World Broadcasting Trust Awards, 1992 + Finalist at BEMA, Okmedia and New York F/Fs

BLOOMING BELLAMY (5 x 30min 16mm)
Dir: John Percival. BBC 1 1993
Series on herbal medicine with David Bellamy.

DEFENDERS OF THE WILD – KEEPER OF THE CONGO (1hr Super16)
Dir: Katrina Murray. Discovery Channel (US) / Channel 4 1993
Dr. Oko and his guards fight to protect the endangered chimps, gorillas and forest elephants from poacher's rifles.

LOCOMOTION – TRACK TO THE FUTURE (1hr 16mm)
Dir: Timothy Copestake. BBC 1993
World history of the railways. The future – Japan's 'Bullet' Train and the hovering 'Maglev'.

21st. CENTURY AIRPORT [part] (3x1hr Betacam NTSC)
Dir: Chris Hale. Channel 4 1994
Three years documenting the design by Renzo Piano and the building of the Kansai Airport on a man-made island in Osaka Bay, Japan.

STATE OF THE ARK – ZOOS THAT TIME FORGOT (1hr 16mm)
Dir: Kate Broom. BBC 2 1994
Eastern Bloc zoos struggle for survival through severe winters, lack of funds and crippling bureaucracies.

TURNING POINT – D-DAY (90min Betacam NTSC)
Dir: Steve York / Rudy Bednar. ABC (US) 1994
Allied invasion at Normandy, fifty years on with Peter Jennings.
1994 Gold Hugo at the Chicago IFF + 1995 Cine Golden Eagle Award

CUTTING EDGE – FOR RICHER FOR POORER [part] (1hr 16mm)
Dir: Lucy Sandys-Wynch. Channel 4 1995
Three very different weddings – Rich, nouveau-riche and poor.

Filmography

PHARAOHS & KINGS – A BIBLICAL QUEST (3 x 1hr Super16) Discovery
Dir: Timothy Copestake. Channel (US) / Channel 4 1995
Egyptologist David Rohl re-examines the chronology of ancient Egyptian and biblical history.

EQUINOX – IT RUNS ON WATER (1hr Betacam)
Dir: Lawrence Simanowitz. Channel 4 1995
Inventors v. Scientists. Imagine a world fuelled by water.

DANCING IN THE STREETS – NO FUN [part] (1 hr Super16)
Dir: Hugh Thompson. BBC 1 1996
A Rock and Roll history. The Punk era and anarchy.

IN THE BLOOD – LOST TRIBES (1hr Super16)
Dir: Chris Hale. BBC 2 1996
Mormons to the Lemba Jews of Southern Africa – A genetic search for 'Lost Tribes of Israel', With Prof. Steve Jones.

ZULU WARS [half] (3 x 1hr Super16)
Dir: Richard Wawman. Learning Channel (US) 1996
Dramatised historical reconstruction of the rise of the Zulu nation under the great warrior Shaka and its fall under Cetshwayo.

SECRET HISTORY – THE WHITECHAPEL MURDERS (1hr Super16)
Dir: Stephen White. CH. 4 1996
Docudrama. The ongoing investigation into the identity of Jack the Ripper. Was it an American quack, Dr. Tumblety?

WARRIOR ISLAND – KOROWAI (1hr Super16)
Dir/Cam: Colin Clarke. Discovery Channel (US) 1996
Study of a remote, tree house dwelling tribe in the New Guinea rainforest, with tales of sorcery and cannibalism.

TIMEWATCH – LENIN'S SECRET FILES (1hr Super16)
Dir: William Cran. BBC 2 1997
With the help of a recently accessed archive, a new perspective on the final years of Lenin's life.

FLIGHTS OF COURAGE (1hr Super16)
Dir: Elizabeth Dobson/Greg Barker. Channel 4 1997
1918 – Pioneer fliers cross a continent against all odds to give birth to the US Airmail.

CUTTING EDGE – WOMEN DRIVERS [half] (1hr Super 16)
Dir: Ella Behair. CH. 4 1997

EQUINOX – RESURRECTING THE MAMMOTH (1 hr Digibeta)
Dir: Chis Swayne. Channel 4 1998
Japanese expedition to Siberia in search of frozen mammoth sperm with which to impregnate an elephant!

SECRET HISTORY – THE PURPLE SECRET (1hr Digibeta)
Dir: Stephen White. Channel 4 1998
Dramatised documentary revealing the horrors of the rare genetic disease, Porphyria, that has plagued the British (and consequently, Eastern European) royal family since Mary Queen of Scots.

QUEST FOR THE LOST CIVILISATION (3x1hr Super16) Discovery Dir: Timothy Copestake. Channel (US) / Channel 4 1998
A highly developed civilisation with advanced knowledge of astronomy and maths predating the Egyptians and Sumerians by many thousands of years? Graham Hancock looks at worldwide evidence for their existence.

TIMEWATCH – GREY OWL [part] (1 hr Digibeta)
Dir: Richard Bradley. BBC 2 1999
1930s – He was an 'Apache' eco-warrior and a superstar, but he was also the man who conned a generation.

SECRET HISTORY – MAU MAU (1hr Super16/DVC Pro)
Dir: Elizabeth Dobson. Channel 4 1999
A fresh look at colonial Kenya's Mau Mau uprising in the 1950s, which cost 12,000 lives – only thirty-two were European.

RED FILES – SECRET SOVIET MOON MISSION / SOVIET SPORTS WARS (2 x 1hr Super16)
Dir: Greg Barker. PBS (US) 1999
Winner -*Best Limited Series'* International Documentary Assc.
Cold War politics of the 'space race' and 'sport' from the USSR perspective.

SECRET HISTORY – THE PEOPLE'S DUCHESS (1hr Digibeta)
Dir: Justin Hardy. Channel 4 1999
Dramatised life story of the influential and scandalous Georgiana Duchess of Devonshire – 18th C. period reconstruction.

SOLDIER POETS (1hr Digibeta)
Dir: Richard Bradley. Channel 4 2000
The poets of World War Two remembered by Tom Paulin.

ENDS OF THE EARTH – DEATH, DECEIT AND THE NILE (1hr Digibeta)
Dir: Stephen White. Channel 4 2000
Retracing the steps of Sir Richard Burton's Victorian expedition across Africa in search of the source of the Nile.

Filmography

KINGS & BEASTS (1hr Digibeta)
Dir: Richard Bradley. BBC 2 2000
Drama doc. A history of royal menageries, starting with the 12th-century Lion Tower at The Tower of London.

ROAD TO RICHES (2 of 6x1hr Digibeta)
Dir: Charles Bruce. BBC 2 2000
History of world economics, from Babylonian times to the present. Presented by Peter Jay.

THE SCIENCE OF SECRECY – HIEROGLYPHICS (30 mins. Digibeta)
Dir: Timothy Copestake. Channel 4 2000
The story behind the early deciphering of ancient Egyptian hieroglyphics as investigated by Simon Singh.

THE REAL CRACKER [part] (5 xI hr Digibeta)
Dir: Patrick Forbes. Channel 4 2001
Verité series following a psychologist and a psychiatrist working with the police on offender profiles.

DISCOVERING THE REAL WORLD OF HARRY POTTER (1hr Digibeta)
Dir: Shaun Trevisic. PBS(US)/Channel 4 2001
Drama doc. The real-life places, people and practices that inspired J.K. Rowling.

EAT LIKE A KING: HENRY VIII (1hr Digibeta)
Dir: Shaun Trevisick. History Channel (US) 2002
The extraordinary diet of the Tudor monarchs and the elaborate rituals that surrounded the king's daily feasts recreated at Kentwell Hall and Hampton Court Palace,

CUTTING EDGE – BOYS ALONE [half] (1hr Digibeta)
Dir: Kim Flitcroft. Channel 4 2002
Ten eleven-year-old boys are left unsupervised & without adult intervention in a large house for five days. The result ...

MY SPERM DONOR DAD [half] (1hr Digibeta NTSC)
Dir: Barry Stevens. CBC (Canada) / 'Storyville' BBC 4 2002
Conceived through artificial insemination in 1952, Barry searches for the identity of his biological father. Amsterdam Audience Award, 2001

UNDERWORLD – FLOODED KINGDOMS OF THE ICE AGE (3 x 1hr Super16/Digibeta)
Dir: Tim Copestake. Discovery Channel (US) / Channel 4 2002
Graham Hancock takes his search for evidence of lost civilisations underwater by exploring the world's oceans.

JACKIE CHAN'S HONG KONG (1hr Digibeta)
Dir: Justin Wickham. Discovery Channel (US) 2002
The Hollywood & Hong Kong martial arts superstar and film director presents his take on his home country.

WHO KILLED TUTANKHAMUN [Drama segment} (2hr Super16 / Digibeta)
Dir: Shaun Trevisick. Discovery Channel (US) CH. 5 2002
New theories about the cause of his death.

THE MYSTERY OF THE THREE KINGS (1hr Digibeta)
Dir: Giles Llewellyn-Thomas. PBS (US) / BBC 2 2002
Drama Doc. An investigation into the truth behind the story and the ethnic identity of the Maji.

A SHADOW OVER EUROPE (1hr Digibeta) Dir: Tony Stark. BBC 4 2002
WW2 Nazi atrocities against the Czechoslovakians and ensuing retributions against the Sudetan Germans. Charles Wheeler investigates how this affects the Czech Republic's entry into the EU.

COMMANDING HEIGHTS [part] (5x1hr Digibeta)
Dir: Greg Barker/Bill Cran. WGBH (US) 2002 / BBC4 2003
Battle for the World Economy. How globalisation has developed and changed the world. Based on the book by Daniel Yergin.

THE HOLY LANCE (1hr Digibeta)
Dir: Shaun Trevisick. Discovery Channel (US) / CH. 5 2003
In the Vienna Museum is a spear that is believed to have pierced Christ on the cross, and it has an intriguing history.

THE REAL JASON & THE ARGONAUTS [documentary section] (1hr Digibeta) Dir: Shaun Trevisick. Discovery Channel (US) / CH. 5 2003
Retracing Jason's journey & looking for any truth behind the myth.

BRITAIN B.C. (2 x 1hr Digibeta) Dir: Timothy Copestake. CH. 4 2003
Frances Pryor delves into prehistoric British history.

WHO KILLED JULIUS CAESAR? (1hr Super16/Digibeta)
Dir: Mathew Wortman. Discovery Channel (US) / CH. 5 2003
Documentary with drama reconstruction. Head of the Italian Carabinieri forensics dept. re-investigates Caesar's assassination using contemporary methods. BAFTA nominated

Filmography

PARTY MAESTRO (1hr Digibeta) [part]
Dir: Malcolm Brinkworth. BBC 2 2003
Verité film follows party organiser Johnny Roxburgh, who sets up events for royalty, the rich, and the famous.

OPERATUNITY – THE WINNERS' STORY (1hr Digibeta) [part]
Dir: Michael Waldman. BBC 1 2003
One year later. Following the winners while recording a Christmas album at Abbey Road Studios.

THE TRUE GLADIATORS [documentary section] (1hr Super16 / Digibeta)
Dir: Shaun Trevisick.
Discovery Channel (US) / CH. 5 2004
Gladiator bones discovered at the Ephesus archaeological site are scientifically analysed to discover new information about their diet, medical practices, lifestyle, weapons used and much more.

BRITAIN A.D. (3 x 1hr Digibeta) Dir: Timothy Copestake. Channel 4 2004
Frances Pryor challenges the concept that Britain sank into 'The Dark Ages' after the Romans left.

HORIZON – KING SOLOMON'S STONE (1hr Digibeta)
Dir: Sean Smith. BBC 2 2004
The 'Johash Stone' bears an ancient Hebrew inscription verifying the existence of the Old Testament's First Temple on the site of Jerusalem's Temple Mount. Is it Israel's most significant archaeological find or a damaging, sophisticated fake?

NEFERTITI – SEARCH FOR THE LOST MUMMY (2hr Super16 / Digibeta)
Dir: Mathew Wortman. Discovery Channel (US) / CH. 5 2004
Documentary with drama reconstruction. The mummy of history's first lady, Queen Nefertiti, ancient Egypt's only female Pharaoh and legendary beauty, is 'discovered' in a tomb in the Valley of the Kings.

WIFE SWAP USA (half 1hr DVcam) Dir: Juan Zaldivar. ABC (US) 2005
'Reality' TV in the US Deep South.

SILENT VOICES (1hr Digibeta) Dir: Charles Harris. Community Channel 2005
Harrowing dramatisation based on real-life cases of physical abuse within the family.

WHEN THE MOORS RULED IN EUROPE (2hr Digibeta)
Dir: Timothy Copestake. Channel 4 2005
Bettany Hughes explores the history, art & culture of the mysterious and misunderstood Moors.

GRANDEST DESIGNS – EL CAJON (1hr. HDcam)
Dir: Adrian Sibley. Discovery Channel (US) 2005
Character-led documentary documenting the construction of the massive 'El Cajon' Dam in Mexico.

SPIRIT OF THE ARTS – KIRI TE KENAWA (30min Digibeta)
SPIRIT OF THE ARTS – CECILIA BARTOLI (30min Digibeta)
SPIRIT OF THE ARTS – RENEE FLEMING (30min Digibeta)
Dir: Safi Schlicht. International distribution 2006
Profiles, both professional & personal, of leading opera singers.

PAUL MERTON – SILENT CLOWNS [part] (DVcam)
Dir: Kate Broom / Tom Cholmondeley. BBC 2 2006
Documentary series with Paul Merton & friends enthusing over the delights of comedy films from cinema's silent era.

FOUNDING FATHERS (2hr Digibeta) Dir: Tim Copestake. Channel 4 2007
Tony Robinson investigates conspiracy theories relating to alternative versions of the founding of the USA.

ATHENS – THE TRUTH ABOUT DEMOCRACY (2 x 1hr Digibeta)
Dir: Tim Copestake. Channel 4 2007
Bettany Hughes presents the story of the world's first great democracy & the philosophers of classical Greece.

THE GREAT WALL OF CHINA [2nd unit] (2hr Varicam HD)
Dir: Nic Young. Channel 4 2007
Docudrama. The Story of General Qi and the building of The Great Wall.

SOLOMON STONE: THE FALLOUT (1hr HDcam)
Dir: Robert Eagle. National Geographic TV 2007
An investigation into the authenticity of Israel's most controversial Biblical archaeological artefacts.

DICKENS & THE INVENTION OF CHRISTMAS (1hr Digibeta)
Dir: Paul Tilzey. BBC 1 2007
Drama-doc about Charles Dickens' influence on the way we celebrate Christmas today.
Written & presented by Griff Rhys Jones.

CLASSICAL DESTINATIONS Series 2 (13x30min HDcam) BBC Worldwide + Sky HD 2008
Simon Callow introduces the great classical composers, their music and the cities that nurtured them.

Filmography

FRONTLINE – BLACK MONEY (1hr HDX) Dir: Oriana Zill. PBS (US) 2009
Lowell Bergman investigates corruption & bribery in the international arms industry.

AMONG THE RIGHTEOUS [part] (1hr HDcam)
Dir: William Cran. Channel 4 / PBS (US) 2009
A search for Arabs who helped Jews escape from WW2 Nazi concentration camps in North Africa.

SERGIO [Documentary section] (90min HDcam)
Dir: Greg Barker. HBO / Storyville BBC / NETFLIX 2009
Drama Doc. The inspirational story of UN legend Sergio Viera de Mello and the attempts to rescue him from the rubble of his bombed HQ in Baghdad. Screened at the Sundance Festival 2009 & The London Film Festival 2009

SUCHET'S MUSIC HALL HERO – SID FIELD [part] (1hr DVcam)
Dir: Tom Cholmondeley. BBC 4 2010
David Suchet traces the history and career of music hall star Sid Field.

IMAGINE – GROWING OLD DISGRACEFULLY (1hr Digibeta)
Dir: Jill Nicholls. BBC 1 2010
Alan Yentob profiles Diana Athill, the best-selling author whose frank memoir brought her celebrity at the age of 92.

IMAGINE – THE WEIRD WORLD OF EDWARD MUYBRIDGE [Part]
(1hr HDX) Dir: Jill Nicholls. BBC 1 2010
The life story of the pioneering photographer best known for his multiple camera studies of animals in motion. With Alan Yentob.

NOVA – ICEMAN MURDER MYSTERY (1hr Varicam HD)
Dir: Brando Quilici. National Geographic TV / PBS (US) 2011
Twenty years after his discovery beneath a Tyrolian glacier, 5,300-year-old Ötzi' is briefly thawed for new scientific research.

THE REAL KING'S SPEECH [Drama section] (1hr HDcam)
Dir: David Barrie. Channel 4 2011
The story behind King George VI's struggle to overcome his stammer.

DOGS 101 – WORK WITH CHEETAHS (10min HDcam)
Dir: Joe Sousa. Animal Planet (US) 2012
In Namibia, specially trained Anatolian Shepherd Dogs protect goat herds from attack by cheetahs.

TABOO – PRIVATE SPERM DONOR (10 min XDcam)
Dir: Bernice Toni. National Geographic TV (US) 2012
He runs his operation from home on his terms and has fathered about 90 children.

FRONTLINE – THE REGIME RESPONDS [part] (1hr HDX)
Dir: Marcela Gaveria. PBS (US) 2012
Investigation into how Syrian President Bashar al-Assad has managed to hold onto power for so long.

NOVA – BUILDING PHARAOHS CHARIOT (1hr HDX)
Dir: Martin O'Collins. Amazon Prime / PBS (US) 2012
Drama doc. Experts research & build replica Ancient Egyptian chariots, test them & the weaponry + recon of battles.

THE OUTCAST COMIC (1hr 4K) Dir: Wael Dabbous. Sky Arts 2016
Stand-up comic Andrew Lawrence outraged the British industry by challenging political correctness and 'coming out' as right wing.

CHURCHILL AND THE MOVIE MOGUL (1hr 4K)
Dir: John Fleet. BFI / Storyville BBC 4 2019
Drama-doc. In 1934, Top film producer Alexander Korda collaborates with Winston Churchill as a screenwriter and historical advisor.

Pop Promos *Artists include:*

MADNESS (x2), BELLE STARS (x3), BOOM TOWN RATS (x2), TRACY ULLMAN, ROBERT PLANT, YAZOO, STATUS QUO, BUCKS FIZZ, MAX BYGRAVES, MUSICAL YOUTH, ALED JONES, JOAN ARMATRADING, ALVIN STARDUST, MARILYN (x2), EVELYN KING, LENE LOVICH, THE UNTOUCHABLES.

Rock Concerts & Jam sessions *Artists include:*

ERIC CLAPTON, JOHN MARTYN, PETE TOWNSEND, DAVID GILMORE, RINGO STARR, MADNESS, HOWARD JONES, TEARS FOR FEARS, DEPECHE MODE, ELVIS COSTELLO.

TV Commercials

POWER STOUT. Beer. Mirage Prods. (60 sec 35mm)
DOUBLE CROWN. Beer. Mirage Prods. (60 sec 35mm)

Filmography

TELSTAR RECORDS. Music. Rhode Island Films. (10 x 30 sec 16mm)
REVLON. Cosmetics. Rhode Island Films. (30 sec 16mm)
SAMSON BATTERIES. Car batteries. Rhode Island Films. (90 sec 35mm)
COTTERS TOURS. Euro-Tour Co. Peter Isaac Prods. (30 sec 16mm)
REVELATIONS. Board games. William Clark Prods. (2 x 30 sec 16mm)
ACTION GAMES [operating] Company Three Productions. (12x30 sec 35mm)

Film Shorts and Corporate Promotion:

'WICKED' E.P.K. (15min HDcam) Dir: Greg Barker.
Electronic Press Kit for the London Production of the Broadway hit musical.

MALLET! (16mm) Dir: Bob Laurie.
Gruesome 'alternative' action pic. with prosthetics Ultimat and special FX.

TIME PASSING – 9 O'CLOCK (10min 16mm)
Dir: Charles Garrad. *A surreal look at time.*

DIARY OF A LITTLE SOD (8min Betacam) Series pilot
Dir: Shirley Sheeman.
Comedy from Simon Brett's book, shot from baby's POV. Voiced by Rick Mayal.

THE HEALING TOUCH (40min 16mm)
Dir: Richard Wawman. *A spiritual perspective on love, sex and touch.*

THE SUN (16mm)
Dir: Malcolm Taylor. *Comedy, promoting advertising in the Sun newspaper.*
Gold Medal '*Best Promotional Film*' New York Film Festival 1988

SUNDAY TIMES CLASSIFIED (16mm)
Dir: Malcolm Taylor. *Comedy in the city with a power-driven executive chair.*

ATM (1inch C Format. 3 cameras mounted together + Ultimat)
Dir: Peter Claridge.
Three-screen comedy routine with Punt and Dennis, for display in the Science Museum, demonstrating the complexities of ATM cash dispensers.

PLAYBACK (16mm) Dir: Charles Harris.
Recruitment film for Nat West Bank. Sceptical kids are caught up in a time travel adventure while producing a school video project.

COMPUTER MARRIAGE (Betacam) Dir: Malcolm Taylor.
Comedy set in the office of a marriage guidance counsellor for computers – Communication problems? The answer is Pirelli – Focon fibre optic and copper cables.

KEEP SAFETY FIRST 1, 2 & 3 (3 x 30min Betacam) Dir: John Gow.
Drama reconstructions of fatal on-track accidents and 'near misses' for railway workers' safety training.

WELCOME TO THE WORLD OF RHONE POULENC (Betacam) Dir: Timothy Burkinshaw.
Stylised office drama explaining May and Baker's corporate identity change.

THE MAN WHO SAID 'YES' (BVU) Dir: Charles Harris.
Espionage comedy explaining commercial positioning to TSB staff.

BUY OUT (BVU) Dir: Charles Harris.
Drama of a company going through a management buyout, produced for the 3 'T's.

THE FLOOR IS YOURS 2 (16mm) Dir: Jim Goulding.
Situation drama for training in the giving of presentations and public speaking. Prod. co: Gower Publishing.

SPIRIT OF THE FOREST (20min Super16 printed 35mm) Dir: Malcolm Taylor.
A rainforest awareness promo to raise funds from governments and industry for WWF projects.

FELIXSTOWE (4min Super16)
Dir: Sam Wallis. *Fast-moving sales promo for Felixstowe container docks.*

FARADAY INSERTS (20min Betacam) Dir: Chris Tuff.
Reconstructed historical electrical experiments for projection at 1994 Faraday lectures.

TOTAL – THE BUILDING OF AN OIL PLATFORM (30min 35mm)
Dir: Roland Brinton. *French cinema short, shot over four years.*

LOHNRO 1989 [part] (40min 16mm) Dir: Malcolm Taylor.
'Home movies' for Tiny Roland, primarily gold mines.

HOOGOVENS ON THE MOVE (3 min 16mm,)
Dir: Ian McNaulty. *Corporate promo for Dutch steel company.*

Filmography

TASTE OF O.S.L. (30min Betacam) Dir: Ian Lewis.
A culinary tour of the Algarve, Dordogne and Tuscany, with
Roy Ackerman. Gold Medal 'Best Tourism Film' New York Film Festival 1992.

NATWEST SPONSORSHIP (40min 16mm.) Dir: Martin Rosenblaum.
A catalogue of the banks' sponsorship programme, from the arts to third World medicine.

THE QUEENS AWARDS FOR EXPORT 1993 (30min Betacam)
Dir: Charles Harris. *The award winners at work.*